HANGED

Hanged

A History of Idaho's Executions

Kathy Deinhardt Hill

Big Mallard Books
McCall, Idaho

Published in 2010 by Big Mallard Books
McCall, Idaho
Printed in the United States of America
Prepared for print by cflinn.com

ISBN   978-0-9717256-3-8
LCCN 2010906958

*You'll get a fair trial followed
by a first class hanging.*

Judge Roy Bean

Contents

Preface 1

History of Idaho Justice 2

1. For Love

James Sidney Larkins 6

William H. H. Bond 15

Fred Seward 27

2. For Fortune

Herman St. Clair 38

Michael Mooney 49

Henry McDonald 56

Edward Rice 70

Noah Arnold 82

Kuok Wah Choi 94

Simeon Walters 100

Ernest Walrath, Troy Powell 110

James Romain, David Renton, Christopher Lower 129

3. For Honor

Alex Woods 144

George Pierson 152

John Jurko 163

4. In Desperation

Tambiago. 173

James Ellington. 179

William L. Reynolds, aka Frank Williams. 187

Theodore Warlich 195

5. The Demon Rum

James Conners. 203

Anthony McBride 208

Timothy O'Conner 215

6. Murder Most Foul

Raymond A. Snowden. 225

Acknowledgments. 237

About the Author 239

Sources. 240

Index 263

Preface

In its history, Idaho has hanged twenty-six men. This book tells their stories. It recreates their lives, their crimes, their trials, and their deaths. It gives insight into Idaho's territorial and state court systems and how they treated those who had taken the lives of others. While some were truly bad men whose despicable crimes shocked communities and outraged the populace, others were just men madly in love, down on their luck, or stuck in unfortunate circumstances.

This book is not meant to be a commentary on the death penalty— its right or wrong place in a civil society. It is just the stories of men who were given the ultimate punishment for their crimes. But in researching this book, I found it disquieting that for every man who was hanged, more were not, even for the same crime, often in similar situations.

We would like to believe that the ultimate punishment is reserved for the worst offenders, those men and women who are so morally corrupt, their offenses so horrific, that they must pay for their crimes with their lives. We also want and expect our court system to be fair, our judges honorable and enlightened, our prosecutors diligent but even-handed, and our jurors honest and impartial, unswayed by personal bias and prejudice. But what we want or expect is often not what we receive.

Why some faced the gallows and others did not is unclear. Some of the men who were hanged spoke with accents; some did not. Most were poor. They all were responsible for the death of another human being, but whether they deserved to hang is debatable, especially in light of countless others who were found guilty of murder and spared.

The reader can decide if justice was served.

History of Idaho Justice

Through the mid-1850s, Idaho was not a destination. It was just a place people passed through on their way to Oregon or California. But when gold was discovered in the Clearwater region in 1860, that changed. After rich claims were found in the Salmon River country, fortune seekers swarmed to the area establishing the towns of Florence and Warren. When gold was found in the Boise Basin in 1862, the rush was officially on. By the summer of 1863, 14,000 people—miners, merchants, blacksmiths, barkeepers, doctors, druggists, lawyers, and law-breakers—filled the streets of Placerville and Idaho City, the two largest towns in the basin. According to an article in the *Sacramento Daily Union*, life in the basin was good, especially because of the "vigilance of our officers, who leave no stone unturned to ferret out and bring to justice offenders against law and order."

The influx of people most certainly brought criminals, and in Idaho's ruggedness, it was easy for people to commit crimes and then escape. Robbery was the most prevalent crime, followed by claim jumping and murder. Miner's courts and vigilante groups were the first attempts at law and order, but few rules governed their actions. For the most part, those who broke the unwritten laws were banished. Those whose crimes were deemed reprehensible were hanged.

How many actually hanged during Idaho's early days is unknown. Chinese immigrants and Native Americans faced the hangman's noose at will, and few of these events were recorded, although some were briefly mentioned in the weekly newspapers of the various mining towns. One of the most notorious incidents occurred in 1885 near Pierce City in north central Idaho when the murder of a merchant led to the arrest of five Chinamen. After some arm-twisting, the Chinese admitted their involvement, and sheriff deputies loaded them on a wagon to take them to trial in Murray, the county seat of Shoshone County. Just two miles out of Pierce, vigilantes attacked the wagon. The vigilantes hanged all five prisoners on the spot. Clearly, the hanging of Chinese immigrants and Indians had little to do with justice and much more to do with the prejudices of the day. Even when court systems were established, little was done to stop this type of "justice."

In the early 1860s, territorial courts under the jurisdiction of Washington and Oregon Territories were established in Idaho in an attempt to limit vigilantes and self-appointed sheriffs from establishing their own laws. The territories also allowed for the creation of justices of the peace and probate courts to give the mining camps a semblance of order. Then in 1863, Idaho became a territory in its own right and three district courts were established throughout the territory. The county jails of Idaho City and Lewiston became the territorial prisons.

But these early district courts were ineffective. The first judges were from the East and Midwest, appointed because of their loyalty to the Republican Party. They had no desire to call Idaho home. They were also not welcome, as Idaho was home to thousands of confederate sympathizers, Democrats all who had little need for Republican carpetbaggers. Also, the sheer size of Idaho Territory discouraged judges. Each judicial district covered one-third of the territory. Holding court at a time and place when needed was sometimes impossible. In addition to their district court duties, these early judges also served as Supreme Court justices, adding to their travel and workload. The problems created a high turnover rate for judges and little judicial continuity in Idaho's early history.

To offset the problems of the district courts, the Idaho Territorial Legislature created probate and justice courts and gave them increased jurisdiction. These courts handled both civil and criminal cases, although they were limited to misdemeanor crimes. However, they filled the void until the district courts in Idaho became better organized.

The district courts handled the murder cases in the counties where the murders occurred. In the event a judge handed down a death sentence, the hanging was carried out in the county of the crime under the direction of the sheriff. Each sheriff set his own protocol including construction of the gallows, time of execution, and number of guests to view the proceedings. The completion of the Idaho Territorial Prison in Boise in 1872 did little to change the hanging venues. Even after Idaho's statehood in 1890, authorized hangings continued to take place at the county level. Finally, in 1899 legislators passed a law that stipulated all executions take place at the Idaho State Penitentiary in Boise. Two years later, Ed Rice was hanged in the prison rose garden, the first official execution performed by the state.

The last hanging took place in 1957 when Raymond Snowden was dropped to his death in the gallows of Cell House 5, the only execution to take place in the room specifically designed for death.

In the 1960s, the climate of the country changed and the death penalty came under fire. In 1961, a group of Idaho legislators attempted to repeal Idaho's death penalty statutes, but conservatives in the Senate soundly defeated the bill on a 37-7 vote. However, the United States Supreme Court began whittling away at death penalty laws, and its rulings would directly affect Idaho. In the 1972 landmark case *Furman v. Georgia*, the court ruled that state statutes which gave juries complete sentencing discretion were unconstitutional. Idaho was one such state. In 1973, state legislators rewrote the death penalty statutes to pass constitutional muster, making the death penalty mandatory for any first-degree murder conviction. Then, in 1976, Idaho death penalty statutes were once again struck down by the Supreme Court, which ruled mandatory death sentences for certain crimes were unconstitutional. In 1977, Idaho legislators overwhelmingly passed a new death penalty law that followed the court's guidelines. At the time, hanging remained the method of execution.

That changed in 1978 when Senator Jim Risch, a Republican, and Mike Black, a Democrat, joined forces to change the way Idaho carried out its death sentences. The men were polar opposites in their feelings about state sponsored executions—Risch advocated the death penalty while Black strongly opposed it—but both wanted executions to be performed as humanely as possible. As a result of their legislation, hangings were outlawed and lethal injection became the preferred method of execution. Such an injection was used on Keith Wells in January 1994.

Idaho's death penalty law came under fire once again in 2002 after the Supreme Court voted down an Arizona law that allowed judges, not juries, to determine mitigating factors in justifying death sentences (*Ring v. Arizona*). Since Idaho's law was similar, legislators scrambled to rewrite the statute to bring it into compliance. It was signed into law by Governor Dirk Kempthorne in February 2003.

Idaho also allowed a firing squad to be used as a method of execution, if lethal injection proved "impractical." But in 2009, the Idaho Legislature removed that option. In the future, any execution in Idaho will be carried out with a needle.

1. For Love

James Sidney Larkins

Idaho Falls, December 25, 1895
Blackfoot, April 29, 1897

Tell me thy company, and I'll tell thee what thou art.
—Miguel De Cervantes

In a court of law, the behavior of the victim, no matter how reprehensible or vile, is not to be taken into consideration. Victims, by definition, bear no fault in the commission of the crimes against them. But the court of public opinion does not follow the same principles, so when James Sidney Larkins shot and killed Josie Hill on Christmas Day, 1895, some say she had it coming. But Sid Larkins learned the hard way that Lady Justice is blind, and she hanged him for the crime in the spring of 1897.

Larkins was born in Salt Lake in 1860, the son of W. J. and Caroline Larkins. His parents were immigrants from England, who made their way to Utah to farm. Life was difficult for young Larkins, whose mother suffered from bouts of mental instability. As a young boy, he was sent with his mother to live with an aunt in Nevada. But his mother's condition worsened, and eventually she became a patient at the Nevada State Insane Asylum in Reno, where she would spend the rest of her life. Young Larkins was sent back to Utah to live with his father.

At eighteen, Larkins left home to work for the Central Pacific Railroad, first as a freight conductor, then as a fireman. When he was in his early 20's, he fell from a train, striking his head on an engine pilot. The resulting headaches were so severe that he left railroading. He traveled to Idaho where he took up ranching in the Gentile Valley, southeast of Pocatello. Here he remained for three years.

When he found that ranching did not suit him, he returned to the railroad business. He traveled to Portland and went to work for the Northern Pacific Railroad as a brakeman and eventually a passenger conductor. After several years with Northern Pacific, he traveled to the Midwest, where he found employment with the Milwaukee and St. Paul Railroad. Larkins never gave a reason why he left the railroad the second time, but in the early 1890s he returned to Salt Lake. He later admitted it was the mistake of his life.

In Salt Lake, Larkins became acquainted with a man he described only as a "gentleman gambler." The man was "smooth and polished," and Larkins was taken with the lifestyle, the thrill of the cards. He claimed the man taught him to play "on the square," and over time he became a skilled card player. Eventually, he went to work for others, playing and dealing cards for a regular salary. His specialties were poker and faro, a popular gambling game of the 19th century.

The gambling houses of Salt Lake City were intertwined with the brothels. Although both were illegal, in the early 1890s the city fathers tolerated the activities as long as they were limited to Commercial Street and Franklin Avenue located in the heart of the city. To show the moral citizenry they were doing their jobs, city officials would raid the sporting houses once a month, collect fines, examine the prostitutes for illness, and then let them continue about their business. It was here that Larkins began dealing cards for Fred Hinkle, who was well known in the area and had paid his fair share of fines.

In June 1891, scandal rocked the brothels and clubs of Franklin Avenue when Ed Callahan, a rich businessman from Salida, Colorado, was brutally murdered. Callahan, who had amassed his fortune running gambling houses, had arrived in Salt Lake in early May and spent several weeks leading a life of "pleasure and debauchery," mostly on Franklin Avenue. In particular, he spent time at a brothel kept by Lottie Lawrence Miner. He was especially taken with a young woman named Josie Hill; Josie Hill was taken with the size of Callahan's bankroll.

Hill was an attractive, fine-figured young woman who had arrived in Salt Lake City from Boston in the spring of 1890. She was well mannered, intelligent, and vivacious; she never "languished for the want of masculine attention." But, as the *Salt Lake Tribune* reported, she was a "woman with a history," one with many aliases who could not be trusted. Working for Lottie Miner, she brought in many clients.

On June 3, Callahan and several friends visited Miner's brothel. After drinking most of the afternoon, Callahan sought out Josie, paid for her services, then spent the rest of the night with her. They awoke late and spent the entire next day together. Josie kept him well supplied with drink, and by late evening he was clearly intoxicated. After midnight, Josie procured a buggy and the two went for a ride, Josie at the reins, their destination unknown. After a short stop at a roadhouse where Callahan had four drinks, they drove on, straight into an ambush. Shots rang out, the horse reared, and Callahan fell from the wagon. Josie remained in the wagon, regained control, and went back to find Callahan. Finding him gasping for life, she jumped back into the wagon and proceeded to town to find help. When police arrived at the scene, Callahan was dead, his bankroll gone.

Suspicion immediately fell on Josie and Clarence Bean, a hack driver who had helped Josie procure the wagon. The police theorized the two planned the ambush, with Josie driving to a prearranged spot and Bean carrying out the deed. Both were arrested the day after the murder.

As soon as word of Josie's arrest was out, benefactors began arriving at the jail. Lottie Miner visited and offered money to pay for a lawyer. Anonymous admirers sent flowers and food. And Sid Larkins, at the request of his employer Fred Hinkle, paid a visit bringing her cash. It was the first time Larkins had met Josie, and he was smitten. She, too, was interested in the handsome young card-dealer who had his sights on owning his own club.

Officials held an inquest into Callahan's death. They did not find any evidence against Bean and released him, but they kept Josie in jail. They also took away her visitation rights, hoping the loss of outside influence would break her. It did not. She refused to answer any questions and stuck firmly to her story that she had absolutely nothing to do with the murder. She was bound over to district court to await a decision by the grand jury, which eventually refused to bring charges against her. After two weeks in jail, she was released.

She and Larkins immediately became a couple, Larkins admitting that his "whole being was wrapped up in her." He claimed that he convinced her to give up her former life, and although they were never married, they lived together as husband and wife.

This relationship would lead to Larkins' arrest. Salt Lake prosecutors never doubted Josie had a hand in killing Callahan, so in January 1892, they claimed to have new witnesses that would lead to her conviction. Police arrested Josie, Lottie Miner, "Coyote Dick" Edwards, and Larkins, charging them with the murder of Callahan. But Larkins' arrest was a ruse; prosecutors hoped they could use Larkins to pry a confession out of Josie. It didn't work, and when the new witnesses could not be produced for the grand jury, all the accused were released. No one would ever be tried for the murder of Callahan.

It is unclear how long Larkins and Josie remained in Salt Lake, but eventually they moved to Boise. Larkins would claim they were very happy until Josie's mother showed up on their doorstep. Josie's mother, also a prostitute, encouraged Josie to return to her former life. To get rid of her, Larkins paid her fare to return to her homeland of Ireland. For a year, they lived without her interference. But she returned and shortly after, Josie went back to work, using her own home as her brothel. Larkins' life spiraled downhill after that. He was especially undone when Josie began a relationship with a prominent Boise man whom Larkins refused to identify.

His jealousy dictated his behavior to the point of masochism. He would sneak into their bedroom and hide behind a dresser. Then he would watch as various men would use her services. His drinking increased; his mental condition deteriorated. In the spring of 1895, he attempted suicide by drinking poison. He was rescued by a friend who found him unconscious and rushed him to a hospital where he recovered. Josie was unfazed by his behavior and planned her escape.

In the summer of 1895 with the urging of her mother, Josie moved to Idaho Falls and took up residence in a house historically known for prostitution. Larkins followed and went to work tending bar and dealing cards for Frank DeKay and Daniel Dee, among others. He was well known to all the bartenders in Idaho Falls and had earned the nickname "Crazy Horse Sid" for his erratic behavior, especially when drunk. People who saw him on a regular basis described him as "pretty full" most of the time.

For a while Larkins stayed with Josie, but eventually she wanted him out of her life and told him so. For Larkins, it was the final blow. He moved into a hotel owned by Benjamin Jenne and began drinking nonstop. He lost his jobs—first at Dee's establishment, then at DeKay's. Both felt Larkins had become incompetent, losing money intentionally when dealing cards, allowing people to take money even though they had lost. Larkins also became extremely vocal and threatening toward Josie, telling anyone who would listen that Josie "could not throw me over."

In mid-December, Larkins showed up at Josie's door. When she wouldn't let him in, he kicked down the door. A fight commenced and Larkins attacked her. Others in the house separated the two, and he was arrested for disturbing the peace. He spent a few nights in jail but was released when two of his friends posted bail. The next day, he was back at Josie's; he wanted the clothes he kept there. Josie refused to let him in,

This sketch of Sid Larkins and Josie Hill appeared in the Salt Lake Tribune on May 1, 1897.

throwing the clothes out the back door. Larkins pleaded with her to let him in, and she relented, only because other men were present. Josie refused to talk to him, so Larkins made conversation with James Kerr, a regular at Josie's establishment. Kerr would later recall that Larkins had been drinking and made numerous threats against Josie and another gentleman who had captured Josie's favors.

On December 22, Larkins was sitting at the bar in Frank DeKay's saloon when he saw a nickel-plated American Bulldog revolver on the counter. The gun belonged to a young bartender, and Larkins asked to borrow it. Two nights later, Larkins was at the same bar, and asked DeKay if he could borrow five dollars. DeKay loaned him the money and questioned Larkins about the gun. Larkins admitted he had it. He left the bar telling DeKay he had a "dirty piece of business" to do that night. DeKay would later recall that Larkins was "comfortable full" when he left.

From the saloon, Larkins made his way to Josie's establishment, arriving sometime around 3 a.m. Christmas morning. Larkins knocked at the door and Josie answered. He asked to speak to George Colter, a gambler who earlier had told him he was going to Josie's place for the evening. Colter came to door and the two talked briefly. Larkins specifically wanted to know who was in the house. Colter told him and then asked

Larkins to leave, but Larkins followed him back into the house. He asked Josie if he could buy some beer, but Josie refused, telling him she could not take his money because he did not have any. For the next two hours, the couple quarreled over a variety of issues. Two other witnesses, Nellie Vernon, another prostitute, and William Thomas, her guest, recalled that sometimes the quarreling was "friendly" but most of the time it was not.

Around 5:30, Colter and Thomas decided to return to town. Josie and Nellie wanted to go with them, so they gathered their coats. But after a short conversation with Larkins, Josie changed her mind. Instead she told her visitors, "It's Christmas. We can well as celebrate here as up in town."

Nellie was unwilling to leave Josie and convinced Colter and Thomas to stay. They shared two bottles of beer and a bottle of blackberry brandy. Then Thomas decided to leave. He would recall that when he left, Larkins was extremely drunk.

It was just before dawn and all of them were in Josie's bedroom. Josie was brushing her hair and getting ready for bed. Colter planned to join her. Larkins was beside himself. He harangued Josie about how badly she had treated him. He reminded her that he had threatened to kill her, and he meant it. Josie mocked him.

"If I have to die," she told him, "I might as well die one time as another, so shoot."

Larkins obliged. He pulled a small handgun out of his back pocket and fired. When she saw the gun, Josie turned away, and the bullet struck her in the back. Then Larkins turned the gun on himself, fired, and fell backward.

Larkins was less than four feet away from Josie when he pulled the trigger, so the muzzle blast caught her dress on fire. Colter put out the fire and then turned to help Larkins. But Larkins managed to stagger to his feet on his own and went outside. He showed no interest in Josie's condition.

Josie was bleeding heavily from the wound in her back. Colter went out and found Dr. L.T. Mitchell and Dr. Franklin LaRue. When they returned, Larkins was gone and Josie was dying. The bullet had passed through her right kidney, perforated her stomach, and lodged in her abdominal wall. The doctors were certain she would not survive, and her death would be slow and painful.

The doctors contacted Bingham County Sheriff John Boyes and Constable Dan Clyne. They organized a posse and later that morning found Larkins four miles north of Idaho Falls, following the Snake River. He was cold and bloody from a large wound in his neck. The officers returned him to Idaho Falls where he was treated by Dr. Mitchell and then locked in the Idaho Falls jail.

For the next two weeks, Larkins would stay in legal limbo. He was not charged with any crime; officials were waiting for Josie to die before they proceeded. He did appear before Justice of the Peace C. B. Wheeler and waived his right to a preliminary hearing. Wheeler then set his bail at $2500 dollars and ordered him to the county jail in Blackfoot. Finally, Josie died on January 7, 1896. A coroner's inquest concluded that her death was caused by a gunshot fired by Sid Larkins.

The Bingham County court system seemed remiss in its dealing with Larkins. No formal murder charges were brought against him until March 16, 1896, at his arraignment in front of Judge D. W. Standrod in the Fifth District Court of Bingham County. The next day he entered a plea of not guilty.

Larkins had a difficult time finding an attorney. At his arraignment he was represented by J. Edward Smith, but it is unclear whether Smith was hired or appointed by the court. Concerned that his brother would not get an adequate defense, William Larkins contacted James Hawley, a prominent Boise attorney. Hawley, who had been working a trial in Cassia County, did not reach Blackfoot until the morning of March 19, the opening day of the trial. Both Smith and Hawley were woefully unprepared. The prosecution, led by attorney Alfred Budge, had turned nothing over to the defense, and Larkins was of no help because he could not remember anything before or after the murder. Although Smith had requested a continuance, it was not even considered, as the judge was to be in Bannock County on March 23 to start that court term. It seems Larkins' trial was just a formality, an expedient attempt to say justice had been served.

Trying to buy time, Hawley and Smith made a motion to quash the information filed against Larkins, based on the lack of a preliminary hearing. The motion was overruled, and the trial began.

The prosecution had eyewitness testimony from Colter and Nellie. They had the murder weapon; they had witnesses who testified to all of Larkins' threats against Josie. It was a clear-cut case of premeditated murder. The fact that Larkins may have been drunk when he committed the crime did not matter.

There was no denying that Larkins shot Josie, so Smith and Hawley had only one defense: insanity. They brought in witness after witness who claimed that in the weeks prior to the murder, Larkins behaved like a crazy man. They discussed his excessive drinking and how it intensified his erratic behavior. They put his father on the stand to describe the insanity of his wife and the similar qualities he saw in his son. They brought in a doctor who discussed that both heredity and excessive alcohol use over time could cause insanity. Finally, they put Larkins on the stand. He could not remember the last time he had seen Josie, but could say there had been "no trouble" between them. He added that when he was drinking, "I am not competent to do anything."

The jury received its instructions at 6 p.m. March 21, returning in three hours with a guilty verdict. Judge Standrod called for a short recess to consider the punishment. It didn't take him long. At 11 p.m. he sentenced Larkins to hang and set the execution for May 15. Larkins was to spend the rest of his days in the Blackfoot County Jail.

Smith and Hawley wasted no time in filing a motion for a new trial. By the first week of May they had collected new witnesses who would testify to Larkins' insanity. They would argue that they did not have enough time to prepare a proper defense. Judge Standrod agreed to hear the motion, granted a stay of execution, and set a hearing date of May 25. The lawyers also filed an appeal of the judgment to the Idaho Supreme Court. Then when Judge Standrod denied the motion for a new trial, they appealed this decision too.

It took eight months for the supreme court to hear the appeal. They found no errors of law, no prejudice against Larkins. In the court's opinion, "The evidence showed conclusively that the defendant committed the homicide." The court also felt that "at the time of the homicide the defendant was capable of distinguishing between right and wrong."

With the decision, Judge Standrod reset the execution date to April 29, 1897. Larkins' last hope was the Idaho State Board of Pardons, but it refused to take action. Time had run out.

Throughout his incarceration, Larkins was a model prisoner. His jailers were sympathetic, and they went out of their way to make his last days comfortable. He had open visitation and regularly received both men and women. He gave several newspaper interviews in which he warned young men to "flee from whiskey drinking, bad women, game, and deceit. These all lead along the same road to ruin." He admitted he killed Josie, but until the end blamed it on the booze. "But for the craze of strong drink, I should never have killed Josie," he said. "I would not be hanged."

On the morning of the execution, Larkins walked to the gallows unassisted. As he stood in front of a crowd of forty spectators, he addressed them with a newfound faith: "My friends, a savior died on the cross for you and me. Accept him as your savior. I believe he is mine. I bid you all a long farewell." With that, the trap was sprung and eight minutes later, Larkins was dead.

While in jail, Larkins was questioned extensively about the Callahan murder. He denied any involvement, and while he could not say for certain, he believed Josie was also not involved. But in May of 1895, a dying Coyote Dick Edwards gave a full confession, claiming that he had shot Callahan, but it was an accident, the result of a robbery gone bad. While he never implicated Josie, he admitted he and an accomplice were waiting for Josie and Callahan to drive by a prearranged spot. After the shooting, Josie drove Edwards back to Salt Lake, dropped him off in town, and then proceeded to notify the police. Her refusal to tell the police entirely what happened can only be indicative of her guilt.

William H. H. Bond

Boise, October 5, 1904
Boise, August 10, 1906

Sitting in his jail cell, William Henry Hicks Bond must have regretted the day he met Jennie Daly. The young beauty with auburn hair and hazel eyes had lured him in, and she played him, like she played others, feigning vulnerability and innocence. Her husband was dead, and Bond, the man found guilty of his murder, would soon face the gallows. She stood at the center of it all, blood on her apron and a beguiling smile on her face.

Also known as Fred Bond, William Bond was an Englishman, born in Cornwall, England in 1879. He claimed he was born in a workhouse and came to the United States in 1900 to find prosperity. How he came to Idaho is unknown, but he probably arrived in 1903 to work in the mines at Delamar, near Silver City. He was joined there by a brother and the two traveled to Mackay where he continued to mine. In early 1904, Bond arrived in Boise and took a room at a boarding house owned by Katie Richards. It is not clear how he supported himself, although one report had him working at the sanitarium, where he was described as in "destitute condition."

If Bond was destitute, he hid it well. He was a slight but handsome young man at 5'1" with dark hair and eyes and a trimmed mustache. Described as "dapper," he appealed to the ladies as both well mannered and well dressed. He caught the eye of Jennie Daly, who with her husband Charles, moved into Richards' boarding house in July 1904.

The Dalys were an odd couple. From Missouri, Charles Daly was in his fifties, bald and overweight. Jennie, still in her teens, was petite and striking. Her looks, however, belied her harsh upbringing and ulterior motives. Born in Illinois or Missouri—she claimed both—she was forced by her mother to beg in the streets until eventually, she became a ward of the state and was sent to reform school. At some point she moved in with relatives in St. Louis. There she was employed by Daly as a housekeeper. After just three days in his home, they married. Only fifteen, she later admitted she married him to escape a miserable life of poverty.

Life with Daly, however, was "considerable trouble," according to Jennie. While at times she admitted he was a good provider, other times she had to beg for every dollar. She claimed he was abusive from the start, treating her like a prisoner and striking her at will. After the birth of their daughter, Charlotte, the cruelty intensified. Jennie claimed she was terrified of Daly and feared for her life. On numerous occasions, he choked her, whipped her with a belt, and threatened to kill her.

The family moved to Boise where Daly had lined up employment with the Boise Gas Company. Their stay at the boarding house was to be temporary until Daly found them a place of their own. For Jennie, the move was an opportunity to start over, and she wasted little time in getting to know her neighbors. Bond was more than happy to oblige.

From the very beginning, the relationship between Bond and the Dalys was peculiar. While Bond befriended the couple and offered to show them around Boise, Charles was more interested in having someone escort Jennie. Jennie was demanding of his time; she wanted to go out every evening to the park or a show. Daly had neither the desire nor the stamina to keep up with his young wife. Bond seemed to be his way out, so he encouraged their friendship. On occasion, he would even pay Bond to entertain his wife, one time giving him ten dollars to take her to a carnival.

Jennie Daly

The arrangement suited them, and when Daly was ready to move his family to a home on 414 N. Third Street, he asked Bond to join him. At first Bond refused, but after Daly offered him a job at the gas company in return for living with the family, Bond accepted. As part of the arrangement, Bond paid a dollar a week for his room, but he did not pay for his meals. In a bizarre twist, Bond and Daly shared a bedroom, while Jennie and the baby slept in the other.

Through the rest of the summer of 1904, the relationship between Bond and Jennie strengthened until it was obvious the two were much more than friends. They were often seen arm in arm, pushing the baby in her stroller. They frequented city parks, the circus, and the theatre. Almost every evening, Bond, Jennie and the baby went out to Joy's Ice Cream Place for treats. If Bond worked for the gas company, it must have been very limited, for he spent most of his time with Jennie and the baby. Only when Daly was home did Bond withdraw from the family, taking Jennie's company only at Daly's request.

Whether Daly was blind to what was happening under his own roof, or he just didn't care, is unclear. But in early September, the bizarre relationship finally came apart when Daly's acquaintances

William H. H. Bond

began commenting on Bond's attention to Jenny. One went so far as to tell Daly that Bond and Jennie made a handsome couple. Daly, perhaps fearing that Jennie was about to leave him, ordered Bond out of the house. Bond at first refused to go, claiming he was in love with Jenny and would "sleep out on the front yard" before he would leave her. But knowing Daly's propensity for violence, Jenny convinced Bond it would be better if he left. He spent the next two weeks living in a tent in Riverside Park.

What transpired in the Daly household during those two weeks is unknown, but at some point, Daly had a change of heart. When Bond returned to pick up his belongings, Daly let him stay. While Jennie told several different versions of why he changed his mind, her most consistent reason was Daly felt bad for putting Bond on the street. By the end of September, Bond was back in the Daly household, sharing a room with Daly and accompanying his wife at his request. The decision would ultimately lead to his death.

No one will ever know who instigated Daly's murder or who actually pulled the trigger. We do know that on the afternoon of Wednesday, October 5, Jennie and Bond, walked downtown, with the baby. They went to the grocery store, drugstore, and ice cream parlor. Their last stop was Loree's Hardware Store. While Bond waited outside with the baby, Jennie approached James Loree and asked to rent a revolver. He showed her a "girl gun" and gave her instructions on how to hold it, placing it in her hand. She asked him to load the gun for her and he did. After paying 70 cents for two days' rental and a partial box of cartridges, she left. The gun would be used that night to kill Daly.

Early the next morning, Bond found Boise police officer John H. Brough and told him "a woman has killed her husband at 414 N. Third Street." Bond led Brough and another officer to the house where they found Daly's blood-covered body in the living room. They also found Jennie Daly and the baby. They did a quick examination of the scene and arrested Jennie on the spot. At that point, Bond tried to leave, but he was arrested also. The police hauled Jennie, Bond, and the baby to jail.

On the way to the police station, at the police station, and on the way to the coroner's inquest, Jennie confessed to the crime. According to Elias Marseters, a deputy sheriff who accompanied Jennie to the inquest, she told him, "I guess I'm in for it. I don't know which would have been the worst, for me to have killed him or him to kill me." At the police station, Jennie produced Daly's life insurance policy and asked Sheriff J. D. Agnew how she could collect on the $250 policy. She also stated directly to Agnew, "I shot my husband."

The coroner's inquest convened at 11 a.m. on October 6. A calm, confident Jennie was called as the first witness, and she testified she had killed her husband. She stated that Daly had come home late on October 5, smelling of whisky. She was feeding the baby, and he began to berate her for being up so late. They argued, and Daly rushed her yelling, "I will kill you." Jennie then grabbed the gun and shot Daly several times; according to her testimony "he groaned for quite awhile," but she thought he was dead and went to bed.

Incredibly, about three hours later, Daly struggled to his feet and once again threatened Jennie. This time, she shot him at close range through the heart, and then for good measure, hit him over the head with a hatchet she had retrieved from the outhouse. Certain he was now dead, she went back to bed with the baby.

Bond was the next witness and confirmed Jennie's story. He was in his bedroom when he first heard Daly scolding her. When he heard the first shot, he rushed to the living room but Jennie barred his way, revolver in hand. Frightened, he returned to his room where he wrote a letter to a brother. After this he went back to bed. He was awakened by a gunshot around 3 a.m. Again, he got up to check, and Jennie let him into the parlor, where he saw the body of Daly lying on the floor. When Bond was asked why he did not interfere, he claimed Jennie threatened him. He also stated, "Mrs. Daly wanted some rest," which is why he did not report the crime until morning.

Following Bond's statement, a series of witnesses testified to what they saw at the Daly house the morning after the murder. Dr. George Collister, who performed the autopsy, explained that Daly had been shot four times, including once at close range in the diaphragm. He also described four head wounds, all of which were caused by a blunt instrument. He believed they could have been caused by a hatchet, but added that none of those wounds were fatal, describing them as having been delivered by "light blows." Collister was followed by James Loree who identified Jennie as a woman to whom he had rented a revolver the previous day.

The inquest adjourned in the late afternoon and resumed that evening. What transpired during the recess can only be described as witness tampering. During the break, Jennie was approached by an acquaintance named Hooper. He told Jennie "that she was getting herself into trouble," and the inquest was her "last chance" to tell her story. But even more bizarre was the behavior of Ada County Assistant Prosecuting Attorney Frank Kinyon, who was in charge of the inquest. While he later denied urging Jennie to lie, he admitted turning her against Bond. Jennie would later testify at Bond's trial that these two men influenced her to change her story.

Change it she did. When the inquest resumed, a now tearful, hesitant Jennie was recalled to the stand where she recanted her confession. Sobbing, she claimed that she and Bond had plotted the murder together, but in the end, Bond carried it out on his own. When Bond was recalled to the stand, he stuck to his original story, stating he was but an innocent bystander to a horrible domestic dispute. No one listened. When he was through, the jury decided there was enough evidence to send both Bond and Jennie to the district court and decreed the following:

> *We the jury find that the deceased came to his death by means of being foully murdered by gunshot wounds and hatchet strokes by the hand of Fred Bond, Mrs. Daly being accessory to the crime through the undue influence of Fred Bond.*

Justice of the Peace William Dunbar charged both with first degree murder and set the next day for Bond's preliminary hearing. He scheduled

Jennie's hearing for the following week. Then Bond and Jennie were hauled back to the Ada County Jail. Charlotte was taken to the home of Frank Kinyon.

At Bond's hearing, only two witnesses were called—Officer Brough and Jennie. Jennie was on the stand for five hours, a figure of composure and self control who elaborated on the events leading up to the shooting, Bond's power over her, and the cover up. She was led adeptly by Kinyon, whose questions led to answers that implicated Bond as the mastermind and sole instigator of the murder. When Bond's attorney Silas Moody tried to cross-examine Jennie, he was interrupted by both Kinyon and John J. Blake, Jennie's lawyer, who continuously advised her not to answer questions that would incriminate her. Moody argued with the judge that Jennie be ordered to answer the questions, but he was overruled. At the conclusion of the hearing, Judge William Dunbar found sufficient evidence to hold Bond for the murder of Daly and bound him over to the district court.

While the judge handed down his decision, Jennie was talking and laughing with Kinyon, sharing stories about little Charlotte. She seemed indifferent to the proceedings and her situation, complaining only to her jailers that Bond would neither look at her nor speak to her anymore.

On October 14, Jennie faced her own preliminary hearing, where she listened to witnesses discuss her confession and behavior following her arrest. While she smiled and waved to the crowd as she entered the courtroom, she was not smiling when she left, as Judge Dunbar also bound her over to the district court to stand trial for her husband's murder.

Both Bond and Daly appeared together before Judge George Stewart of Idaho's Third District Court on January 26, 1905. At that time, the prosecutor Charles Koelsch requested the two be tried separately, and Stewart granted his motion.

Kirtland Perky, a fiery attorney, joined Moody to defend Bond. At Bond's arraignment, Perky asked that the information provided by Jennie Daly be set aside. That motion was denied, and Bond then entered a plea of not guilty. His trial was set for February 6.

Over 200 women and half as many men crowded the courtroom at the start of Bond's trial. Koelsch set the stage in his opening statement, blaming the murder on Bond and making Jennie out to be an infatuated, easily-influenced young woman who, when it counted, refused to kill her husband. During the first two days of testimony, he entered into evidence the revolver, the hatchet, Bond's bloody shoes, and a sealed envelope. He examined the coroner, the undertaker, the police photographer, the two police officers who were the first on the crime scene, several other county officials who investigated the case, and Frank Kinyon, the prosecutor who had turned Jennie against Bond.

Perky attacked the state's witnesses immediately. He focused on two areas: the chain of evidence and Jennie's honesty. Perky got every police official to admit that the Daly home was never secured. During the two days following the murder, people were allowed to come and go in the residence, including Jennie Daly. Perky was especially ruthless with Kinyon. Under cross-examination, he made Kinyon admit that he did not secure Jennie's bloody apron as evidence, even though he had seen it hanging in the kitchen, and Jennie had confessed to wearing it the night of the murder. He also admitted that he allowed Jennie to return to the house to gather clothes and other items, including some of Bond's, all unsupervised. In a heated exchange, Kinyon acknowledged telling Jennie the contents of Bond's testimony at the inquest in hopes of turning her against Bond.

The state's main witness, Jennie, took the stand on the third day. She was dressed in black, and the *Idaho Daily Statesman* described her as a "school girl who had just recovered from an illness." Prosecutor Koelsch guided her through her testimony as she calmly recounted the murder of her husband.

According to Jennie, Daly often beat her, and she was afraid for her life. The night before his murder, Daly had threatened to whip her with his belt, and only the intervention of Bond prevented it. The next morning, Bond advised Jennie to get a gun for protection, and she did, renting the revolver at the hardware store. When she reached home, she hid the gun in Bond's trunk.

Daly came home for dinner that evening around 7 p.m. and then went out again. After he left, Bond advised Jennie to get the gun, in the event she might need it when Daly returned. Jennie testified she did what she was told, getting the gun and placing it in her apron pocket.

When Daly arrived home around midnight, Jennie was in the kitchen feeding the baby. She joined her husband in the living room, where he removed his shoes and top shirt. Jennie and Daly then began arguing about offensive comments he had been making about Jennie at work. Daly denied them, blamed Bond for their marital problems, and when Bond appeared in the living room, threatened to break his neck. Daly ordered Bond out of the house, but Bond refused to leave, instead offering Daly a dollar to cover his rent for the next three days.

Daly then asked Jennie if she loved Bond. She replied that she did. He then asked Bond if he loved Jennie. When Bond said that he did, Daly replied, "I guess my wife has no more use for me then." At that point, Jennie said both she and Bond went back to the kitchen, where Bond wrestled the gun away from her, telling her, "If you ain't going to use it, then I will." Bond went back into the living room with the gun, followed by Jennie who was holding the baby. According to Jennie, she took a seat in the rocking chair and watched as Bond approached her husband and shot him twice. At that point, Jennie ran from the living room into the kitchen. Bond retreated to the kitchen, grabbed the hatchet, and charged back into the living room, where he proceeded to hit Daly with the hatchet and shoot him at least one more time.

With Daly mortally wounded, Bond went to the kitchen where Jennie said she washed the gun and laid it on the table. Jennie testified that Bond instructed her to write a letter to a relative, admitting she had killed her husband. Then Bond concocted the story Jennie was to tell the police the next morning. Bond told her, "you go and give yourself up tomorrow and say you done it, and you will get out of it all right, but if I go and say I done it, I won't get out." With their stories straight, they went to bed.

Perky's cross-examination of Jennie was brutal, attacking her honesty at every turn. Jennie admitted she lied about her age to get married; she lied at the police station; she lied at the inquest. He even caught her in several lies on the witness stand, including one when she first stated that after the murder she lay down to rest, and then later said she had not. When he crossed her up, Jennie became belligerent, refusing to answer the questions or simply stating "I don't remember."

But more damning than the lies was Jennie's acknowledgment that she "would have killed my husband if I knew I wouldn't get in trouble." Also, three days prior to the murder, she confided to the butcher that she would "kill my husband the next time he abused me." Jennie also admitted her testimony was influenced by the men at the inquest and that she would hold back information on the stand if Prosecuting Attorney Koelsch wanted. Finally, Jennie confessed to changing her dress following the shooting and returning to the crime scene twice after her arrest. There she took the bloody apron, a trunk filled with her clothing, and unnamed items out of Bond's trunk, none of which were produced at the trial.

If Perky and Bond were feeling confident after exposing Jennie as an unbelievable, self-serving witness, their hopes were dashed when Sheriff J. D. Agnew took the stand. First Agnew was asked to verify Bond's signature, which he did. He was then asked to examine a letter and envelope, which he also identified as written in Bond's hand. Koelsch then asked to place the letter and envelope into evidence. Perky vehemently objected, but he was overruled. The letter was then read in open court.

> *September 23, 1904*
>
> *Dear Sister and Brothers*
>
> *Just a line or too to let you know how i am or where i am living or dead. It is a long time since i heard from you, which i would be glad to hear from. I am still living got good health and i wish you all the same i hope Susan is still living i hope to meet all of you next spring i am married got a little French girl my family is one girl i don't have to·work hard i am in a office Gas office living in a City where it is always fine weather never no snow here I hope Nettie is not mad with me I want to be friends with her she knows i respects her and always shall I wonder where she married or not tell me Reuben or where she is sparking I hope she have a nice fellow I married the Bell of St. Louis she can sing or dance we do take on to all the theatres that come here I went to Ringling Bros with her and everywhere else I shall be satisfied with her till spring and then it will be goodbye to her She would soon bust up a millionare if she had her way Now if you respect me and write me i will send a picture of me and her and baby I would like Nettie to write me But try one of you to write me I am so anscous to hear from you Give my kind love to Fred and Annie Pedlar Harry you promise me you would write a line or two to me We will have a good time Harry when we meet Reuben and Harry and Nettie try to write a good long letter goodbye remember to the girls from your own loving Brother*
>
> *Fred Bond*
>
> *414 No. Third Street*

After the presentation of the letter, Koelsch rested his case. Perky called witnesses to counter Jennie's testimony, but the damage had been done. Perky rested his case without calling Bond to the stand.

In their closings, prosecuting attorneys Koelsch and H. L. Fisher argued that even if Mrs. Daly's testimony were thrown out, there was still enough evidence to convict Bond. Fisher went so far to say that even if

Bond "did not fire the fatal shots himself, he at least influenced Mrs. Daly to do so," and therefore should not be spared in the least.

Perky's closing focused on Jennie's lies, calling her an "unscrupulous, unreliable woman who had no conception of the sanctity of an oath," who was "liable to swear to anything at any time," especially when her own life was in danger. As for the Bond's letter, Perky dismissed it as the writings of a "garrulous" young man, attempting to put himself in a favorable light to his family. Perky told the jury that the physical evidence did not connect Bond to the crime in any way.

In his instructions to the jury, Judge Stewart told them that even if Bond did not fire the fatal shots, he was still guilty if he encouraged or assisted another person to do so. He also told them they had four choices in their verdict: first degree murder, second degree murder, manslaughter, or not guilty.

The jury deliberated for three hours, and then sent the foreman to ask the judge about penalties for each verdict. Stewart informed him that penalties were set by the court, and that the jury should concern itself solely on the guilt or innocence of the defendant. A half an hour later, the jury returned with verdict of guilty in the first degree.

Bond stood before Judge Stewart on February 18 to hear his sentence. Stewart read the charges and the jury's verdict, and then sentenced Bond to death. His execution was scheduled for April 14, 1905. He was then taken to the Idaho State Penitentiary to await his fate while his attorneys immediately appealed the verdict and asked for a new trial.

The trial for Jennie Daly began on February 21. It drew less attention than Bond's but contained much of the same testimony, put forth without any fanfare by Prosecutor Koelsch. In Jennie's defense, her attorney John Blake blamed her predicament on her impoverished upbringing where she was taught to be a beggar and never learned the difference between right and wrong. He laid the guilt totally on Bond, calling Jennie a "victim of a designing man." To add to the drama, Jennie's daughter was brought into the courtroom during Blake's closing statement. According to the *Idaho Daily Statesman*, young Charlotte dried her mother's tears as Blake proclaimed her innocence.

Jennie's jury deliberated for ten hours before returning a verdict of manslaughter. Upon hearing the verdict, Judge Stewart was clearly annoyed and admonished the jury.

"I cannot help but question your process of reasoning," Stewart told the jurors. "How you concluded that Mrs. Daly killed her husband without premeditation, malice, or revenge is beyond me." He went on to tell the jurors that it was the job of both the court and the jurors "to see that laws were enforced impartially," but in this case "this verdict was of the jury," and he wanted no part of it.

When it came time for sentencing, Judge Stewart made his dissatisfaction clear as he sentenced Jennie to ten years in prison, the maximum allowed for the crime. Jennie received the sentence with a smile, and reporters noted that she appeared delighted in the judgment. "Making allowance for my good behavior, I will only be in prison for six years and three months," she said as they led her from the courtroom. "I will still be a young woman when I get out."

Jennie became the belle of the Idaho State Prison, at times the only woman in the facility. Whether she ever came in contact with Bond is unknown. For his part, Bond kept to himself, waiting and fretting over news of his appeal.

Bond's attorneys appeared before Judge Stewart on February 23 to ask for a new trial. Perhaps still fuming over Jennie's escape from the hangman, Stewart agreed to hear the motion. He set August 1, 1905 as the time to hear arguments. As a result, the supreme court stayed Bond's execution, pending the outcome of the hearing.

At the hearing, Bond's attorneys listed sixty-three reasons for a new trial. Many of their complaints centered on Jennie Daly, whose tainted testimony and lies were all that tied Bond to the crime. Stewart listened, but in the end, refused to grant the motion for a new trial.

Undeterred, they appealed to the Idaho Supreme Court. On June 19, 1906, Moody stood before the justices to argue there was no corroborating evidence to support Jennie's claims. Thus, there was no evidence to convict Bond. He also questioned the admissibility of the letter Bond wrote to his family. In the end, the court was not convinced and upheld the verdict and the judgment. On June 30, Judge Stewart reaffirmed his original sentence. He rescheduled the execution for August 10, 1906.

Perky and Moody had little hope, but they continued their efforts to save Bond. They went so far as to contact Jennie, in hopes they could convince her to admit she had committed perjury at Bond's trial. But Jennie remained faithful to herself and refused to meet with the lawyers. When that failed, they asked Governor Gooding to grant Bond a reprieve. Gooding,

Judge George Stewart

however, would not interfere, and Bond's fate was sealed.

In his final hours, Bond wrote a letter to a brother, met with his spiritual advisor Dr. D. L. Roach, read his Bible, and ate his last meal—ham, fried eggs, toast, potatoes, sliced tomatoes, pie, and coffee. Then, in the early morning of August 10, Warden E. L. Whitney went to his cell and read the death warrant. The two men shook hands, and then Whitney led him to the scaffold.

A small crowd gathered in the prison yard to bear witness. Among them were Charles Koelsch and Frank Kinyon, who were instrumental in condemning Bond to his fate. As Bond stood on the trap door, Warden Whitney asked him if he had anything to say.

"I am guilty of a whole lot, but not all," Bond said. "God bless you all. May the Lord have mercy upon my soul."

With that, Warden Whitney sprang the trap, and William Henry Hicks Bond fell to his death. He was buried in the prison cemetery.

Jennie Daly walked out of the Idaho State Prison on May 25, 1911. Just as she had predicted, she served just six years and three months of her sentence. Upon her release, she moved in with some friends on Thatcher Street. Whether she reunited with her daughter is unknown.

Fred Seward

Moscow, October 19, 1908
Boise, May 7, 1909

In 1908 moral fervor beat wildly in the hearts of Moscow, Idaho civic leaders. They passed ordinances restricting the sale of alcohol in the city limits. With their "Bawdy House Ordinance," they cracked down on local prostitutes by raising fines and giving jail sentences to men and women involved in the sale of sex. In July, an arsonist destroyed the Moscow Brewery, and in August, city officials refused to renew the licenses of the three surviving saloons, prompting the local newspaper to declare the town "completely dry." Moscow was so clean that by 1909, a college investigator declared Moscow a moral town, fit for the sons and daughters of Idaho's noble citizens. So enthusiastic was Mr. Badly, the investigator, he declared, "in all my life I have never seen any city where the moral conditions were better than those in Moscow." But it wasn't always so. In fact, just one year before Badly made his flattering remarks, Moscow was the scene of a sensational murder, when star-crossed lover Fred Seward killed his prostitute girlfriend Clara O'Neill.

That Seward committed the crime was never in question as he freely admitted his guilt. But the moral outrage of Moscow's citizen, along with a colorful parade of dubious prosecution witnesses, led Seward to the gallows.

Fred Seward was born January 11, 1881, near Palouse, Washington, the oldest son of John and Della Seward. Hindered by learning problems and family poverty, he had little schooling and spent his early years working on the family farm. When he was thirteen, he went to work on his uncle's farm, and from there traveled around northeastern Washington taking odd jobs. He spent time in Republic, Kettle Falls, and Spokane. It was during these travels, in 1902, that he married Iva Cook, aged sixteen. Shortly after, they had a son.

What became of the Seward's wife and child is unknown. Seward revealed little information about this relationship, and even that was contradictory. During his trial, he testified he had been trying to save money for a divorce and later he told Idaho prison officials he was married and had one child. Then, just hours before his execution, he confided to the prison chaplain that he was divorced and had a five-year-old son. What is clear is that when Seward returned to Palouse in the fall of 1907, he was alone and led the life of a single man.

Palouse was no booming metropolis, but it still offered its citizens activities to meet their various vices. Seward hired on as barkeeper at a saloon in Palouse, and within a short time found himself captivated by a young prostitute who called herself Grace Wilson.

Wilson, whose real name was Clara Reece, arrived in Palouse in 1907. Census records show that in 1900 she was 16 and lived with her father and several brothers and sisters in Wallace, Idaho, where her father worked in the mines. In Wallace Clara met William O'Neill, a watchmaker. They were married and in 1906, Clara gave birth to Pearl O'Neill. Pearl was sickly, her exact illness unknown, but shortly after her birth, Clara fled her husband and Wallace. She took Pearl to Spokane and left her in the care of an aunt. She then moved to Palouse where she went to work in a brothel operated by Grace Fleming.

Fleming was a well-known madame in the area, operating houses in Palouse City, Moscow, and possibly Pullman. Under the guise of offering assistance, she sought young women down on their luck and alone. Before long, Clara was one of Fleming's girls and attracting the attention of a variety of clients, among them Fred Seward.

In March of 1908, Seward paid a visit to Fleming's "sporting house" where he was serviced by O'Neill. He would later admit that he fell in love with her almost immediately. Neither her profession nor her marriage deterred him, and within a month the two were living together. Seward encouraged her to divorce her husband and give up prostitution, which she promised to do. He began saving money for his own divorce. He envisioned them settling down in Palouse and raising a family. From his prison cell he would later lament, "I always thought that she intended to marry me and greatly desired that she live a decent life as my wife."

Grace Fleming, however, painted quite a different picture. According to Fleming, Seward's interest in O'Neill was all business. Fleming would be a damning witness at Seward's trial, claiming that he wanted Clara to "rustle" for him so he could live off her earnings.

In late spring of 1908, Fleming closed her establishment in Palouse and moved back to Moscow. There she ran her business out of a house known simply as "222" near present day A or Almon Streets. On June 16 she was arrested for violating the city's prostitution laws, a move the local newspaper

Fred Seward

reported as an attempt to measure public sentiment toward the new ordinances. The case seemed to matter little to Fleming; between April of 1894 and June 1908 she had been arrested nineteen times for prostitution-related crimes. Each time she had paid a fine and went on her way. She expected this time to be no different. As soon as she was released, Fleming was back in business.

When Fleming left Palouse, it is not clear if O'Neill continued to work as a prostitute. What is clear is that the relationship between Seward and O'Neill soured. Seward became increasingly miserable, asking her to leave the community because he "could not work if she was there," indicative of her continued work as a prostitute. In midsummer, O'Neill did move to Spokane, and Seward, taking the advice of his friends, convinced himself to end the relationship.

In September, O'Neill called Seward and invited him to Spokane. He was wary of the offer, but eventually accepted, and went to the city with the sole intent of "quitting her," as he would later tell police. Clara did not take the news well, swearing vengeance on him and threatening to follow him wherever he went. Seward softened and agreed to stay in the relationship if Clara promised to stay away from Palouse where her occupation was well known. He urged her to move to Boise, Idaho, where he would join her. This she promised to do, and Seward returned home.

To Seward's dismay, Clara showed up in Palouse four days later. He begged her to move to Boise where she could start over, where she could find honest employment, but Clara refused. Instead, she went to Moscow where she returned to work hustling for Grace Fleming. Seward would later blame Fleming for turning Clara against him.

For three days, Seward stewed over the situation. Then on the night of October 16, he traveled to Moscow. He later told police that on his arrival, he spent the night at Fleming's establishment, but not with Clara.

The following day, he checked into the DuMonte Hotel, where Clara joined him. Over the next two days, they would go out, sometimes alone, sometimes in the company of Hattie Caldwell and T. J. Ziegan. Caldwell was a prostitute who worked for Fleming. Ziegan, who may also have used the name Fred Zeigler, was a probable client of both O'Neill and Caldwell.

Over the weekend, Clara and Seward were anything but a happy couple. Seward begged her to leave Moscow, but Clara only laughed at him, telling him she planned to expand her services to Pullman, where she could make a lot of money with the boys at Washington State University. Seward told her that if she did, he "would go back to Palouse and quit her, that she could go her way and I would go my way."

On Sunday night, October 18, the two separated. Clara worked at Fleming's and Seward stayed alone at the DuMonte hotel. The next day around noon, Seward walked down to the house at 222, a gun tucked in his belt. He planned to end the relationship, one way or another.

He found Clara in the kitchen and the two quarreled. Fleming, Caldwell, and another girl were also in the kitchen, hanging on every word, so Seward suggested that he and Clara continue their discussion on the back porch. Once outside, they passed a small storage shed in the alley. As it was cold, Seward pushed open the door to the shed, and the two went inside. They fought. Fifteen minutes later, Clara was dead.

When the police arrived at the scene, they found the body of Clara on the floor of the shed. She had been shot. Near her body lay the gun and Seward, who after shooting Clara, had attempted to kill himself. He had wounds to his left arm and face, and a large gash crossed his throat. Grant Robbins, Latah County deputy sheriff and the first officer on the scene, found the carnage so great he believed both were dead. Then Seward sat up and told him, "I am not dead, but I have fixed the girl."

Seward would tell two versions of what happened. One involved self-defense. In his first statement to the police and at his trial, he claimed Clara attacked him. Angry because he planned to leave her, she used the ruse of straightening his tie to slash his throat with a small penknife. At that point, Seward took out his gun and shot her. Then believing he would die from the profusely bleeding neck wound, he turned the gun on himself to hasten his end.

The signed confession given from his hospital bed stated otherwise. Seward admitted that he killed Clara in a fit of anger and then attempted to kill himself. During the argument in the shed, Seward once and for all told Clara it was over. Enraged, she screamed, "If you do go and leave me after all this, I will kill you." Seward responded with, "By God, I'll beat you to it." Then he shot her.

Seward's first shot hit Clara in the chest at close range. As she crumpled to the floor, Seward grabbed her and shot again. This bullet passed through Clara's torso and into Seward's left arm. He then fired one more shot into her head before turning the gun on himself. He put the gun to his right temple and fired but only managed to shoot out his right eye. Desperate, he took a knife from his pocket and slashed his throat, then fell next to his prostitute lover.

Police rushed Seward to the Inland Hospital. While the wounds to his forehead and eye were ghastly, they were not life threatening. In the days following the shooting, police questioned him extensively, eventually eliciting a signed confession. Upon his release from the hospital, he was confined in the Latah County Jail.

From the beginning of the investigation, Seward's chances of escaping the ultimate punishment were slim. Although the Moscow newspaper, *The Star Mirror*, described him as one "who wore a good countenance" and not a "bad man," county prosecutor William Stillinger saw him differently. Seward had soiled Moscow's reputation, and he planned to make Seward pay. Although Seward's friends and family were hopeful a charge of second degree murder would be made in the case, Stillinger saw the shooting as premeditated and filed first degree murder charges. To convince a jury, he would turn to the testimony of some strange bedfellows, among them Grace Fleming, who would become his star witness.

Seward appeared for his preliminary hearing on November 28 in front of Judge Henry Cummings and was bound over to the district court. On December 7, Seward's case got underway before Judge Edgar C. Steele of Idaho's Second Judicial District. When Seward told the court he was without counsel, Steele appointed Warren Truitt to represent him. Truitt was given only two days to prepare a defense. On December 9, they were back in court where Seward pleaded not guilty to the charge of first-degree murder.

On the afternoon of December 14, with the jury sworn and seated, Stillinger called his first witness, Hattie Caldwell. Hattie's contempt for Seward was so clear that a reporter for the *Moscow Star Mirror* reported her testimony was "ladened with lemon juice." She described how Clara and

Seward had fought throughout the weekend until the two left Fleming's establishment together minutes before the murder. When defense attorney Truitt tried to discredit her testimony, hinting that she worked as a prostitute for Grace Fleming, Hattie claimed her business with Fleming was "sewing."

Caldwell's statements were collaborated by Ziegan and Fleming. Fleming's testimony was especially spiteful. She called Seward a "tin-horn, dinner pail, saloon swamper" who had lived off Clara's earnings. All three claimed that Seward was the one pushing Clara into prostitution, wanting her to hustle for him in Boville, Idaho, and when she refused, Seward shot her.

The prosecution's most damning evidence came from Seward himself—his signed confession taken just two days after the murder. Although Truitt argued it had been coerced and taken under duress, and thus inadmissible, the judge allowed it. With its entry into the public record, the prosecution rested its case.

Truitt had little defense to offer. He called on character witnesses to show that the murder was one of passion, that Seward was not a cold-blooded killer. Seward's employer in Palouse, C.B. Eslick, testified that Seward was a good, hard-working man who got caught up with the wrong group of people. But the fact remained that Seward had pulled the trigger three times, and on the stand he was forced to admit it. Although he claimed that Clara had threatened to kill him, and it was she who had cut his throat under the pretense of straightening his tie, he was ultimately responsible for her death.

The jury made quick work of a verdict. After deliberating less than two hours, they found Seward guilty of first-degree murder. Truitt motioned for an arrest of judgment to give him time to file an appeal of the verdict. He returned to court on December 28, at which time Judge Steele denied his motion and sentenced Seward to die on February 19, 1909.

Seward was transferred to the Idaho State Penitentiary. Prison records indicate he stood 5' 6" and weighed 162 pounds, with light brown curly hair and light brown eyes. He was also described as "quite hairy." He bore the scars of the shooting, with prison officials noting the powder burns around his right temple and his missing right eye.

Truitt indicated he planned to appeal the verdict and ask for a new trial. However, there are no court records indicating any appeal. In fact, by

February, Truitt seems to be no longer involved in the case. Instead, Edwin Snow, a Boise lawyer, had taken up Seward's cause.

In February, Seward's friends and family rallied to his defense. His father, along with several other friends and relatives, traveled to Boise to petition the Idaho Board of Pardons for a commutation of Seward's sentence. This fight was led in part by F.A. Shaw, Chief Clerk of the Idaho State Senate. But with the execution date fast approaching, they needed the help of newly elected Governor James Brady to stay the execution. Brady met with Seward's father and reviewed the court transcript. On February 17, stating that "Good and sufficient reasons have become known to me," Brady granted Seward a reprieve until April 7, the next scheduled meeting of the board of pardons. Lawyer Snow, who the previous day had mailed his appeal for a new trial to the district court in Moscow, telegrammed the clerk of the court: "Mailed you yesterday notice of appeal Fred Seward. Governor this morning postponed execution. Do not file appeal."

Why Snow never filed the appeal is unknown. Perhaps he thought that with the governor's support, Seward's sentence would be commuted. Whatever the reason, after the reprieve was granted, no other court action took place on behalf of Seward. His lawyer did not appeal to the district court, which meant there would be no appeal before the Idaho Supreme Court. Seward and his lawyer, it seemed, put all of their faith in the governor and the pardons board.

It was a bad decision. The fervor of morality that had swept Moscow in 1908 was now alive in the Idaho Capitol. Led by the Republican majority who were encouraged by Governor Brady to "remember the pledge," the legislature approved a measure that would allow county commissioners to decide if their constituents would reside in a "wet or dry" county. In this prelude to prohibition, Idaho lawmakers were determined to protect Idaho's citizens from themselves and the demon rum. For Seward, whose life rested in the hands of three Republicans—Governor Brady, Attorney General Daniel McDougal, and Secretary of State Robert Lansdon—it was not a good omen.

Throughout the month of March, Seward stayed upbeat, writing letters to his family, making friends with his guards. He became acquainted with the prison chaplain, Reverend Charles Chalfant; however, he made it clear he would not need any spiritual advice. He truly believed his sentence would be commuted.

On April 7, the board of pardons met to discuss Seward's request for commutation of his sentence. Board members listened to testimony and then decided an additional hearing would be needed. They would meet April 26 to make a final decision on the matter. They reset Seward's hanging for May 7, 1909, and told prison warden E.L. Whitney to proceed with the execution on that date unless "in the meantime you shall otherwise be ordered by this Board."

Seward was optimistic that this second reprieve would lead to the commutation of his sentence to life in prison. When his second hearing took place, his lawyer presented depositions from former classmates and acquaintances who all claimed Seward was not mentally responsible for his act. Others spoke of his good character, his clean record. All supported a commutation of his sentence to life in prison.

The arguments were for naught. While no transcripts of the hearing remain, minutes indicate the final decision: "After due consideration, the application for commutation was denied."

Warden John Snook broke the news to the condemned man. Seward put on a strong front at first, daring the state officials to "shoot their wad." But his bravado soon turned to dismay when he learned that May 7 would be his last day on Earth. For Snook, the execution was to be his first test as warden. He had replaced a well-respected Whitney on April 19, and all eyes were on him to see if he could manage the job.

While curious reporters, law enforcement officials, and criminal psychologists clamored to examine Seward, Snook protected his prisoner. Seward spent his remaining days in the company of Rev. Chalfant. He granted no interviews but did give a signed statement to the *Idaho Daily Statesman*. In it, he admitted killing Clara but denied it was done with premeditation. He did agree, however, that the state "has a moral, as well as legal right to exact the penalty for my deed."

As the execution date approached, Snook readied the scaffold and tested the trap door; Seward prepared himself for his fate. Meeting with Chalfant, he claimed that he was ready to go and worried that the execution "will be worse for my aged father, mother, sister, and brothers than for me."

On the morning of May 7, Seward told Chalfant he would say nothing on the scaffold. Instead, he asked the reverend to make a statement for him after he was gone. "Tell them," he said, "that while I have made a failure of this life, I have hope for the life to come. God has forgiven me and I have peace."

Shortly after 8 a.m., Warden Snook arrived at Seward's cell to read the death warrant. Then accompanied by Guard Dan Ackley and Deputy Warden D. P. Rich, Snook led Seward out of the building to the gallows. A crowd of about fifty awaited them. As Seward passed, all in the crowd tipped their hats and bowed their heads.

Seward mounted the scaffold unaided and was led to the trap door, where the guards bound his hands and feet. Snook asked him if had any final words, but Seward shook his head. Instead, he turned to Deputy Rich and asked if he was in the proper place, to which Rich nodded affirmatively. Then, as if fearing a prolonged end, Seward looked Rich in the eye and told him, "Make a good job of it." With that Rich adjusted the noose and placed a black cap over Seward's head. At 8:09, Rich nodded to Snook, and Snook, as he had practiced, released the trap. Six minutes later, Seward was dead. He had not cried out; he had been solid to the end.

The gallows, Idaho Statesman, *May 8, 1909*

Rich cut the rope and with the aid of two other prison guards lowered Seward's body and placed it into an awaiting coffin. They loaded it onto a wagon and then led the procession to the prison cemetery. Rev Chalfant said a few prayers over the grave and Seward was settled into his final resting place. The affair was over in less than an hour.

Later, Warden Snook recorded in his accounts book a payment of twenty dollars to Schreiber and Sidenfaden for the purchase of a pine coffin.

After the tragedy, the bawdy houses of Moscow apparently closed their doors. Grace Fleming's charge and anticipated trial for prostitution faded away, the court record left neatly and inexplicably blank. The murder of Clara O'Neill and Seward's execution did what no law could do; it made prostitution a crime of the heart, and with that, the brothels of Moscow turned out their lights and went quiet.

2. For Fortune

HERMAN ST. CLAIR

VANWYCK, OCTOBER 21, 1897
IDAHO CITY, JUNE 24, 1898

"I hope to God there are no damned dogs or chickens where I am going."

Whether Herman St. Clair's dying wish came true is uncertain. What we do know is his life, along with his colorful stories, came to end on the gallows of Idaho City on June 24, 1898.

To trace the life of St. Clair is to follow the web of a spider. The tales he told of his early days—his life as an Indian scout for the army, his adventures as a sailor on the USS Hartford during the battle of New Orleans, his foray into overseas travel—are all questionable and, at this time, unfounded. He painted a life of intrigue and danger, claiming responsibility for crimes he didn't commit while firmly denying those he apparently did. In the end, all we know for sure is that in the fall of 1897, he committed murder near Van Wyck and paid the ultimate price for his crime.

St. Clair told Idaho officials he was born in 1850, but California prison records put the year closer to 1860. He claimed two areas of origin, Oklahoma and Texas. His surname of St. Clair is doubtful as he hinted it was an alias, one of many he used. We do know he showed up in Idaho in 1879 where he hired on as an Indian scout for the 1st Cavalry under Captain Reuben Bernard. While no official record of his military service exists, an eyewitness does have him in the Central Idaho mountains searching for Sheepeater Indians. The Sheepeaters, also known as the Mountain Shoshoni, were accused of several attacks on miners in the Salmon River Mountains, specifically on Loon Creek and the South Fork of the Salmon River. Captain Bernard and his cavalry were dispatched to find the instigators, and they engaged the Sheepeaters in several small skirmishes. St. Clair claimed to have been injured in the ambush that killed Private Harry Eagan (Egan) whose grave lies on Soldier Bar on Big Creek. However, Orlando Robbins, chief of the scouts, remembered that when the fighting began, St. Clair deserted, stealing his military-issue horse. Robbins and St. Clair would meet twenty years later in Idaho City, where Robbins served as chief of police.

St. Clair drifted into the Wood River area
there he traveled to California where he imm...
trouble. From 1883 to 1894 he spent time in
prisons for perjury, robbery, and grand larcen...
aliases: Eugene St. Clair, Homer Woolsey, ar...
release, he traveled north, spending time in S...
camps in British Columbia. He was in Washington ...
Decker. The two formed a partnership, according to St. Clair, and mad...
plans to travel to Mexico together.

How they ended up in the town of Van Wyck, Idaho, which was
located approximately one mile west of present-day Cascade, is unknown.
Although one of the largest communities of Long Valley in the late 1890s
with general stores, saloons, and hotels, it was not easily accessed. A part
of Boise County, travelers reached Van Wyck from the south on the Ola
Road while those from the north followed the Packer John Trail. Perhaps
Van Wyck's isolation gave St. Clair confidence that he could commit the
perfect murder.

On October 19, 1897, Decker and St. Clair left the gold camp of
Warren north of McCall and traveled south along the Warren Wagon Road.
Driving a light spring wagon pulled by two bay horses, their contrasting
appearances made people take notice. Decker was "heavy and low," about
5'8", 190 pounds, with a dark complexion and dark hair. St. Clair was tall
with a sturdy, athletic build. He was unforgettable with his bright red hair
and thick red mustache.

The two stopped for the night approximately twelve miles north
of McCall, along the North Fork of the Payette River. Camped nearby
was A. L. Rinearson, who had spent the day fishing. St. Clair introduced
himself and Decker and told Rinearson they were heading to Mexico. As
Decker tended to the horses, St. Clair bent Rinearson's ear with stories of
his exploits in British Columbia.

The next day, the pair reached McCall where they stayed at
the establishment of Anneas "Jewsharp Jack" Wyatt, an early McCall
entrepreneur who had the first party boat on Payette Lake. Wyatt would
later recall that while St. Clair did most of the talking, Decker was in
charge of the purse strings. He bought coffee, bread, and hay, paying his
bill in silver coins taken from a small, black clasp purse. Decker also sought
information concerning the road to Boise.

*St. Clair's mug shot
from San Quentin*

Decker and St. Clair arrived in Van Wyck on the afternoon of October 21 and stopped at the general store owned by Henry Cross. Decker bought supplies and found a place to stay—the vacant cabin of Jerry Lester, two miles southeast of Van Wyck. As they headed to the cabin, they visited the farm of Levi Kimball. St. Clair remained in the wagon while Decker negotiated for some hay, timothy mixed with pigweed. He paid in silver taken from the black clasp purse and tied the hay in a bundle using a short rope with a loop in one end. They left Kimball and continued to the cabin. St. Clair would later recall that Decker fed and tethered the horses then took some of the hay inside where he made a bed.

The next morning St. Clair hitched the horses to the wagon and traveled alone back to Van Wyck. He passed only one person before he arrived around 8 a.m. He put the team in Cross's barn and proceeded to Groom's Saloon where he offered to buy everyone a drink. When two men, one of them Cross, refused, St. Clair picked up a shotgun and pointed it at Cross, claiming, "This is the way we make them drink in Texas." Then, realizing he was drawing attention to himself, he apologized.

Cross was immediately suspicious of St. Clair. He quizzed the boisterous redhead about the whereabouts of his partner. St. Clair claimed he had sent Decker on to Boise with a freight team the previous evening, but Cross knew the most recent freight team was on its way to Warren, not Boise. St. Clair also began throwing money around, taking it from a small, black clasp purse. He bought candy and chewing gum for little children and drinks for everyone at the saloon. When St. Clair pulled out his .38 Smith and Wesson and asked if anyone was interested in a trade, Cross was sure something bad had happened to Decker. He was even more convinced when he learned the gun was missing four rounds, two of them recently fired.

Another person who became suspicious of St. Clair was Joseph J. Robbins. Robbins wandered into Groom's Saloon around 5 p.m. and found St. Clair sitting at the bar drinking whiskey. They struck up a conversation and before long St. Clair had a new best friend. Robbins, however, was not so sure. "I made him for a liar, right off," Robbins would later testify. "He (St. Clair) was from British Columbia and every other place I ever spoke of." St. Clair told Robbins he was in Van Wyck to do some "telegraphing." He was in the process of buying mines for an English and American Company, and he was gathering provisions for workers he left at a mine near Florence. Still the free-flowing whisky made Robbins put down his guard, and at evening's end, he invited St. Clair to spend the night at his ranch.

The following day St. Clair retrieved his wagon from town and returned to Robbins' home. He removed a bundle of clothes and gave it to Robbins, claiming he had more at his sister's home in Boise. He also offered Robbins the spring wagon, if he would accompany him to Boise where he was going to pick up his other, "better" wagon. For Robbins' hospitality, St. Clair showered his family with money. In return, Robbins loaned St. Clair an overcoat and a shotgun. When the conversation turned to St Clair's pistol, he claimed a half-breed woman had discarded it after killing a man. While that may bother some, St. Clair claimed, "it made no difference."

At the same time St. Clair was dealing with Robbins, he was also doing some behind the scene negotiations with others, looking for someone to accompany him to Mexico. He offered Charles Stockum forty dollars a month to accompany him, promising him a "good time." When Stockum questioned St. Clair's honesty in dealing with Robbins—he had apparently made him a business proposition too—St. Clair told him, "To hell with Robbins and other people. You pay no attention to what I tell them. I am liable to tell them anything. You see this overcoat and gun I borrowed from Robbins? They are mine now. I ain't coming back."

While St. Clair was making plans to leave Van Wyck, Cross gathered William McCall and Tom Worthington to discuss his suspicions. On the morning of October 24, the three rode to the Lester cabin in search of John Decker. They found fresh hay, both in and around the cabin, and wagon tracks that led across the road and into the woods. They followed the tracks to the bottom of a hill and there found a body, wrapped in a bloodstained

Main Street, Van Wyck in the 1890s

blanket, secured by a short rope with a loop in one end. Another rope, apparently used to drag the body to the spot, was wrapped around its neck.

Upon the discovery, the three men returned to Van Wyck, Cross and McCall cutting through the woods in search of evidence, Worthington following the road. At the time, Van Wyck had no law enforcement officials, so they took it upon themselves to arrest St. Clair. Once in Van Wyck, they gathered a group of approximately twenty men and sought him out. They arrested him and confiscated his pistol, a watch, and a small, black clasp purse, which contained $120. Then they took him to the spot where they had found the body. Worthington removed the blanket from the face of the dead man, and St. Clair identified him as John Decker. Cross and McCall loaded the body onto a wagon and returned to Van Wyck while Worthington handled St. Clair. As they passed through the woods heading back to the road, Worthington commented on the nice timber in the area. St. Clair's response was all bravado: "You can hang me, you sons of bitches," he said. "I am a bad man from Texas and I saw ropes before I saw any of you."

Worthington took first watch over St. Clair. Others gathered evidence, including the items left with Joseph Robbins. These included bloodstained clothes and a black, bell-crowned hat. The ropes and blanket from the murder scene were also collected. All items were turned over to Dr. James T. Beers, a pharmacist from Crawford, who arrived in Van Wyck on October 26 to conduct a coroner's inquest.

St. Clair remained in the custody of the Van Wyck citizens as he awaited the results of the inquest. They kept him well-fed and well-supplied with liquor. While he never admitted killing Decker, he made several statements implicating two others, a man and a woman. During his first night in custody after a few drinks loosened his tongue, he told Worthington, "I plead guilty to knowing who killed John Decker: there was a man and a woman interested besides myself." But no matter how much whisky Worthington gave him, St. Clair would not give up their names.

The inquest took three days. Dr. Beers examined Decker's body and found two gunshot wounds on the left side of his head, one at the temple. Either would have been fatal. Both were marked by powder burns, leaving Beers to conclude that Decker had been shot while he was sleeping. Beers took testimony of witnesses who identified the clothing and possessions of Decker. Others told of St. Clair's behavior following Decker's disappearance. At the end of the inquest, the jury chose to charge Herman St. Clair with the murder of John Decker.

Boise County Deputy Sheriff Clay Mosher traveled to Van Wyck to take St. Clair into custody. They returned to Idaho City on November 1, and St. Clair was confined to the Boise County Jail. Prosecuting Attorney Charles Hays examined the information from the inquest and decided a probate hearing was in order before proceeding to the district court. He also realized that to get a conviction, he would need the bullets that killed

St. Clair as Homer Woolsey at Folsom Prison

Decker. He contacted Beers and directed him to exhume the body and retrieve them. Beers reluctantly followed his orders. On November 7, he performed an autopsy on Decker, recovering one of the bullets, which he determined to be a .38 caliber. He attempted to find the other, but the task was so gruesome—"very unpleasant," according to Beers—that he gave up. He told Hays one bullet would have to do.

Probate Judge Thomas S. Hart found sufficient evidence to send St. Clair on to the district court. St. Clair appeared before Judge George H. Stewart in the District Court of the Third Judicial District on November 11 where he was charged with "willful, deliberate, premeditated murder," a charge he vehemently denied. The judge then set November 15 as the trial date and appointed L. E. Workman and Karl Paine to defend St. Clair.

On the opening day of the trial, St. Clair asked for a continuance. He submitted an affidavit naming five men in British Columbia and Oregon who would testify that the wagon, horses, money purse, and watch rightfully belonged to him, not Decker, as the prosecution claimed. St. Clair's lawyers needed time to find these witnesses. His lawyers also asked for a continuance because they needed more time to prepare their case. Finally, they asked for a change of venue. St. Clair claimed that while in Van Wyck he was threatened on several occasions; he did not believe the people of Boise County would give him a fair trial. Judge Stewart listened to the requests and then denied them all.

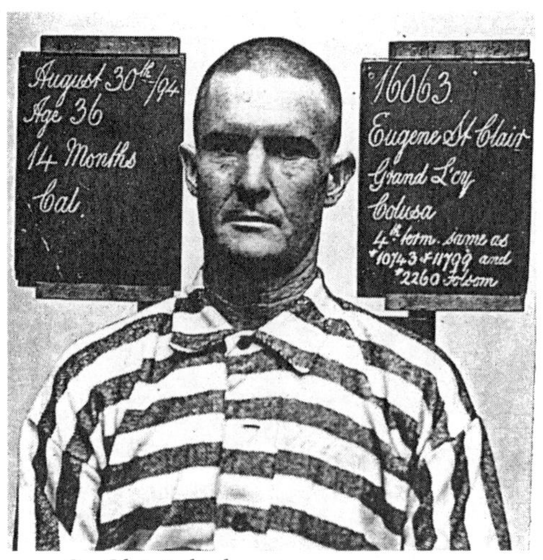

St. Clair in his last stay in a California prison

The trial took three days—one for jury selection, one for testimony, one for closing arguments. The prosecution called witnesses who saw St. Clair and Decker together. They identified Decker's clothing that St. Clair had given to Robbins. They discussed St. Clair's brazen behavior following Decker's disappearance, and they related comments St. Clair had made concerning the murder. Prosecutor Hays presented the gun, bullet, watch, ropes, and black purse as evidence pointing strongly against St. Clair.

In his defense of St. Clair, Workman tried to implicate Robbins, hinting that St. Clair was so generous with Robbins because the two had worked together to commit the crime. Robbins adamantly denied the accusation. Workman also questioned the analysis of the bullet which the prosecution claimed came from St. Clair's gun. But Workman had little to exculpate St. Clair. When it came time for him to put on a defense, he simply submitted the affidavit St. Clair had filed in asking for the continuance. He called no other witnesses, not even St. Clair.

The jury deliberated just forty-five minutes before declaring St. Clair guilty. He listened passively as the verdict was announced and made no comment as he was returned to his cell. On November 20, Judge Stewart sentenced him to hang at "some convenient private place" in the county and set the execution for January 14, 1898. St. Clair's lawyers gave notice that they would appeal the verdict. They were given thirty days to present their case.

During the trial, St. Clair appeared ill. He had lost weight and looked frail, collapsing at trial before the verdict was read. Dr. Beers would testify that St. Clair suffered from delirium tremens, while Boise County Sheriff Jotham Lippincott believed St. Clair had a heart condition. St. Clair's confidence also seemed to dwindle as the days passed. He asked that a light be left burning at night in his cell to keep away "visions." He also asked if someone could spend the night with him in his cell. However, Lippincott was suspect of St. Clair's motives and denied his requests. His suspicions would eventually be justified.

Workman and Paine stood before Judge Stewart on January 3, 1898, to argue for a new trial. They claimed the judge had erred in failing to grant the continuance. They insisted no sane man would have stayed in Van Wyck after committing murder, as St. Clair had done. Finally they contended no proof had been offered that the murdered man—who at first was known as John Doe—was really John Decker. Stewart was unconvinced and denied the request. On January 10, just four days before the scheduled execution, St. Clair's lawyers filed an appeal before the Idaho State Supreme Court. With the appeal, St. Clair was granted a stay of execution.

The Boise County Jail, where St. Clair was incarcerated, had once served as the Idaho Territorial Prison. Built in the 1860s of hand-hewn logs, it was notorious for the daring escape attempts of its prisoners. With that in mind, Boise County officials considered moving St. Clair to the Ada County Jail, which they believed was more secure. But the decision went unmade, and St. Clair spent the first several months of 1898 in the company of Sheriff Lippincott and his jailer James McQuillan. He learned his appeal had been filed with the supreme court and a decision would be rendered in May.

McQuillan came to know St. Clair well. During the long evening hours in the jailhouse, St. Clair would entertain him with "strange and improbable stories" of his life at sea. St. Clair showed him his elaborate tattoos—a weeping willow, a full-length Japanese girl, a red heart pierced by a dagger, two wreaths of flowers surrounding each knee cap—all supposedly acquired at various exotic seaports. McQuillan was impressed by his prisoner's vast knowledge, right down to his ability to knit scarves and hats. McQuillan went so far as to conclude, "St. Clair was not so bad as he was supposed to be." So it was to McQuillan's surprise when on April 22, 1898, he found himself at the end of a double-barreled shotgun with St. Clair at the trigger.

As he did every morning, McQuillan had left the jail to take the guard dogs for a drink at a creek located a short distance from the stockade. When he left, St. Clair was in his unlocked cell, but still in the locked section of the jail called the "bullpen." Two large iron lattice doors—one that led to the front of the jail, the other led to the outside—secured the bullpen and the jailer's quarters. Somehow, St. Clair had secured a file and knife and loosened the bolts on the back door enough make his escape. Then, rather than leaving the area, he went to the front of the jail, entered the jailer's quarters and stole the shotgun and a pistol. He was leaving through the front door when he ran into McQuillan.

"Put up your hands, Jim, and go inside the jail," St. Clair ordered, "or I shall have to kill you."

McQuillan's response was to start talking. He argued with St. Clair that he could not get away; for sure he would be captured and killed. And as he talked he inched closer until he was within six feet of St. Clair. Then, St. Clair heard a wagon passing and the voices of men approaching. When he turned his head toward the sound, McQuillan made his move.

McQuillan jumped St. Clair, nailing him hard with a left hook to the jaw. Off balance, St. Clair fired the shotgun, but both charges went over McQuillan's head. St. Clair discarded the shotgun and pulled the pistol from his waistband. With a dog attacking his leg, he took aim at McQuillan, but the jailer was able to grab the barrel of the gun, and the shot missed its mark. Then with his free hand, McQuillan grabbed a bowie knife he always carried and brought it down hard on St. Clair's wrist, causing him to drop the gun. McQuillan then grabbed the pistol and shot St. Clair in the jaw. For good measure, he hit St. Clair in the head with the pistol as his model prisoner fell to the floor.

St. Clair was in bad shape. The bullet to the jaw took out three teeth and some of his tongue; it also hit his shoulder. The bullet fired while he grappled with McQuillan had struck him in the hand. In all, he had nine knife wounds, the one on his wrist being the most serious.

St. Clair was taken to his cell where Dr. Warren Newell dressed his wounds, predicting St. Clair would survive. He did, but he was in sorry shape. He couldn't eat because of the wound to his jaw. This was then exacerbated by an infection. The fingers of his right hand were swollen and useless. When he learned that the supreme court had turned down his appeal, he was resigned to his fate. "I might as well die," St Clair told a reporter. "I am not going to live long anyway."

On June 14, St. Clair appeared before Judge Stewart. Although weak and thin, he was determined to walk to the courtroom, a distance of about 300 yards, to hear the judge set a new execution date: June 24. Judge Stewart, distressed by St. Clair's condition, allowed him to sit through the proceedings.

As the day of the execution neared, St. Clair was philosophical, but not repentant. To the end he claimed he had not killed Decker. He was appreciative of his lawyers, Dr. Newell, and even his jailers. He held no hard feeling for McQuillan, claiming the deputy had been more than kind to him in jail. As far as the injuries he suffered in the escape attempt, he simply stated that McQuillan, "did his duty as a guard. He did what was expected of him."

Although he refused to accept responsibility for Decker's murder, he was willing to admit that he had not always lived a good life. Even then, he blamed outside influences. "Whiskey, cards, and fast women are a combination that will bring almost any man down, as they brought me down," St. Clair said. "He may get along all right with one or two of these vices, but with the three mixed, hell is the final windup."

St. Clair seemed to have only one fear as the day of the execution neared; he wanted to make sure he would die quickly. On several occasions he asked Sheriff Lippincott to give him "plenty of drop." The sheriff promised he would and lengthened the rope for a six-foot fall.

On the morning of his execution, St. Clair enjoyed a final meal of coffee, poached eggs, and strawberries and cream. Shortly before 10 a.m., Dr. Newell gave him a whisky toddy and a small dose of morphine. Then at 10:23, Lippincott told St. Clair the time had come. St. Clair emerged from the jail looking corpse-like, his new suit hanging loosely on his emaciated body. When Lippincott and deputies McQuillan, Elder Smith and Clay Mosher offered to assist him to the scaffold, he told them, "Never mind. I can walk up there." And so he did.

St. Clair was calm. He complained only once, when Mosher placed the noose around his neck. St. Clair moved his head from side to side and told him, "You are choking me." Mosher loosened the noose. Then he put the black cap over St. Clair's head, at which point St. Clair firmly said, "Goodbye, everybody." With that, Mosher gave the signal, and both Smith and Lippincott pulled the levers that sprung the trap. St. Clair would have been pleased; the drop was sufficient.

St. Clair was buried later that day just outside the fence of the Idaho City Cemetery. His grave was marked with a wooden headboard that recorded his crime. The

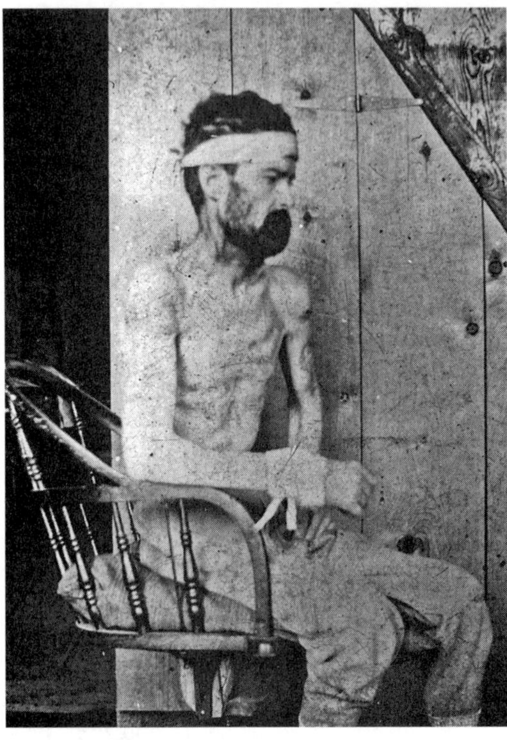

St. Clair in the territorial prison at Idaho City shortly before his execution

headboard has since been lost, and his grave now is unmarked.

For months following his death, stories continued to circulate about St. Clair's life of crime. He supposedly robbed a post office in Weiser, held up a train in the Midwest, and killed a man in Texas. The stories were as colorful as the ones St. Clair told himself. The man who once swore he was afraid of no one, not even the devil, would have been pleased.

MICHAEL MOONEY

FRANKLIN, OCTOBER 27, 1881
MALAD, DECEMBER 29, 1882

In the southeast corner of Idaho, a little over a mile from the Utah border, sits the town of Franklin. Established in April 1860 by thirteen Mormon families, the little community on the northern end of Cache Valley flourished immediately. By the fall of 1860, over sixty Mormon families called it home, establishing the first white settlement in Idaho.

With the settlement came the railroad. With the urging of Mormon leader Brigham Young and to the delight of the Mormon settlers who did most of the work, the Utah Northern Railroad pushed into Franklin on May 4, 1874 and began regular runs between Franklin and Ogden. For the next four years, Franklin was the northern terminus for the short-gauged line, and the town became a center of trade and commerce. Franklin held this place of importance until 1878, when Utah Northern filed for bankruptcy. The company was taken over by the Utah & Northern Railway, an offshoot of Union Pacific, which pushed the railroad north toward Pocatello. Franklin's fortunes faded soon after. Still, Utah & Northern continued to operate the Franklin station, where on October 27, 1881, Michael Mooney shot and killed Joel Hinckley.

Hinckley, just twenty-one, was the station manager. One of eighteen children of Arza Hinckley, a practicing polygamist with three wives, Joel moved north to Franklin from Cove Creek, Utah, where he worked as a telegraph operator. He was well-liked and described as a "pleasant, boyish young man." Once in Franklin, he was introduced to fifteen-year-old Lucy Woodward, daughter of William Woodward, one of the founding fathers of Franklin and also a thrice-married polygamist. Over Woodward's objections, Joel and Lucy married in March 1881 and moved into the Franklin station.

On the night of October 27, 1881, Joel and Lucy walked the half-mile to visit her sister and brother-in-law Alexander and Zina Stocker (Stalker). They spent the evening talking and playing cards. The girls were especially excited about Lucy's pregnancy. Around 9:30, Joel and Lucy started the ten-minute walk back to the station following the railroad tracks. On the way, they saw two men walking aimlessly on the road that led from the

Franklin Co-op to the station house. They were not alarmed; Franklin was a quiet, peaceful place.

When they reached the station, Lucy unlocked the main door, which opened into the waiting room. Joel took some packages into the freight room on the north end of the building, and Lucy followed bringing him a lamp. When he was finished, they went to the office, which adjoined their living quarters on the south end of the building. There, they were joined by James Stocker, the mail carrier, who slept at the station. The three talked briefly, and James retired to the waiting room where he made his bed. Lucy went into her bedroom while Joel stayed in the office to wash.

Stocker heard footsteps on the north end of the station platform and saw two men looking through a window into the waiting room. Lucy also heard the footsteps and asked Joel to close the blind on the office window, which he did. A few moments later, two masked men burst into the waiting room with guns drawn. They moved toward the office where they confronted Joel.

"Throw up your hands," the first one yelled, pointing his gun at Joel's head. But before Joel could respond, the gun discharged, the bullet striking him full force in the chin. He slumped against the wall, then slid to the floor mortally wounded.

The men fled north from the depot. Stocker, who had watched the scene unfold, chased them for about fifty yards. Lucy, who had hidden behind her bedroom door, summoned the courage to check on her husband. She spoke to him, and while his lips moved, he could not speak. In her stocking feet, Lucy rushed to the home of section manager Peter Bowcut, who enlisted the aid of one other railroad worker. They went to the station and found Joel alive, still sitting up against an office wall. They laid him out on the floor, and he died a short time later.

Stocker could give only vague descriptions of the assailants. The shooter, the first to enter the room, stood about six feet tall and weighed 180 pounds. He was clean-shaved with dark skin and hair. The second man was shorter, about 5'8", with a stockier build at 160 pounds.

Oneida County Sheriff W. H. Homer had been traveling on business when he happened to stop at the Oneida Railroad Station. There he learned of the murder in Franklin. Railroad telegraphers sent messages up and down the line, informing all station managers of the deadly attack. The railroad manager at Fort Hall dispatched an engine, caboose, and telegraph agent to Oneida for Homer's use. He sought assistance from sheriffs in

Box Elder, Weber, and Logan, Utah. He also organized posses to scour the area north of Franklin. He was sure the suspects would be traveling north to the rugged and less populated area of the Bear River or Cariboo ranges. To help, the Utah & Northern Railroad offered a $1,000 reward for the capture of the murderers.

For five days the fugitives, Michael Mooney and Frank Barnes, eluded capture. Then on the afternoon of November 2, tired and hungry, Mooney approached Don Sager at his ranch in Portneuf Valley near Soda Springs and asked if he could buy some bread. Aware of the murder in Franklin, Sager questioned Mooney and became suspicious of his answers. While Mooney claimed he had come from Cariboo, he could not name one person he knew there. Sager tried to detain him, asking Mooney in for supper, but he refused, claiming his partner was waiting for him in an abandoned cabin down the road. They planned to stay there for the night. Sager gave him some bread and watched him walk away. He sent word to Sheriff Homer who was camped nearby, and then took his wagon to the cabin where he found Barnes and Mooney. Sager invited both men to spend the evening at his house, but they declined. He then offered them a ride to Blackfoot, which they accepted, but instead of traveling toward Blackfoot, he took an alternate road back to his ranch where Sheriff Homer was waiting to arrest the suspects.

Homer and his deputies transported the prisoners by wagon to the rail station at Oneida. While there, a mob stormed the station platform demanding immediate justice. Sheriff Homer diffused the crowd, telling the people they lived "under a civilized form of government." He asked for their help to guard and protect the prisoners so they might have a fair trial. Heeding his message, the crowd dispersed, and Homer and his party continued by rail to Franklin.

At Franklin, Barnes and Mooney stood before Justice of the Peace W. L. Webster. He found cause to hold the men on murder charges. He ordered the sheriff to take them to Malad where they would be confined to the county jail to await the findings of a grand jury.

On the trip to Malad, Barnes was more than happy to talk to anyone who would listen. Claiming it was Mooney's idea to rob the station, he went along because he needed money. They had no intention of shooting anyone; the gun accidentally discharged when Mooney pointed it at Hinckley.

Mooney spoke of the affair only once. He confided to his guard and Sheriff Homer that he and Barnes had gone to the station to rob the safe

and Barnes panicked and accidentally shot Hinckley. "I had my pistol on the mail boy," Mooney claimed. "Had I had it on the poor boy, he would have been alive today." Later in his jail cell, he was overheard to ask Barnes, "How can you sleep with the blood of an innocent man on your hands?"

The grand jury convened on November 16, 1881. Prosecutor Willard Crawford relied heavily on the testimony of Lucy who claimed to have heard someone yell, "There, damn you, you have done it," immediately after the shooting. Crawford placed Barnes behind a partition and had him repeat the phrase, and Lucy identified the voice as the one she had heard. Crawford also presented Barnes' confession and the testimony of Stocker. It was enough for the grand jury to indict Mooney and Barnes for first-degree murder.

On November 18, Mooney and Barnes appeared before Judge John T. Morgan in the Third District Court of Idaho Territory where they both pleaded not guilty. Morgan appointed H. M. Bennett to defend them. They would be tried separately, and Mooney would go first on November 21.

After a day of jury selection, trial testimony began. Crawford set out to convince the jury that Mooney was the killer. He called Stocker to testify that the taller of the two men, Mooney, had fired the shot. He put Lucy on the stand to identify the voice she heard after the shot: it belonged to Barnes, not Mooney. Crawford also questioned Sheriff Homer who had found a fully loaded gun on Barnes, but no gun on Mooney. According to Homer, Mooney admitted the shooter's gun had been thrown away as they fled the station. Since Barnes still had his gun, the shooter must have been Mooney.

Mooney took the stand in his own defense and insisted the shooting of Hinckley was an accident. Their plan was to rob the safe, and they pulled their guns to convince Hinckley to open it. Barnes in his nervousness pulled the trigger.

The victim,
Joel Hinckley

Defense attorney Bennett put Barnes on the stand as his last witness, which proved to be Mooney's demise. While Barnes agreed with his partner that the shooting of Hinckley was an accident, he put the blame of the entire incident on Mooney. According to Barnes, Mooney was the mastermind behind the robbery, and he fired the fatal shot.

In his instructions to the jury, Judge Morgan clarified the different levels of murder. He also told the jury that if two men were engaged in a robbery and a murder occurred, it was "immaterial as to who fired the fatal shot." The jury listened and in two hours decided that Mooney was guilty of murder in the first degree. Judge Morgan would pronounce sentence on November 28.

While Mooney awaited his sentencing, Barnes went to trial. Jury selection began on the morning of November 25, and when the jury pool was depleted, Judge Morgan recessed the proceedings until the afternoon. During the break, counsel from both sides met to discuss a plea bargain. When the court reconvened, Prosecutor Crawford withdrew the first-degree murder charge, leaving a charge of second-degree murder to which Barnes pleaded guilty. Morgan advised Barnes that even with his plea, the judge had the final determination as to the degree of guilt, which could be murder in the first degree. Barnes was unswayed.

The prosecution laid out its case, the same as presented against Mooney. In his defense, Barnes continued to blame Mooney for the shooting but reiterated that it was an accident. They had no intent to harm anyone; Mooney only pointed the gun at Hinckley to make him open the safe.

On November 28, both Mooney and Barnes were back before Judge Morgan to hear their sentences. Mooney went first and learned he was to be hanged on January 20, 1882. He showed no reaction. Barnes was sentenced to fifteen years in the territorial prison. He broke down and had to be helped from the courtroom.

Mooney's attorney filed an appeal for a new trial, based on errors of the court, including the seating of a deaf juror who had to be removed. Judge Morgan listened to the argument but on November 30 ruled there were no grounds for a new trial, and the verdict and sentence would stand. Bennett then appealed to the territorial supreme court, and Morgan granted a stay of execution until the appeal could be heard.

Barnes was transferred to the Idaho Territorial Prison while Mooney remained in the Oneida County Jail in Malad. He kept mostly to himself and gave few details of his life. He claimed he was born in Australia in 1852 and immigrated to America in 1869. He worked as a miner and spent some time in British Columbia, Washington, and Oregon before traveling to Lemhi County in Idaho in the late summer of 1881. There he met Barnes and they decided to travel south to Utah to spend the winter. Out of money, they sold their horses near Crystal City, a mining camp near Challis, and continued on foot. They had been in Franklin less than two hours when they decided to rob the railroad station.

The supreme court heard Mooney's appeal in September 1882. Bennett's argument centered on Judge Morgan's refusal to instruct the jury concerning intent. Bennett believed the evidence needed to prove Mooney's intent to kill Hinckley was part of the robbery, and he wanted the judge to inform the jurors that if Mooney acted without intent, he could not be convicted of first-degree murder. But Morgan refused, and the supreme court affirmed his position. Idaho statutes stated that any murder committed in the attempt or perpetration of a robbery was murder in the first degree. Mooney's conviction and sentence were upheld, and Judge Morgan reset his execution for December 8, 1882.

The decision was a setback to those in Malad who were convinced Mooney was not the triggerman. Led by Dr. J. W. Morgan, a group of citizens circulated a petition asking Governor John Neil to commute Mooney's sentence to life in prison. Neil granted a reprieve of twenty days, during which time he would consider the appeal. But as the days passed, with no word from the governor, Sheriff Homer began preparations for the execution.

With the execution days away, Homer asked Mooney if would like any spiritual advice, but he rejected the offer, telling the sheriff, "I don't want any damn preacher's prayers for me." Instead he preferred the company of Dr. Morgan, who remained with him until the end. He made no comments about his family or past life and had only one regret: he did not kill Barnes before he opened his mouth.

On December 28, Sheriff Homer informed both Mooney and Morgan that no word had been sent from the governor; the execution would go on as planned. Mooney watched from his cell as Homer directed the construction of the scaffold, which was completed that night.

The next morning, Mooney ate his usual breakfast and had a shave and a haircut. He put on a white linen shirt, a new black suit, and a pair of black slippers. Dr. Morgan held out hope that a message from the governor might still arrive, but Mooney was resigned to his fate. By noon a crowd had begun to gather, scaling the fence around the jail to get a better view of the proceedings. Sheriff Homer, who was uncomfortable in his role as executioner, had his deputies clear the area. Only a handful of witnesses were allowed in the jail yard to view the proceedings.

At 1:45, Homer, accompanied by Mooney's lawyer, entered the condemned man's cell to read the death warrant. Then, as they made their way to the scaffold, a light snow began to fall. Mooney ascended the steps unassisted and took his place on the trap door. Turning to Homer, who had once saved him from a lynch mob, Mooney told him, "Homer, God damn you, don't get excited over this thing. Do it right." He turned and nodded to several men on the scaffold and once again addressed the sheriff, "Do this as quick as Christ will let you, if there is any Christ." Then he added, "I don't care any more for dying that I would for going to a dance."

His legs were bound and his arms were tied behind his back. As the black mask was drawn over his head he spoke to under-sheriff Benjamin Evans. "Goodbye, Benny," he said. "Thanks for your kindness to me in jail." They were the last words he spoke. At 2:17, his body was taken down and turned over to the city sexton who was instructed to bury Mooney outside the cemetery gates.

In May 1882, Lucy Hinckley gave birth to a girl, Ann. The baby did not survive and was buried next to her father. Lucy remarried in 1883 and had five more children. She died in Oregon in 1948.

At the territorial prison, Frank Barnes was a model prisoner. Although Governor George Shoup denied his request for a pardon in June of 1889, Warden E. W. Beemer reduced his sentence by six years and three months for good behavior. He was released on September 12, 1890.

Henry McDonald

Pilgrim Station, September 28, 1880
Silver City, October 14, 1881

Henry McDonald had a problem—he was unable to tell the truth. He told so many lies that when it came time for him to set the record straight, he could not remember what it was. Had he told one story and stuck with it, he may have escaped the hangman. Instead, in the end, no one—not the jury, nor the judge, nor the public, nor the press—believed one word he said.

McDonald was born in Scotland in 1853. In the late 1870s, he was living in Kelton, Utah with his young wife Emma and his son Henry. He was good with stock and worked for wages and board for various freighters. His goal was to own his own team and haul freight on the Kelton Road.

With the completion of the transcontinental railroad in 1869, stage and freight companies scrambled to establish new trade routes into Idaho territory. One of those ran from Kelton to Boise. Established by John Hailey, a well-known Idaho businessman, the 240-mile route took forty hours to complete. Throughout the 1870s and early 1880s, the Kelton Road was the major stage and freight line into Idaho. People had their goods shipped by railway to Kelton and then freighted to Boise by teams. The price of freight was four to six cents a pound. The population of Kelton during the boom was 700, many of them involved in the freighting business.

One of those freighters was George Myers. Although he called Boise home, he made frequent trips to Kelton and was well known among the station managers and ferry operators along the way. He was easily recognized by his full, white beard. Born in Pennsylvania in 1825, he made his way west to the mining booms in California, Nevada, and Idaho where he earned his living with his wagons and mules. While other teamsters respected him, describing him as quiet and industrious, he could also be somewhat ill-tempered, especially when it came to business. He was also known to drink on occasion, and when he did, he could be extremely unreasonable.

McDonald also made frequent trips on the Kelton road, driving teams for others. He would stay in Boise working odd jobs until he could hire on to drive a team back to Kelton. It was on a return trip to Boise where he met Myers. According to McDonald, in August 1880, the two met on the road at Goose Creek, and during their conversation, Myers indicated he was ready to sell his team—two wagons, eight mules, and one saddle horse—for $1400. He wanted one-half down and good security for the rest. However, no agreement was made, and Myers continued to Kelton while McDonald went on to Boise.

While waiting for Myers to return, McDonald worked as a laborer and a butcher. On September 1, he met with Myers, and they once again discussed the sale of the team. Myers told McDonald he would be leaving Boise to return to Kelton mid-month. McDonald, who was driving freight for a Mr. Horne (Hoven), had deliveries to make before he could go. Myers had no intention of waiting for McDonald and left Boise, probably on September 23.

On September 24, McDonald quit his job with Horne, bought a ticket to Soul's Rest on the Overland Stage, and went after Myers. Upon reaching Soul's Rest, he found Myers had already passed, so he purchased additional fare and continued the ride until he caught up with Myers on September 26. Myers welcomed the young man onto his wagon, and they made their way to Rattlesnake and the ranch of Augustus Rikewine, where they put up some grain for their return trip. The following day they continued to Little Canyon Creek, near present-day Glenns Ferry. Here they stopped at the saloon of William Ramsdell where Myers had a conversation with Gus

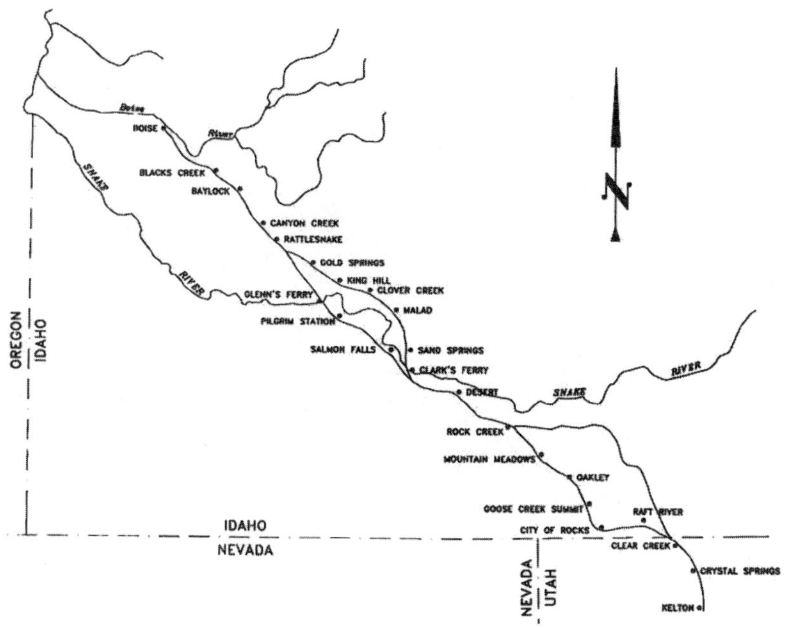

Glenn, whose ferry led to the founding of Glenns Ferry. Glenn tried to convince Myers to use his ferry on this trip, but Myers declined, preferring to use the ferry of Len Lewis further down the road. Shortly after crossing the Snake River, the two stopped to camp.

The next morning, approximately two miles east of Pilgrim Station, they met another teamster, Edward Guard. In passing, McDonald told Guard he had bought Myers' team, with $500 down. Knowing McDonald had always worked for wages, he was suspicious of the claim. When he asked Myers if he had sold his team to McDonald, Myers answered with an emphatic, "No, I have not."

We have only McDonald's stories on what may have happened the rest of the day, and because they changed so much, it is impossible to discern the truth. No one saw McDonald or Myers on the road after they passed Guard. What is true is that McDonald, driving Myer's team, pulled into the Salmon Falls Station alone on the evening of September 28. Several men noticed the absence of Myers and questioned McDonald. He told them that Myers had gone ahead to purchase a pair of mules.

The next day, McDonald awoke to find most of the team missing. He borrowed a horse from Matt O'Conner and spent the rest of the day tracking them back down the trail. He arrived at Pilgrim Station that evening and still had not found the stock. He spent the night at the station, and the next

Loaded freighters at Silver City

day he offered freighter John Howell $2.50 if he would find the animals. Howell agreed. McDonald drove Howell's team on to Salmon Falls and that night, Howell arrived, mules in tow. The next morning, McDonald left for Kelton ahead of the other teamsters.

McDonald finished his trip and over the next two weeks let freight agents know he had purchased Myers' team and was looking for a load to take back to Boise. In his work, he ran into E. S. Clark, a freighter from Boise. Clark, who had known Myers for years, asked about the whereabouts of his old friend. McDonald told him that Myers had gone to Birch Creek to pick up a horse. He added that he had purchased the team from Myers for $1400—$900 down with the balance due in July.

Clark and McDonald left Kelton at the same time for the return trip to Boise. On October 23, they stopped at Pilgrim Station for the night. There, McDonald wrote a letter to William Marlatt, signed it with Myers' name, and posted it. The next day he left for Boise, stopping at Rikewine's ranch for the grain he and Myers had left for the return trip. Rikewine was leery, but gave him the feed, as he recognized the team and the wagons. He asked McDonald about Myers' whereabouts, and McDonald told him he had left Myers behind to hunt for some mules. McDonald moved on, and Rikewine spent the rest of the evening waiting for Myers. He never arrived

Back in Boise, McDonald went to see Marlatt, a good friend of Myers. By then, Marlatt had received the letter, which he found suspicious. Myers had boarded with Marlatt over the years, and Marlatt was well acquainted with his handwriting. He was sure that the letter he had received from Pilgrim Station was not in Myers' hand. He was also suspect of the content.

Salmon Falls, Oct. 23rd, 1880

Mister William Marlatt—Sir

I have sold my team too Henry McDonald, and I have got track
of that horse of mine and I am going to find him. I may go down
to Portland, Oregon, if I don't find him, and come back by Kelton.
I want too go down there on business. I am going down with some
folks that is acquainted down there and I will get a team from
McDonald to come home if he don't load there. Mister Marlatt, I
want you too git that colt that is halter broke and let McDonald
have him. I want him broke too work and I can drive him back.

I will give him a order for him and I want you to look out for the
horses till I get back.

George Myers.

McDonald asked for the horse. Wary, Marlatt asked for a bill of sale, knowing Myers would not have turned over the horse without it. McDonald promised he would produce one, and reluctantly, Marlatt gave up the horse. He questioned McDonald about Myers' team, but McDonald declined to give any information. After McDonald left with the horse, Marlatt turned the letter over to Ada County Sheriff Joe Oldham.

To provide a bill of sale for the horse, McDonald once again put pencil to paper and produced another letter, this one to himself, purportedly from Myers

Willow Creek, 1st, 1880

Mister Henry McDonald

I am now at Willow Creek. I have bought a span of mules
and wagon and want to traid for the horses if you want to trade
them—well I hope that yo got the colt—all rite I will pay Mister
Marlatt for gitting him for yo—I may go too the Dallas and I may
go too the rail road and if yo want the mules yo can have them. Well
I have not much too say this time. I hope yo had a good trip will rite
too. Well I did not get the horse I herd of him at the Bridge on Jon
Days and I am goin thare and thin I will start home or else I will
come down too the railroad and I will see yo their. Rite and direct to
Jon Days Bridge.

Yours truely

George Myers.

McDonald went to visit Russ Walters, a former employer. He told Walters about losing the bill of sale for Myers' horse, and then pulled out the letter he claimed to have received from Myers. He asked Walters to help him read it, which he did. Afterwards, Walters told him the letter would stand in place of a bill of sale. McDonald left the letter with Walters, asking him to give it to Marlatt. This letter was also turned over to the sheriff.

Suspicion continued to mount against McDonald, who told conflicting accounts of how much he paid for Myers' team. He also began telling people that Myers had gone to Oregon—Baker City, Willow Creek, John Day, The Dalles—to look for a horse with old friends he had met on the Kelton Road. But when Myers' friends sent letters attempting to contact him in those different locations, the letters were returned. A search for Myers along the trail between Pilgrim Station and Salmon Falls came up empty.

Finally, the case caught the attention of John Hailey, whose business depended on keeping the stage and freight road safe. He contacted Thomas Cahalan, deputy district attorney of Ada County, and urged him to look into the case. Although Cahalan had no proof that a crime had been committed, he decided to confront McDonald. In mid-November, he directed Sheriff Oldham to arrest McDonald. Oldham found his suspect returning from a freight trip to the Wood River mines and confined him to the Ada County Jail.

Cahalan learned that McDonald liked to talk, so he invited several of Myers' friends to the jail to visit him. McDonald stuck with his story that Myers had met some old friends on the road and decided to go to Oregon with them to look for a horse. But he added a twist: he had been out rounding up stock on the morning Myers and his friends had gone, so he assumed they

Henry McDonald

had left for Oregon. However, waiting for him at camp were two men who robbed him at gunpoint. They took most of his money, told him to keep quiet, and then let him go. He identified the two as Frank Kellet and Gus Glenn, the ferryman. According to McDonald, if anyone killed Myers, it must have been them.

McDonald was not implicating himself. Cahalan needed solid proof to keep him in jail, so he enlisted the aid of William Glines, McDonald's cellmate. Glines, who was facing charges of horse stealing, was told to elicit as much information as he could. He was happy to oblige as he was promised "special liberties" for his efforts.

McDonald repeated the story that Kellet and Glenn murdered Myers, claiming they had promised to come to his aid if he were arrested. Since they had not kept up their end of the deal, he decided to tell the "truth." But the more McDonald talked, the more he implicated himself. He was sure he could not be convicted unless a body was found. When Glines told him a search party was looking for the remains of Myers, McDonald claimed they were going on a "wild goose chase." McDonald said he was positive they could not find the body unless "they were better hunters than he was a cacher." He added that "anybody could find old bones and clothes along the road" but no one could identify them as belonging to Myers.

But it was McDonald's penchant for writing letters that gave the prosecutor his first concrete evidence. On the night of November 18, McDonald composed a letter to George Rodgers, a bartender from Kelton. Needing to prove that Myers was alive, McDonald gave Rodgers specific instructions on how to write three letters, all of them supposedly coming from Myers. McDonald seemed desperate, acknowledging if he remained in jail for a grand jury hearing, he was doomed.

> *Boise City, Nov. 18, 1880*
>
> *Mister George Rodgers*
>
> *Sir:*
>
> *I am now in a tite place and you are the only friend I know of that I can trust. George I have not got any money, jest now, but take this letter to my wife and see if she has, and, if not, get some and go down to Taris or farther if you can and copy this on the other side and send back to me. Tell my wife I am well, I think I will be out in a short time. George, don't show this letter too anyone; or don't delay, for if I have to stay till the grand jorai I am gone for good.*
>
> *George, now doe mee this favor, for this does depend on my life and I will make it all-rite with you when I see you...*
>
> *George, don't be afraid of the money; I am going to sell a span of mules as soon as I can and I will send the money to my wife, but George, don't wait till I send the money, go rite away, now you can go and tell my wife, and tell her not to fret, nor say anything about this. George, be shure and try and see some of Myers hand rite and sine his name as near a like as yo can. George now don't fall and don't rite anything about the affair between mee and myers; because the sheriff opens letters and read them, and also go and tell my wife to not say anything outside of the family affairs. George don't fail to do this for I am in a bad place at present...beshure Rite what I have*

marked with this pensell and nothing more. Don't show this letter to anyone, for if you do, I am gone too h___ll.

From your friend,
Henry McDonald.

With that advice, McDonald then added the three letters he wanted Rodgers to write. The first letter was to support McDonald's contention that Myers was in Oregon.

Willow Creek n.a. 1st 1880
Mr. Henry McDonald
Sir

I am now at Willow Creek. I have bought a span of mules and wagon and want to traid for the horses if you want to traid for them—Well I hope that yo got the colt—all rite I will pay Mr. Morlatt for gitting him for yo—I may go too the Dallas and I may go too the rail road if you want the mules yo can have them Well I have not mutch too say this time I hope yo had a good trip will rite too Well I did not git the horse I heard of him at the bridge on Jon Days and I am goin thare and thin I will start home thin or else I will come down too the rail road and I will see you their Rite and direct to John Days Bridge

Yours Truely
George Myers.

The second and third letters were to be postmarked from Terrace, Utah. McDonald was aware that people had been looking for Myers in Oregon. He needed to show that Myers could not be found because he had returned to Utah.

Taris November 18th
Mister Henry McDonald
Sir

I am now at Taris and I am a little under the weather and I want to go down too Ward as soon as I can and then I am coming too Kelton and see yo and straiten the business between yo and me and then I am goin to Boisee City. I hope yo had a good trip and got a-long well.

Yours truely
George Myers.

> *Taris November the _____ 1880*
> *Mister Henry McDonald*
> *Sir*
> *I am now near Taris on a ranch with a family. I am a little*
> *under the weather and I am going too Ward as soon as I can and*
> *thin I am coming too Kelton and see yo about the team and draw*
> *the ritings and fix it all rite I hope yo had a good trip and got along*
> *allrite from your friend*
> *George Myers.*

As a final word of advice, McDonald advised Rodgers where he could find copies of Myers' handwriting and once again expressed the urgency of his situation.

> *George this is what I want copied ad sind too mee do this*
> *without fail and don't rite any more than this yo can go and at*
> *Conants and Malery yo can see his hand rite there or at the Jues but*
> *don't let their men know any thing about this for God's sake.*
>
> *Beshure and git his shipment card and see where he signs his*
> *name and git it as near as you can—date the letter—whin yo rite*
> *George I have always been a friend to yo now do me this favor*
> *Youres Truely*
> *Henry McDonald*
> *I shall go to Hell if yo don't do this for me.*

Glines was a willing witness to the letter writing, holding a candle so McDonald could see and giving suggestions when needed. When McDonald asked Glines to mail the letter for him, he was more than happy to give it to jailer L. L. Tyner who passed in on to Cahalan.

The prosecutor continued gathering information. He had several interviews with McDonald, attempting to pin him down on his story. But McDonald was unshakeable. Even though he had no bill of sale, he swore he gave Myers $600 down on his team with an agreement to pay $800 more in installments. When Cahalan pressed him on the location of Myers' grave, McDonald told him he had no idea; the last time he had seen Myers, the old man had been standing in the back of his wagon. He believed Myers had gone to Oregon because that is what he was told by the men who robbed him.

Cahalan's big break in the case came on March 12, 1881, when ranchers Frank Lewis and Henry Robinson happened to find the back of a shirt half buried in loose dirt. Lewis recognized it as a shirt often worn by Myers. They searched the area and discovered what they believed to be a grave, approximately 600 yards north of Kelton Road two miles east of Pilgrim Station. Not wanting to disturb it, they rode to Salmon Falls and posted a letter to Cahalan telling him of their discovery.

Cahalan sent Henry Pierce to investigate. In and around the gravesite Pierce found remnants of an undershirt, a heavy pair of grey pants, and a pair of blue California overalls, the kind typically worn by Myers. As coyotes had ransacked the site, he could find only a few full pieces of bone, and they were spread in various directions from the grave. He was unable to find the skull, but near the grave and in the grave itself he found a large quantity of gray hair. Pierce gathered his findings into a cloth sack and returned to Boise where he presented Cahalan with the last evidence he would need.

Sheriff William Bryon broke the news to McDonald. Still McDonald maintained his innocence, telling the sheriff that he was expecting a large sum of money, and as soon as it arrived, he would hire an attorney and tell what he knew. He also requested a meeting with Cahalan. He gave the prosecutor a list of names claiming they would "prove him clear."

Although he put on a brave front for the authorities, McDonald realized his luck was running out. Escape seemed to be his only option, so in early April, he and another prisoner began digging a tunnel under the jail. They were caught before they could use it. Shortly after, he learned the prosecution had intercepted the letter to Rodgers, and Glines was going to testify against him before the grand jury. The news led to a fight between McDonald and Glines, in which McDonald claimed the testimony would cause him "to swing from the first tree he came to."

Sheriff Bryon kept an eye on McDonald. Twice he had to change the leg irons, as McDonald managed to nearly cut them off. But the extra vigilance was not enough. On May 14, after several weeks of tedious effort, McDonald removed the lock from his cell door and made his way to freedom. His jailers were sitting in the next room.

McDonald took a horse, somehow procured a gun, and traveled northeast toward the mining camp of Atlanta. He was familiar with the area, having freighted there. Once in Atlanta, he shaved his beard, sold the horse, and found a partner who would lead him through the Sawtooth Mountains to Bonanza on the Yankee Fork River.

Jailer Jerry Plume, who was responsible for McDonald's escape, was not about to lose his man. He followed McDonald's trail and on May 22, caught him hiding in a cabin in the Sawtooths.

While McDonald was on the run, the court case against him moved forward. Since the crime had been committed in Owyhee County, the trial would be held at Silver City with Judge Henry E. Prickett presiding. Cahalan remained on the case as a special prosecutor. The determined Boise lawyer would finally bring the case to trial.

On May 27, McDonald stood before Judge Prickett to hear the charges against him. As he had no lawyer, Prickett appointed Henry Martin to represent him. The next day he was back in court to plead not guilty for the murder of George Myers. Prickett set June 7 for the opening date of the trial.

Cahalan was ready. He had gathered twenty-three witnesses and each one added a piece to the murder puzzle. Freighters and ranchers recounted what they had seen on the Kelton Road; Myers' friends recalled conversations with McDonald concerning the purchase of Myer's team. Handwriting experts compared the letters McDonald had written in Myers' name to samples of Myers' handwriting and concluded they were not the same. They all recognized the hair and clothes found on the trail as belonging to Myers. Cahalan produced Gus Glenn, the ferry operator, who denied any involvement in the disappearance of Myers. And no one, not even those who had lived and worked on the Kelton Road for many years, had ever heard of Frank Kellet.

Defense Attorney Martin fought back. He attacked Myers' character, getting witnesses to admit that the old man had an ornery streak and a fondness for whisky. Those same witnesses also claimed that prior to Myers' disappearance, McDonald had always been an industrious and conscientious worker. Martin also questioned the motives of Glines, who admitted he was given special treatment after agreeing to spy on McDonald. Still Martin knew it was not enough; he had no other choice than to put McDonald on the stand.

For two days, McDonald entertained the jury with his remarkable tales. While he stuck to the story that he had purchased the team from Myers, he now claimed the old man's death was an accident. According to McDonald, Myers had a dog that was having trouble keeping up with the wagons. Whenever McDonald would stop to take care of the dog, Myers, who was drunk, would yell at him to keep moving. Eventually, McDonald tied the dog in the back of the trail wagon, only to have it jump out. Unfortunately, the rope was not long enough, so the dog was forced to hop on its back legs to keep up. When McDonald stopped to untie the dog, Myers lost his temper. He told McDonald the dog was none of his affair. The two argued as they walked along, the wagons still moving forward. Then Myers moved to the lead wagon, mounted the rigging, reached into the jockey box, and pulled out a gun. Just then, the wagon hit a chuckhole. Myers was thrown underneath the wagon where he was kicked by the mules and run over with the front wheel of the wagon. McDonald claimed he managed to set the brake, but Myers became caught under the back wheel and was dragged for several feet before the wagon came to a stop. Myers died shortly after.

McDonald also explained why he did not take Myers' body on to Salmon Falls for a proper burial. He claimed that after the accident, Frank Kellet and Len Lewis came upon the wagons. The men told him they would take care of the body, and that he should go on and keep his mouth shut about the accident. If people asked questions, he was to tell them that Myers went to Oregon. They also said that if that story did not hold up, they would blame the old man's disappearance on Gus Glenn.

The more McDonald talked, the bigger the lies became. He did not tell anyone about Myers' death because he was afraid of Lewis. Besides, he said, "I believe it is usual when companies are traveling together and one of them gets killed, to let it go and say nothing about it." As for the letters, he needed the first one to get the horse he had honestly purchased from Myers. The ones from jail were not his doing; Glines had told him exactly what to write. He just did what he was told. While he did admit to lying about being robbed at gunpoint, he swore everything else he said was true.

In rebuttal, and to McDonald's surprise, Cahalan put Len Lewis on the stand where he adamantly denied any involvement in the disappearance of Myers. Looking directly at McDonald, Lewis testified, "What the defendant says about me is false and he knows it. I have never heard of such a man as Frank Kellet. I never had a conversation with the defendant about the death of Myers at no time and at no place."

With that, the case was turned over to the jury. They took just sixty-five minutes to return a verdict of guilty. Two days later, McDonald stood in front of Judge Prickett, who admonished him for committing "one of the most inexcusable and cold-blooded crimes ever committed in this Territory." The judge then sentenced McDonald to hang on August 5, 1881.

John Hailey helped bring McDonald to justice.

Martin appealed the case to the territorial supreme court, claiming Judge Prickett had erred in his instructions to the jury. He also argued that Prickett's tone in giving those instructions reflected the judge's attitude that McDonald was guilty. McDonald received a stay of execution until the court could hear his case. He did not have much of a reprieve. In September, the court rejected his appeal and Judge Prickett reset the execution for October 14.

Waiting in jail for his execution, McDonald continued to proclaim his innocence and laid the blame on Len Lewis. In an article in the *Owyhee Avalanche*, McDonald claimed that he, Lewis, and Frank Kellet originally planned to rob Myers; McDonald would get the team and Lewis and Kellet would take the money. But the plan went awry when Myers fought back. McDonald confessed that he hit Myers one time, but it was Lewis who delivered the fatal blows, adding that in court "anyone could see that he (Lewis) was guilty."

In June, prior to the trial, Prosecutor Cahalan had written to Sheriff Bryon, telling him that McDonald was "digging his own grave by his false statements." On October 14, the lies stopped. In the middle of a heavy snowstorm, Sheriff John Springer and his deputies led McDonald to a waiting wagon. They drove one mile north of Silver City to the Ruby City Cemetery where the gallows and over 300 people waited for the execution. Accompanied by Father Nattini, a Catholic priest, McDonald mounted the scaffold and stood as the death warrant was read. When Springer asked him if had anything to say, McDonald was finally silent. He shook hands with his guards and the priest and took his place on the trap door. A few minutes later he was dead. They placed his body in a plain pine coffin and buried him in the cemetery.

The Kelton Road outlived McDonald by only two years. In 1883, the Short Line Railroad pushed into Shoshone, Idaho, and the road was no longer needed. John Hailey, who had established the freight line and had been instrumental in bringing McDonald to justice, founded the town of Hailey and served as a representative in Idaho's territorial legislature. Between 1899-1901, he was warden of the Idaho State Penitentiary, and in 1910 he published *The History of Idaho*. The book contains no reference to McDonald or his crime.

EDWARD RICE

WALLACE, OCTOBER 1, 1900
BOISE, NOVEMBER 30, 1901

In the early history of Idaho, executions were local affairs, held in the counties where the notorious crimes had been committed, where condemned criminals faced both judge and jury who called for swift justice. Usually, the county sheriff was in charge, and he performed his duties in any way he saw fit. In 1899, in an effort to stop the circus atmosphere that sometimes characterized the hangings and to create uniformity in how the state treated its worst felons, the legislature passed a new law that required all legal executions to be held at the Idaho State Penitentiary, directed by the warden, and hidden from public view. That was probably little consolation to Edward "Baldy" Rice, who in 1901 was the first state prisoner to hang at the Old Idaho Penitentiary.

Rice was born in Baltimore, Maryland in 1858. His father was a German immigrant, while his mother hailed from Pennsylvania. He attended school for only one year and never learned to read or write. As an adult, he signed his name with a simple "X." In 1878, at age 22 and no prospects at hand, he enlisted in the US Army for a five-year tour. He was assigned to the Maryland 2nd Infantry, Company G.

After a short stay in New York, Rice was sent to San Francisco and from there to Vancouver. He had a short deployment at Fort Lapwai near Lewiston, until he was sent to his final assignment at Fort Coeur d'Alene/Fort Sherman. It was here Rice's behavior ran afoul of Army expectations. In a report to his superiors, Captain Charles Keller called Rice "unfit for service" and asked that he be discharged. The cause: Rice wet his bed every night. Army doctors concurred that Rice was incontinent, a problem supposedly caused by a congenital problem, not illness. Still, his incontinence was disruptive, and he received an honorable discharge due to disability. Whether this problem plagued him for the rest of his life is unclear as his prison file is devoid of any mention of it.

Relieved from service, Rice found himself in Umatilla, Oregon where he tried to find work as a cigar maker. He then spent time in Missoula, Montana before moving to Spokane, Washington where he went to work as a bartender. There he met Amelia (Millie) Larsen. In 1890, they married and moved to Wallace, Idaho.

Wallace was probably not the best place to take a new bride. In the late 1890s, men outnumbered women 200 to one, most of them seeking their fortunes in the mines of what is still known as the Silver Valley. So rich in minerals, the area once ranked as one of the top ten mining districts in the world. The town buzzed with activity—not all of it favorable. Gambling, a major source of entertainment, could be

Edward Rice

found in the twenty-eight saloons scattered in Wallace's downtown district. The large male population was also serviced with at least five bordellos, one still in operation into the 1990s. The town attracted all sorts, including its share of ruffians who were not afraid of a good fight. In 1899, when the Bunker Hill and Sullivan Mining Company refused to recognize the miners' union in the area, the miners went on a rampage using dynamite to destroy company buildings and machinery. With one man killed, famed Idaho attorney William Borah was brought in to prosecute those responsible. Federal troops were called to quell the riot and Idaho Governor Frank Steunenberg ordered martial law that remained in effect for two years. The uprising culminated in the murder of Steunenberg in 1905.

In the midst of this mayhem, Edward and Millie started their family. Mabel was born in 1892 followed by Phyllis in 1894. To support his family, Rice went to work in the mines pushing a wheelbarrow for the Union Mills. He also tended bar and cut firewood. During the union riots, he served as a deputy sheriff, a position he held for six months. He also applied for his veteran's pension, which was denied.

Rice not only needed the money to support his family, he also needed it to feed his gambling habits. He could not resist a good game, whether it was black jack, poker, or craps. Millie eventually tired of the struggle and in June 1900, returned to Spokane. She moved in with her parents and filed for a divorce.

Rice was not willing to let her go. According to Rice, between June and October he worked diligently, saving his money so he could contest the divorce. He earned three dollars a day as a bartender at the Bank Saloon and was a partner in a mine on Sherlock Creek. By the end of September, he claimed to have saved at least $200, which he kept hidden under a trunk in his room above the saloon. However, at the same time, he owed people around Wallace at least $200, buying on credit or borrowing money to stake his gambling. He bargained he would be able to pay his debts after he won his divorce case.

Not everyone struggled as much as Rice. Fortunes were made by businessmen and mining executives who invested in the Silver Valley. Merchants who provided for the needs of the miners also found financial success. One such merchant was Matthew Mailey (also Maily, Marley, Meuli), who immigrated to the United States from Switzerland in 1870. He spent some time in Montana before arriving in the Wallace area in 1886 where he staked several successful mining claims near Osborne. In 1896, he established a cigar shop in Wallace selling tobacco and smoking supplies. He did a fair business and was known as "unusually quiet and inoffensive," a kind man who lived by himself in the back of his shop. He had no known enemies, paid his way, and banked most of his money. Records show that on October 1, 1900, he had $2300 in the First National Bank at Wallace. In his store he had a small safe where he would provide change to his neighboring merchants or loan money to his customers if they were in need. He was also known to carry large sums of money—bills in a leather pocketbook and coins, usually gold, in a tobacco pouch. This money would lead to his ruin.

On Sunday night, September 30, 1900, Rice prowled the streets of Wallace. He wandered in and out of several saloons, looking to borrow money from an easy mark. He finally found H. W. Scott who loaned him a five-dollar gold piece. With the money, Rice bought into a poker game. Later, he borrowed money from another man to cover a craps table. Whether he won or lost in either case is unclear. Rice could not remember, claiming, "I didn't pay too much attention to that." Around 11 p.m., he wandered into Sweet & Gaut's Saloon. Sitting at the bar sipping on an Oscar Pepper Whiskey was Mailey. Mailey was considering a trip to Mullan that night, a small mining town six miles east of Wallace. The two men talked for a few minutes, and then Mailey left. Rice followed him out of the bar.

The two made their way to Steers' saloon. Mailey asked Rice to accompany him to Mullan; he had business with Peter Sherlock, Rice's

Sixth Street in Wallace

partner. The two men left the saloon and headed east on Cedar Street, but when they reached the outskirts of Wallace, they turned back. According to Rice, the two went back to Steers' and then parted ways.

Rice spent the rest of the evening continuing his rounds to the various taverns in Wallace. Witnesses would identify him around town into the early morning hours. At around 2:15, he stopped at the dance hall and spoke to Ione (Onie) Rollins who lived above the hall. He confided in her that he and Mailey had been together until about 2 a.m., and they had visited the Corner Bar for a drink. Rollins would later say Rice had money in his pocket, claiming he had "won tonight up at the Corner." He had won enough to pay for a frolic with Onie.

Rice waited for Onie in Room #4 of the Bank Saloon. She arrived at 4 a.m. and an hour later she was sleeping soundly. She would later claim she was unaware of when Rice left the room. She would not see him again until mid-morning when he returned to the room to change his shirt.

Monday morning at 6:20, Rice was at the bar at the Bank Saloon where he had several drinks. Bartender Richard Foley would recall he was agitated and disheveled. He also noticed blood on Rice's knuckles and shirtsleeves. Foley teased him about his appearance, asking him if he'd been "licking his girl." When he asked Rice about the dark-colored stains on his pants, Rice abruptly left the saloon. For the next twelve hours, Rice's behavior would make him the prime suspect in a murder that was about to be discovered.

Mailey opened his cigar shop each morning at 7:15. He and James Layman, a tailor who owned a clothing store next door, often swept the sidewalk together. On this morning, Layman did the sweeping by himself. When Mailey still hadn't opened his shop by nine, Layman became concerned. He peeked into the window of Mailey's shop and saw a human foot protruding from behind the counter. He ran to find the city marshal.

Marshall J. W. McGinnis broke open the front door to the shop. He found a man lying on the floor, a bloody pillowslip pulled over his head. McGinnis immediately sought the help of Shoshone County Sheriff Angus Sutherland. Together they removed the pillowslip and recognized Mailey. His body was still warm.

Mailey had been savagely murdered. His skull had been fractured above his right eye, his throat slashed, and his right hand broken. In all, he suffered seven blows to the head, all on the right side, along with a three-inch wound in his neck that severed his jugular. Two blood-soaked handkerchiefs packed the neck wound. A twenty-inch flat steel bar lay next to the body. Blood was everywhere—on the counter, on the cash registers, on Mailey's still-locked safe.

Sutherland had the shop secured. He collected the evidence—the metal bar and handkerchiefs—and after finding the laundry mark "ED" on one of the handkerchiefs, took them both to the Superior Hand Laundry to be washed. He was hoping to find more laundry marks on the hankies. He then began making the rounds of the saloons in Wallace, gathering information, looking for witnesses.

In the afternoon, the sheriff was back at the tobacco shop where he took an inventory of the safe and cash registers. The safe contained nearly 400 dollars in paper money, checks, and gold and silver coins. One till contained twelve dollars, and the other held a watch, some gold rings, and several diamond stickpins. Then word came that the laundress at the Superior Hand could positively identify the owner of one of the handkerchiefs—Ed Rice. Sheriff Sutherland had his man.

Rice, too, had a busy morning. After his drinks at the Bank Saloon, he went to the OK Clothing Store on Bank Street and bought a new pair of pants using a $20 gold piece. He changed his pants right in the store, rolling up his old ones and taking them with him. He deposited the pants at the laundry. He then made his way to the W.U. Telegraph Company where he sent a telegram to Del Carey Smith, a lawyer in Spokane representing him in his divorce case. Filed at 8:18 a.m., the telegram read, "Be sure that I will be there tomorrow," and was signed by Rice. Around 10 a.m. Rice returned to his room at the Bank Saloon where he saw Onie still in bed. Here he changed his shirt, gathered up some other belongings, and stuffed them in a cubbyhole in Room #9. Later, he would place his laundered pants in the same hiding place.

Wallace was abuzz with Mailey's murder, but Rice seemed oblivious to it. Instead, he was intent that morning to pay off all of his debts, some of them over two years old. From the shoe store to Taylor's General Store, to the barber to friends, Rice seemed to owe everyone money and suddenly he had plenty. His payment of choice was a $20 gold piece, paying at least six debts with the coin. Two other debts were paid with $10 gold pieces, while one other was paid with a ten-dollar bill. His final payment of the day went to Onie Rollins. He paid her a $20 gold piece for services rendered earlier that morning.

While Rice was handing out money, accountants and bookkeepers began going over Mailey's finances. While there was no sign of forced entry or robbery at his store, the numbers in his safe did not add up to the numbers that appeared in his ledgers. In fact, the safe was about $980 short.

By early Monday evening, Sheriff Sutherland had heard and seen enough. Talk on the street was that Baldy Rice was good for the crime. With tensions running high, rumors of a lynching made the rounds in saloons on Sixth and Bank Streets. As a precaution, Sutherland put extra deputies on duty at the jail. He armed himself and made his way to Room # 4 above the Bank Saloon where he found Rice alone. Together they went down the stairs into the saloon. They stopped for a moment, and Rice asked if he could get a cup of coffee in the kitchen. The sheriff didn't object, and Rice disappeared for a few minutes. When he returned, the two men walked to the county jail, where Rice was locked up under heavy guard.

A coroner's inquest on Mailey's death was called for October 3. Witnesses testified as to both Mailey's and Rice's movements prior to the murder. Rice's behavior after the murder was noted for the record. The most damning piece of evidence was Rice's handkerchief at the murder scene. Although one witness, John Hickey, recalled seeing Mailey with a tall, dark man between the hours of five and six the morning of the murder, it was not enough to quell the call for charges against Rice. This information was then turned over to a grand jury who indicted Rice on first-degree murder charges.

On Friday, October 12, Rice, along with his lawyer Charles F. Miller, appeared before Judge Alexander E. Mayhew of Idaho's First Judicial District to hear the charges against him. Shoshone County Attorney Henry F. Samuels served as prosecutor along with Charles W. Beale, a private attorney, who offered his services to the state. Rice asked for a continuance and Mayhew set Oct. 15 as the date to hear his plea. Back in court on Monday, Rice pleaded not guilty and then requested another continuance, this one until the next term of the court. Mayhew agreed to hear cause for the continuance the next day.

The hearing took two days. Rice's attorney argued he needed time to find John Hickey, who suddenly vanished into the hills of Northern Idaho. Hickey, Miller contended, could show another man may have committed the murder. Miller also told the judge it would be impossible for Rice to get a fair trial. A reward had been offered for information leading to the arrest of Mailey's murderer and a mob formed to lynch Rice when he was arrested. The prosecutor had even brought in a private lawyer to help secure a conviction. These added up to a stacked deck against Rice. Only time would lessen the emotion in the case. Still, Judge Mayhew was unconvinced. He denied the motion for a continuance and set October 23 as the opening date of the trial.

Jury selection took two days. On October 25, the prosecution began with a series of witnesses who could place Mailey and Rice together prior to Mailey's murder. One witness, Al Fish, placed Rice in Mailey's store at around 6 a.m. the morning of the murder. This eyewitness testimony was then followed by the introduction of the physical evidence. All pointed to Rice as the killer.

The marked handkerchief found at the murder scene was matched with another found hidden in the kitchen at the Bank Saloon. Rice's laundered pants were found in their hiding place in Room #9. Bartender Foley described Rice's demeanor and appearance, down to his bloody knuckles and stained pants. Sheriff Sutherland described the condition of Rice's long underwear when he undressed at the jail—both knees were stained with blood.

The prosecution also presented a long line of witnesses—twelve in all--who received money from Rice the day of the murder. Defense Attorney Miller objected to these witnesses, claiming no foundation had been laid for their testimonies, nor did they add anything material to the issue. These objections were overruled. Then Prosecutor Samuels called Joseph Whalen, deputy assessor of Shoshone County, who had carefully examined Mailey's bankbooks. Whalen was positive that Mailey's safe was short $996.66, give or take a few dollars. With this information before the jury, the prosecution rested its case.

Rice was clearly in trouble, and Miller knew it. First, he asked the court to disregard statements and evidence concerning Mailey's bank accounts, as they were incomplete, inconsistent, and inadmissible. The judge denied the request. Then Miller again asked to strike all the testimony related to Rice's payment of his debts because there was no proof there had been a robbery at Mailey's business. This request, too, was denied. He had no choice but to put Rice on the stand in his own defense.

Rice claimed his innocence from the beginning and did his best to explain away the evidence against him. He was right-handed; the killer appeared to be left-handed as all the blows to Mailey's head came from the left. He had left Mailey alive around 2 a.m. the morning of the murder. He bought new pants the same morning because his old ones were thin; he needed something warmer for the coming winter. Room # 9 where he stored his clothes was open to everyone; in fact, everyone who lived in the Bank Saloon used Room #9 as a dressing room. He had not seen the two handkerchiefs marked "ED" for months. As for the stain the bartender saw on his pants, that was water he had splashed on himself as he was cleaning up that morning. The blood on his drawers came from open sores on his legs that bled and discharged "corruption." They had flared up prior to the murder, and since he had worn the same drawers for six days prior to his arrest, they were bound to have stains on them. For good measure, he even showed the jury his legs; the legs did have several open sores.

As for his sudden monetary fortune, Rice claimed that on Monday morning he decided to give up on his marriage; he would not go to Spokane and contest the divorce. Instead, he took the money he had been so diligently saving and decided to pay his debts. He even gave names of additional people he had paid off. He maintained he was just trying to settle up with everyone, put his divorce behind him, and start over.

But the prosecutor had the copy of the telegram Rice sent on Monday morning, telling his lawyer he would be in Spokane the following day. Rice argued he had sent the message on Sunday morning, and there truly was some confusion on the date. According to F. Brightman, the telegraph

Bank Street in Wallace

operator, he originally dated the wire September 30, but changed it to October 1 when he realized his mistake. On the stand Brightman testified he was certain that he received the information from Rice at 8:18 a.m. on October 1. He recalled that Rice paid for the telegram with a silver piece, and it was sent at 8:30 a.m. that day.

Samuels' cross-examination of Rice was relentless. He pressed him for details of his gambling, how much he had won in the past month, how much he had earned at his other jobs. He wanted to know why he had given up on the divorce, when for the last three months he saved every penny to fight it. And he wanted to know why, the morning Rice decided to abandon his fight, he felt the urgent need to pay off his debts. Rice had no good answers. He seemed confused, and he contradicted himself. His testimony was filled with long pauses and times when he would simply answer "I really don't know." In the end, he could only say that sometimes he won, sometimes he lost.

With the jury, he lost. On November 1, after closing arguments and the judge's instructions, the twelve men retired to deliberate the case. It took them all of twenty-five minutes to render a verdict of guilty. Five days later, Judge Mayhew sentenced Rice to hang, setting the execution for December 31, 1900. On the same day, a judge in Spokane granted Millie Rice a divorce.

Rice arrived at the Idaho State Penitentiary on November 11. As with all convicts, his physical description was recorded. He stood 5'7" tall and weighed 187 pounds. Doctors noted he had very bad teeth and three tattoos, two of them women, one on each forearm. He had dark hair salted with grey, grey eyes, and a dark complexion. He was placed in a solitary cell to await his fate.

He did not take imprisonment well. Under the rules of solitary confinement, he was allowed no visitors except his lawyer, spiritual advisors, and family. He had no family and even his lawyer was scarce during the first month of his incarceration. The lack of contact made him inclined to fits of weeping, insomnia, and delirium. However, he gave the guards no trouble and was even called an "exemplary prisoner."

Rice firmly expected an appeal to be filed on his behalf and became increasingly frustrated when his lawyer failed to do so. Finally, on December 24, just seven days before the scheduled execution, attorney Miller filed his appeal with the Idaho Supreme Court. The court ordered a stay of execution and agreed to hear the case.

Edward Rice would be the first person hanged at the Idaho State Penitentiary in Boise.

But on New Year's Day, 1901, Rice tried to settle the issue on his own, slashing his throat with a Case knife. Shocked guards quickly called the prison doctor, George Collister, who used twenty-four stitches to close the wound. Rice would not discuss his motive and was embarrassed by the attempt, calling himself a "cussed fool." He claimed the attempt was not an admittance of guilt and his appeal would give him the chance to prove he was innocent.

His appeal would center around several key issues. Rice's lawyer would argue that the handkerchiefs were inadmissible because they had been washed after they were found. There was no proof that the handkerchiefs found at the crime scene were the same that came back from the laundry. There was also the question of the continuance, as the lawyer contended he had not been given ample time to produce an effective defense, nor time to find key witnesses who would be able to exonerate Rice. Finally, Miller would claim that all testimony concerning Mailey's finances and Rice's payment of debts should have been disallowed, since there was no evidence of robbery at Mailey's establishment, only evidence of a murder.

William Borah tried to save Rice.

The Idaho Supreme Court heard the case in April. On June 15, 1901, it rendered its decision. The appeal was denied. While some of Miller's objections may have been valid, they were not enough to make a reasonable jury come to any other conclusion: Rice was indeed the killer. In September, Miller asked for a rehearing, but that request was also rejected. On October 1, under close guard, Rice returned to Wallace to hear his final sentencing. He was to hang on November 30, 1901.

Upon his return to Boise, Rice was kept under constant watch. His behavior was erratic; his insomnia worsened. Miller considered mounting a last minute insanity defense but did not have faith in his ability to prove it. Then an unlikely participant decided to wade into the issue. William Borah, who had met Rice in Wallace during the miners' uprising in 1899, visited Rice in prison. Shocked by his appearance and demeanor, Borah brought in three doctors to examine Rice and determine his sanity. Two of the three—including prison doctor Jessie DuBois—believed Rice was insane. Borah took their findings to Governor Frank Hunt and asked for a reprieve until a more thorough examination of Rice's mental state could be made.

On the evening of November 29, Hunt gathered the board of pardons to consider Borah's request. After hearing all the concerns, including a recant of Dr. Dubois' diagnosis of Rice, who decided Rice wasn't crazy, just a "pervert," the governor announced there would be no intervention on Rice's behalf. The execution would go on as scheduled.

On the morning of November 30, a scaffold stood in the prison yard. Curtains of white muslin surrounded the structure blocking it from view as required by law. Shortly after eight o'clock, accompanied by a Catholic priest, Warden Charles Arney, and four prison guards, Rice made his way to the gallows. He climbed the steps on his own accord and positioned himself on the trap door without any assistance. While he was pale, he stood stoically. As the Warden stepped forward to shake his hand and bid him goodbye, Rice did not seem to grasp his imminent demise.

"Goodbye, Mr. Arney," he said. "I don't think you are doing right to put me out of this world. There is no hurry. There is lots of time."

With that, Rice dropped to his death. He was buried later that day in the prison cemetery. The priest, Warden Arney, and the four prison guards carried him to his final resting place.

Nearly destroyed in the Great Fire of 1910, Wallace rebuilt and remained a colorful, wild west town for most of the 1900s. But it was not without its detractors. In 1973, local and state authorities closed the community's five remaining brothels. Several, however, managed to survive, and one operated until 1990. Gambling flourished until June 23, 1991, when 150 FBI agents raided fifty-eight bars in the area, shutting down their gaming operations. Not surprisingly, the people in Wallace protested the raid, claiming their activities were "no more harmful than bowling on Sundays."

Noah Arnold

Hope, July 16, 1923
Boise, December 19, 1924

Bonner County Sheriff William Kirkpatrick was desperate. He had a murder on his hands and an angry mob at his door. The brash young Negro man sitting in his jail refused to confess, and he taunted the sheriff, giving misleading information on the whereabouts of his accomplice. Kirkpatrick knew he had to appease the crowd, but protect his prisoner at the same time. The ruse he concocted went exactly as planned.

Kirkpatrick directed his deputies to gather the crowd of outraged but controllable citizens to a secluded spot west of Sandpoint and prepare for a staged hanging. Then under the cover of darkness, Kirkpatrick took his prisoner, Noah Arnold, to join them. The mob was ready, and when Arnold arrived, the sheriff led him to a tree from which a rope was suspended. Arnold was then hoisted onto a wooden box and a noose was tightened around his neck. The locals closed the circle around him and swore to hang him if he didn't tell them what they wanted to hear. At that moment, Noah Arnold believed he was going to die, so he told the crowd what it wanted to hear; he confessed to the murder of William Crisp and gave up his accomplice.

They did not hang Arnold in the pine woods of northern Idaho. The sheriff's ploy worked, and the crowd got in enough good licks to satisfy its need for revenge. Roughed up but alive, Arnold was returned to his cell. While he would escape the hangman on that particular night, he was not so lucky with Idaho's court system. He climbed the scaffold at the Idaho State Penitentiary in December 1924 and paid the ultimate price for his crime.

Noah Arnold knew trouble most of his days. To reconstruct his life is to trace an assortment of lies and tall tales, all told by Arnold himself. Involved with the justice system in his early teens, he took several aliases, changed his place of birth, his parentage, and misled police departments across the United States during a sixteen-year crime spree.

Arnold was born on February 14, 1892, in Lowell, Kentucky, to Clayton and Mary Ann (Anna) Arnold. He had at least one older brother, Clayton, and a younger sister, Bettie. Census records specify the family was mulatto, and Noah indicated from time to time that he was one-quarter

American Indian. Descriptions of him support this, as in various prison records and newspaper articles he is described as a "medium" or "chocolate" Negro. Mug shots show him with dark hair, piercing brown eyes, and high cheekbones.

As for schooling, Noah claimed at one time his mother taught him at home, but at other times, he indicated he attended school through the sixth grade. While in both Kentucky and Washington reformatories, he received formal education, and he was able to read and write, although on a remedial level. He left home at thirteen, and whatever education he received from then on came from experience.

Arnold's criminal record began on March 14, 1906, when he was arrested and then convicted for grand larceny. He was sentenced to two years in the Kentucky House of Reform in Greensdale, only to escape on December 30, 1908. He fled to Tennessee, where he was caught riding freight trains near Memphis. He served thirty days in the Shelby County Jail and paid a twenty-five dollar fine.

After his release, Arnold returned to Kentucky where he managed to stay out of trouble for the next four years. But in April 1912, he was arrested and found guilty of second-degree burglary for breaking into a storehouse in Paris, Kentucky. Arnold was sentenced to one to five years in the Kentucky State Reformatory in Frankfort, where he was punished on numerous occasions for fighting and refusing to work. His bad behavior prolonged his stay, and he was not paroled until February 15, 1915.

With his freedom, Arnold traveled west. He eventually made his way to Tacoma, Washington, but not without several stops where he had run-ins with the law. In late 1915 in Chicago, he was arrested for vagrancy and suspicion of murder but was released. In early 1916, he was picked up in Staples, Minnesota, for riding freight trains. He was set free with the admonition to "leave town," which he did, traveling next to Missoula, Montana. There he used an alias, Jack Ford, and was arrested for vagrancy, given a ten-day suspended sentence, and sent packing.

Once in Tacoma, using the name Robert Ford, he went to work in the shipyards. He immediately found himself in trouble, arrested for assault when he shot a man in a fight. He was sentenced to six months in the Pierce County Jail but released after thirty days. Once out, he fired shots at a woman and fled to Seattle to escape arrest.

In Seattle, he made the acquaintance of Mabel Bell. On the night of January 4, 1917, Arnold was alone with Bell in her apartment. Bell's live-in boyfriend, Harry Agie, arrived at the apartment at approximately 11 p.m. and was not pleased to find his girl alone with Arnold. An argument ensued and a few minutes later, Agie was dead. Arnold claimed self-defense, alleging Agie had attacked him with a straight razor. Prosecutors, however, thought otherwise and charged him with second degree murder. Under the alias of Robert Ford, he was found guilty of manslaughter when evidence showed that Agie had been unarmed. According to the prosecuting attorney Frank Helsell, "Ford is the sort of negro who carries a gun and flourishes it upon the slightest provocation and is altogether too willing to shoot."

Arnold was sentenced to not less than two nor more than twenty years in the Washington State Reformatory at Monroe. He arrived at Monroe on May 9, 1917 and wove an elaborate story of his life, claiming he was born in New Orleans, never knew his father, and that prior to arriving in Tacoma, had worked in Chicago for four years as a bartender and shoe shiner. This information

Noah Arnold, alias Robert Ford, at the Washington State Reformatory

was noted by the reformatory chaplain, who also stated that Arnold, as Ford, seemed "frank and respectful to good people. May develop along the right line."

The chaplain's optimism was soon dashed as Arnold's behavior had him in trouble most of the time. In July, he was sentenced to thirty days solitary confinement after he fought and threatened another inmate claiming, "I have killed one man. I can also kill another." Later he lost his yard and movie privileges for talking in his cell. In early November, he was caught smoking in his cell, and spent another fifteen days in confinement. As soon as this punishment was lifted, he again was caught smoking in his cell.

Acknowledging that attempts to reform Arnold were having no effect, Monroe's superintendent, Donald Olsen, recommended Arnold's transfer to the Washington State Prison in Walla Walla. In his letter to the warden, Olsen wrote, "he [Ford] is not, or never was, amenable to reformatory methods." The transfer was approved on December 5, 1917, and two days later, Arnold became prisoner #8432 in the Washington Penitentiary.

Noah Arnold at the Washington State Penitentiary

Arnold, still as Robert Ford, settled into prison life at Walla Walla. How he fared is unknown, but on March 9, 1919, he sent a letter to the prison captain.

"Dear sir. I would like to have an inarview with you please sir on som very importon bisness at your pleasure. Yours very respectably."

No record of what took place at that meeting exists, but on April 1, 1919, the prison's physician and Henry Drum, the prison warden, signed commitment papers that sent Arnold to the Eastern Hospital for the Insane at Medical Lake, Washington. How long he stayed is not known, but he eventually admitted to officials that his real name was Noah Arnold. In a note in his own hand, he indicated,

"This is so call Robert Ford. My right name is Noah Arnold. I have a brother at Cartersville, Kentucky name Claton Arnold and my father is also named Clayton Arnold. He lives at Lowell, Kentucky where I were born in 1892. from Robert Ford, right name, Noah Arnold."

By July 1920, Arnold was back at Walla Walla and looking for his release. Still using the name Robert Ford, he wrote a letter to Washington Governor L. F. Hart concerning the board of pardons. He complained he had yet to have a hearing before the board, even though he had been incarcerated three years and three months, "one year and three months over the specified minimum time decreed by the judge." He asked the governor to intervene and instruct the pardon board to hear his case at its October 1920 meeting. Arnold's request was granted, but he was not paroled at that time and remained in prison for another year. Finally, on December 12,

1921, the pardon board granted his release. By the end of December, he was on his own.

As part of his parole, Arnold was not allowed to leave the state. He was also required to make a monthly report to the chief parole officer at the penitentiary. On January 5, 1922, Arnold reported he was living in Spokane and actively looking for work. By February, he had secured employment as a porter at a barbershop and was earning three dollars a week, along with whatever he could make shining shoes. He wrote his parole officer that, "times is purty hard now but I won't forget our agreement."

By the end of the month, life had improved for Arnold. He was still employed at the barber shop, where he also roomed, and had pocketed $25.50. His report to the parole officer indicated he was looking forward to the coming spring: "I will make good this months as the weather is good here and business is picking up." It was the last report Arnold made. By March, he had abandoned Spokane and his good intentions.

For the next year, Arnold managed to elude parole officers and committed no other crimes for which he was arrested. Then in the summer of 1923, working with an ex-con named Mike Donnelly, Arnold made the ultimate mistake. He killed a white man.

Hope is a quiet little town in Northern Idaho on the shores of Lake Pend Oreille. There, on the night of July 16, 1923, W. A. Crisp was just closing his general store when two Negro men approached the front door. As it was locked, Crisp went to the door to see what they wanted. They asked if they might buy some bread, so Crisp let them in.

Also in the store at the time was James Campbell, Hope's postmaster. Campbell would testify in a preliminary hearing that as soon as Crisp unlocked the door, the two men pushed their way in and pulled guns. The burglars demanded both men get their "hands up." Donnelly confronted Campbell, putting a gun in his back, while Arnold went after Crisp. Unhappy with Crisp's initial response, Arnold yelled at him to, "Get 'em higher or I'll bore you." As Arnold attempted to take the gold watch from Crisp's pocket, Crisp turned to hit Arnold. A shot rang out and Crisp fell first to his knees, then face to the floor, crying, "I'm dead, I'm dead." At that point, Donnelly momentarily left Campbell and attempted to shoot Crisp in the back, but his gun misfired. Campbell went to the aid of his friend, jumping on Donnelly's back to take him down. Angry, Donnelly slammed the butt of his gun into Campbell's head. As Campbell slumped to the floor, Donnelly fired a shot at him but missed.

Campbell lay dazed as both Donnelly and Arnold turned their attention to Crisp. They rifled his pockets and searched the store for cash. With the shooters occupied, Campbell recovered enough to slip outside and hide in the shadows. He watched as Arnold and Donnelly ran from the building and headed west along the Northern Pacific Railroad tracks. He returned to the store to call a doctor who in turn notified the sheriff.

Crisp lay mortally wounded. He was sent by train to a hospital in Spokane, where he died the following morning.

The incident sparked an intense manhunt which lasted over a week. No Negro in northern Idaho was safe from suspicion, and every black man on the road between Spokane and Troy, Montana, was hauled before the Bonner County sheriff for questioning. Canadian border guards locked the borders to all Negro men, and Sheriff William Kirkpatrick offered a $250 reward for the capture of each "bandit." Few men attended Crisp's funeral as every able-bodied man in Hope joined the posse to track down the "black thugs."

The two eluded capture for over a week, hiding in the wooded hills around Hope, Sandpoint, and Bonners Ferry, surviving on food they stole from root cellars. At one point, they found themselves surrounded by over 100 armed men, and still they got away. They began making their way west, following the Pend Oreille River. Emboldened by the posse's inability to catch them, they became less cautious, traveling in plain sight. Arnold was first to be captured. On July 25, he was arrested aboard a passenger train bound for Newport, Washington. He had actually purchased his ticket.

Arnold was taken to the Bonner County Jail. There, under intense interrogation, he gave his captors information on Donnelly's whereabouts. Arnold, however, was less than truthful with his remarks, misleading the sheriff and his deputies, until Kirkpatrick had enough of the lies and Arnold's arrogance.

The people of Hope and Sandpoint cried for swift justice. No black intruder was going to harm one of their own and get away with it without tasting the lash of their vengeance. Arnold had made them look foolish, hiding right under their noses. Now he was comfortable in their county jail, telling them lie after lie about Donnelly, refusing to admit his involvement in the murder. Finally, the sheriff had enough. If Arnold was going to taunt him, turn about was fair play. So under Kirkpatrick's direction, the mob did its work, threatening Arnold with a backwoods lynching. A photo, which has since been lost, shows Arnold surrounded by the armed men, the noose tight around his neck. It did not take long for Arnold to confess to the crime and turn on his accomplice. On the night of July 29, Donnelly was captured crossing a train bridge outside of Priest River, Idaho.

The sheriff's staged hanging and the capture of Donnelly emboldened the locals. They began preparations to lynch both the "Black Bandits," this time in earnest. Kirkpatrick, fearing he could not protect his prisoners, transferred them to the Kootenai County Jail in Coeur d' Alene, Idaho. There they remained until August 4 when they were returned to Sandpoint and arraigned, charged with first-degree murder. Both men pleaded not guilty and were bound over for their preliminary hearing on August 7 in front of Probate Judge Myrvin Davis. At the hearing, Davis heard testimony from Crisp's wife, Josephine; eyewitness Campbell; and Union Pacific signal man H. R. Sage, who had seen both Donnelly and Arnold prior to the murder. Judge Davis found sufficient evidence to send the case to district court and ordered the two men held without bail.

As the men awaited trial, the *Northern Idaho News* detailed the lives of the two defendants, focusing heavily on Donnelly, whose past was riddled with daring robberies and bold escape attempts. Imprisoned in the Washington State Penitentiary for murder, Donnelly had been paroled on May 15, 1923. Whether he knew Arnold from the prison is unknown, but within a month of his release, he and Arnold were suspected of robbing a bank in Plains, Montana. They were also the prime suspects in several robberies in Shelby, Montana, and allegedly robbed a man on a train between Shelby and Sandpoint. Arnold, however, always denied his involvement in those crimes, claiming he did not meet Donnelly until July 16, well after the Montana robberies. He would also claim that he was afraid of Donnelly and forced to do "his bidding." Reporters echoed this, writing that Donnelly was the "more forceful, aggressive character of the two," and had a "dominating personality." The swagger and arrogance Arnold portrayed immediately after he was caught faded with each passing day.

Arnold and Donnelly were kept in solitary confinement under tight security during their stay in the Bonner County Jail. As their district court date neared, Bonner County Prosecuting Attorney Allen P. Asher announced he would not accept a guilty plea from either defendant. Asher wanted the two killers to hang, but he believed only a jury could impose the death penalty. If the two pleaded guilty, there would be no jury to impose the sentence, and the men could only be sentenced to life terms.

Arnold's court-appointed lawyer, A. T. Aronson, agreed with Asher. It was Aronson's opinion that a district court judge did not have the authority to impose a death sentence, and he passed this information on to Arnold. But Aronson also told his nervous client that the judge could take matters into his own hands. Ultimately, the counselor left the decision up to Arnold.

On September 12, 1923, Arnold appeared before Eighth District Court Judge W. F. McNaughton to enter his plea. Although McNaughton warned him a guilty plea might result in a death sentence, Arnold admitted his guilt. Donnelly, represented by Oscar J. Bandelin, also pleaded guilty to the murder charge. Contrary to his earlier statements, Prosecutor Asher sat quietly in the court and filed no objections while the men entered their pleas.

Clearly, prior to the hearing, some backroom agreements had been made which would doom Arnold. Immediately following the guilty pleas, Judge McNaughton shocked the defendants when he announced he had the same latitude as a jury in determining a sentence of life or death. He called on Prosecutor Asher to assemble his witnesses and evidence against the two men and set September 14 for the penalty hearing.

Asher went to work building his case, especially against Arnold. He put James Campbell and Mrs. Crisp on the stand to tell their stories. He also called those involved in the pursuit of Arnold and Donnelly. But his strongest testimony came from Sheriff Kirkpatrick who had collected three bullets—one from Crisp's body and two from the store. According to Kirkpatrick, all three were .45 caliber bullets and came from the gun belonging to Arnold.

To finish his case, Asher produced copies of both Donnelly and Arnold's prison records, suggesting that incarceration had done nothing to improve the morality of the two men. The only punishment suitable for both men, according to Asher, would be death.

Attorneys for Arnold and Donnelly did little in the courtroom. Aronson objected to the admission of the prison records, but he was overruled. In his closing argument for Arnold, Aronson suggested that the shooting of Crisp may have been accidental, caused by the scuffle between Arnold and Crisp. Donnelly's attorney argued that Donnelly had only been an accessory to the crime, and as such should not be sentenced to death. Neither Arnold nor Donnelly spoke in his own defense. They returned to their cells on Thursday afternoon to await their fates. Two days later, they were back in court to hear the judge's decision.

Telling them that the "lives of those criminals who in perpetration of their crimes hold human life cheaply are also held cheaply by the state," McNaughton sentenced Arnold to pay the "extreme penalty of death," and set Nov. 1, 1923 as the date of execution. As for Donnelly, the judge sentenced him to life in prison, claiming his punishment was as far as the court could go.

Arnold showed no emotion when hearing the sentence, but once back in his cell, he cursed the court and the prosecutor. Within hours, he was on his way to the Idaho State Penitentiary in Boise where plans for his execution began. At the same time, Arnold's attorney filed a motion to vacate and set aside the conviction. He asked McNaughton to allow Arnold to withdraw his guilty plea and enter a plea of not guilty. This motion was denied.

In Boise, William M. Morgan, once a Chief Justice of the Idaho State Supreme Court, and J. B. Eldridge, his former partner, learned of Arnold's plight. Morgan had obtained the picture of Arnold in the woods with the angry mob ready to string him up. According to Morgan, Arnold's confession was tainted and under those circumstances he did not understand how "the trial court could impose the death penalty." Morgan planned to contact Sandpoint officials and promised to represent Arnold if necessary. Other prominent Boise attorneys took up the cause, visiting Arnold in prison and offering free legal advice. Their involvement assured another examination of the trial and troubled the people of Hope and Sandpoint. They believed the Boise lawyers were meddling in the case, which had been "misrepresented" in the capital city. They were being cast as uncivilized backwoods vigilantes, an impression they resented.

In October, Aronson, joined by Morgan and Ivan Hiler, appealed Arnold's conviction and sentence before Judge McNaughton. He denied their request for a new trial, and the case moved forward to the Idaho Supreme Court. Arnold received a temporary stay of execution, and his lawyers went to work on his appeal.

Focusing on Arnold's ignorance of the law, his lynch mob experience, and the judge's abuse of power, Aronson and Morgan asked the Supreme Court for a new trial. Appearing before the court on August 2, 1924, they argued Arnold never fully understood his predicament or his lawyer's advice, and when warned by the judge that a guilty plea could lead to his execution, he was too afraid to answer. The lawyers also claimed the lynch-mob confession adversely affected Arnold, as he was convinced anyone who heard his confession would be able to testify against him at his trial. He did not know it was inadmissible, and no one, including his lawyer, told him differently. Finally, the lawyers believed only a jury could sentence a man to death, and the judge had overstepped his authority in sentencing Arnold to hang.

Idaho Attorney General A. H. Conner countered every point, with affidavits from Aronson and Asher, both indicating that Arnold had been made aware of his rights. Asher's affidavit was the most damaging. He claimed Arnold "fully realized that he was guilty of murder in the first degree," and that Arnold had confided in him that he "would rather be hanged than go to the penitentiary for life."

Arnold waited two months to hear his fate. On October 3, the Court issued its ruling supporting the judgment and sentence. In writing for the majority, Justice C. J. McCarthy noted that the "decision of the district court as to the penalty is supported by evidence both competent and sufficient." He added that Arnold "knew he had committed an atrocious murder," and the "judgment should not be set aside merely because he is disappointed in the result." As for the incident in the woods, the court dismissed Arnold's claims. While the episode was despicable, perhaps even criminal, it had no bearing on Arnold's case. Since his confession there had not been used against him in court, he could not use it to ask for a new trial.

With the court's decision rendered, in the early morning hours of October 27, Arnold was taken by train to Sandpoint. There, Judge McNaughton once again sentenced him to death, setting December 19, 1924 as his date of execution. At nightfall, he was back in his cell at the state prison, where he would await the gallows.

While his fate was almost certain, Arnold did not give up hope. He asked the Idaho State Pardon Board to commute his sentence to life in prison. His request included letters from his attorney, support letters from Judge McNaughton, and a statement from Mike Donnelly. Since his execution date was December 19, and the pardon board did not meet until January 7, 1925, Arnold asked for a reprieve, at least until the pardon board could hear his case.

His request met with intense opposition. Asher wrote a letter to the prison warden calling Arnold a "man who makes crime his business." Conner contacted the governor, telling him to deny Arnold's request for a reprieve. Conner wrote that "Arnold is a criminal. He is…a menace to society and there is not the slightest reason why clemency should be extended to him."

Arnold heard nothing from the pardon board and knew he was running out of options. He decided to play the race card and turned to Charlie Young of Pocatello, a representative of the National Association for the Advancement of Colored People. On November 17, Arnold wrote to Young explaining that he was in "ceres trouble." He hoped

Arnold's Idaho prison mug shot

Young could use the influence of his organization to get his case before the pardons board. In his letter, Arnold, not completely truthful, described his near-hanging experience in Sandpoint, claiming the mob extricated a confession from him, changed it "the way they wanted it," and then used it against him in court. He also hinted that his predicament was caused by bad advice from his attorney and a judge who had it out for him. He urged Young to contact attorneys Morgan and Smith in Boise who could give him the whole story. He was sure that once Young was aware of all the facts, he would agree that Arnold was "far from getting Justers."

The NAACP was still in its infancy in 1924, and Arnold was no poster boy for black civil rights. Despite the staged lynching episode, going to bat for a confessed murderer probably would not have been in the organization's best interest. Whether Young tried to intervene on Arnold's behalf is unclear, as no correspondence from him or the organization can be found in Arnold's prison records.

With no help from the NAACP or the governor, Arnold's appointment with the executioner remained on schedule. On December 17, knowing the end was near, he signed over his prison account—$13.99—to W. B. Williams, a minister from the African Methodist Church. Then, on the afternoon of December 18, Arnold ate his last meal: ham and eggs, soup, pudding, toast and coffee. He remained calm throughout the afternoon, talking to his jailor, J. G. Root. He admitted to Root that he had killed at least five men, but William Crisp wasn't one of them. Later that evening, minutes before his execution, he would make the same statement when Warden John Snook asked him if he had any final words.

"I want you all to know that I am not guilty of the murder of William Crisp," he replied with a loud, but quivering voice.

"Who committed the murder?" the Warden asked.

"Mike Donnelly killed Crisp," was his reply.

In the early morning hours of December 19, a small group of reporters, prison guards, and law enforcement officials braved the extreme cold to watch the state finish what the mob in Sandpoint started. They watched as Arnold was led into the northwest corner of the prison yard where the dimly lit scaffold cast eerie shadows against the prison wall. They stood quietly as Arnold climbed the stairs unassisted, and they shivered as his guards bound his legs and ankles and adjusted the noose. They listened as Arnold admonished his guards to carry out their duties well.

"Do a good job of it because I don't want to strangle," he told them.

Still there was a glitch. The trap door mechanism on the scaffold was counter-balanced by a large water bucket, which was filled when Arnold's weight on the trap door opened a faucet. But the night was so cold that before the bucket could fill, the faucet froze. Arnold waited patiently on the scaffold as prison officials thawed the faucet with hot water. The onlookers in the court yard stood silent.

The problem solved, the trap fell. Arnold was reciting a prayer at the time. He was pronounced dead at 12:29 a.m. and was buried that afternoon in the prison cemetery.

Mike Donnelly remained in the Idaho State Penitentiary until January 18, 1943 when he was given a ninety-day parole. As he stayed out of trouble, his parole was extended for one year, with the stipulation that he could not go to Bonner County. On July 18, 1944, after a year of good behavior, Donnelly was pardoned.

In November 1950, Idaho prison officials received a request for Donnelly's prison records. He had been arrested in Deschutes County, Oregon, for larceny. What happened to Donnelly after the arrest is unknown.

Kuok Wah Choi

Atlanta, October 30, 1883
Hailey, September 18, 1884

The execution of Ah Sam (Kuok Wah Choi) at the hands of Idaho's legal system may have been justified; he was tried and convicted of a murder he clearly committed. But while the legal system may have worked in his situation, it failed miserably for thousands of other Chinese living in the mountains of Idaho in the 1800s. No justification, no excuse, exists for the cruelty and discrimination they faced.

When the Chinese arrived in Idaho in the early 1860s, public opinion was already against them, and work was hard to come by. Fueled by derogatory stories and stereotypes disseminated by California newspapers, white miners and settlers in Idaho's early mining camps passed laws prohibiting Chinese from working in any mines or camps or filing any mining claims. Idaho's territorial legislature added to the discrimination, passing legislation in 1864 that levied a monthly four-dollar tax on any Chinese engaged in mining. This was later increased to five dollars. The sheriff of each county was charged with collecting the tax on the first of each month, and if the Chinese miner could not pay, the sheriff could auction his property on as little as one-hour notice.

Besides struggling to make a living, the Chinese also struggled to stay alive. Violence against them was widespread, occurring in every mining camp in the territory. A Chinaman accused of any crime could be hanged; no due process existed for him. Such was the case in Warren when a young Chinese miner was hanged after he stole a pair of boots. In Pierce, five Chinese were accused of killing a shopkeeper. Before they could be taken to trial, they were ambushed and hanged. This vigilante justice won approval at the highest level of government. Idaho Territorial Governor Edward A. Stevenson defended the hangings, claiming, "Many devilish acts have been perpetrated by the Chinese," adding that they had "low, filthy habits" and have "disgusted our people."

Even those who kept to themselves faced violence. In the winter of 1879, nineteen miners were attacked at their winter camp on Loon Creek, near the former gold camp of Orogrande in north-central Idaho. Thirteen died at the hands of white miners dressed up as Indians. In 1882,

Chinese in Idaho mining camp

two vegetable peddlers on the road to Hailey were robbed and killed. No investigation was made into their murders; again, local authorities blamed Indians. In 1887, on the Snake River in Hell's Canyon, thirty-four Chinese miners were killed by a group of young men from Oregon. Although one confessed to the crime, a jury failed to convict three others, and no one was ever punished. In 2005, the site of the slaughter was officially recognized as Chinese Massacre Cove.

The inability of the Chinese to find justice in Idaho's courts came from laws that barred them from testifying, giving evidence, or bringing lawsuits against white men. Thus, when white men committed crimes against the Chinese, they were untouchable. Along the same lines, a Chinaman accused of a crime by a white man was not allowed to testify in defense of himself or have other Chinamen testify on his behalf. Frontier justice for the Chinese was no justice at all.

Despite efforts to keep them out of the territory, by the late 1870s, thirty-seven percent of Idaho's population was Chinese. They provided cheap labor for construction projects, offered domestic services for white settlers, and revived many of the mining communities that had collapsed when gold fields declined and fortune-seekers moved on. White miners, ignoring the laws, sold their claims to the Chinese, who worked them diligently and found the gold left behind. Many of them built successful businesses and some did earn the respect of white residents. But they never fit in, and they never escaped the blatant discrimination practiced against them every day. Whites refused to accept their culture and made no attempt to learn their language, even their names.

As a result, generic names were given to the Chinese in place of their birth names. The prefix "ah" which means "that person is called" would be added to any part of a Chinaman's name, real or imagined. As a result, monikers such as Ah Wait, Ah Say, Ah Yet, and Ah Boo were common in every mining camp. The 1870 federal census lists over ten Ah Sam's living in Idaho Territory, five of them in Idaho City alone. Whether one of them was Kuok Wah Choi, who became the only Chinaman legally hanged in Idaho, is unknown.

Kuok arrived in Alturas County in 1878 and earned his living as a cook in the various mining camps. When he committed his crime, he was thirty-seven-years-old and well-known to his countrymen. He had never been in trouble with the law. At the end of October 1883, Kuok left his job in one of the mining camps and moved to Atlanta. He boarded with Tot Kee, a doctor and merchant, who had lived in the area for over thirteen years. Located on the edge of town, Tot's cabin was one of four occupied by Chinese.

On the night of October 29, Kuok spent time with friends Ah Loop and Bow Kee before retiring to Tot's cabin. The next morning, sometime between eight and nine, Kuok had breakfast with his friends, then returned to his cabin where Tot was still in bed. Kuok took out a pistol and shot Tot in the head. He then left the cabin, pistol still in hand.

Ah Loop and Ah Bow watched as Kuok exited the cabin. They saw him throw the pistol in a nearby ditch and then leave the scene, walking down Main Street. Ah Loop caught up with Kuok and asked him what he had done. " I killed Tot Kee," he said. "It is all right. It was my right to kill him."

Ah Loop, Ah Bow, and Ah Tim took Kuok to Deputy Sheriff Patrick Furey. It is unclear how they communicated, but Furey asked Kuok if he had killed a man. He responded "I killed a man, and if you want to hang me, do it right away." Furey locked Kuok in a cell, and accompanied by both white men and Chinese, he went to Tot's house to survey the crime scene.

Tot was not yet dead. According to Furey, when they entered the room, he gave one last gasp, then died. Furey examined the body and found what he believed to be a large bullet wound on the right side of Tot's head. He would later testify that Tot had been shot while he was sleeping.

Kuok remained in the Atlanta jail for two days. Then Furey took him to Rocky Bar, where he appeared before Justice of the Peace Sol Newcomer. Furey asked that a warrant be granted for Kuok's arrest for the murder of Tot Kee, and the judge agreed. He ordered Kuok to be held until a grand jury could hear the case. On June 13, the grand jury found enough evidence to indict him on first-degree murder charges.

Kuok appeared in Hailey before Second District Court Judge Case Broderick on June 14. Broderick appointed G. L. Waters to serve as defense attorney while John Huston would prosecute the case. On June 16, Kuok pleaded not guilty. Because Kuok clearly had difficulty with the English language, Broderick hired an interpreter. The interpreter would also be needed for the Chinese witnesses who would be allowed to testify against one of their countrymen.

The trial took only one day. Prosecutor Huston called Ah Loop, Ah Bow, and Ah Tim to the stand. Even with an interpreter, language was a problem, as they often did not answer the questions they were asked or contradicted their own testimony. Still, all three agreed they saw Kuok with a gun after the shooting, and all heard him confess to the crime. Sheriff Furey also testified, giving the prosecution motive. According to Furey, Kuok claimed that Tot owed him twenty dollars, and for room and board, Tot was taking Kuok's money "as fast as he earned it."

Defense attorney Waters tried to shake the testimony of the Chinamen and place the blame on others living in the area, but he had no success. He had no defense witnesses and could not place Kuok on the stand, as he continued to claim that he had the right to kill Tot. The jury quickly returned a guilty verdict.

On July 8, Waters was back in court to argue for new trial. On July 14, his motion was denied. Judge Broderick then sentenced Kuok to hang, setting the execution for September 5, 1884. In his comments, unlike other judges, Broderick did not ask God to have mercy on Kuok's soul.

Waters immediately appealed the conviction and the judgment. On July 30, John T. Morgan, chief justice of the Idaho Territorial Supreme Court, stayed the execution. Kuok would remain locked in the Alturas County jail in Hailey until the court heard his case.

The case went before the supreme court in January 1885. Waters argued that Judge Broderick had erred in his rulings on when the defense's peremptory challenges could be used against jurors. Idaho statutes were unclear on this issue, so Waters felt he had just cause for a new trial. But the judges, Broderick among them, believed the intent of the law was followed, and they could find no error in the record. The judgment against Kuok was affirmed. The justices ordered the district court to set a new date to carry out the execution.

Waters, however, was not finished in his fight to save Kuok. On May 21, 1885, he filed an affidavit asking Judge Broderick to suspend the judgment against Kuok and order a competency hearing. Waters believed his client was insane and had found a doctor, N. J. Brown, who would support that claim. Broderick agreed and appointed three doctors to examine Kuok. He scheduled a sanity hearing for the morning of August 4.

The transcript of that hearing has been lost, but court records show that six people testified, including Dr. Brown, Sheriff Furey and Charley Sing, a Chinaman who visited Kuok. After closing arguments, the case was given to the jury. Although they deliberated the rest of the day, they were unable to reach a decision.

The next morning they were back in court, where Judge Broderick urged them to continue their work. After several more hours, they returned and asked permission to question Dr. Brown, who had originally supported Waters' request for a sanity hearing. They asked him but one question and returned to their deliberations. Shortly after, they returned to the courtroom to announce, "We, the jury, do find that the said defendant is sane."

Waters immediately asked for a new trial. On August 6, he and Kuok appeared before Judge Broderick. The judge denied the motion for a new trial and set Kuok's execution for September 18, 1885. There would be no more appeals.

Kuok was put under a suicide watch. According to the *Wood River Times*, the Chinese looked upon death by hanging as "disgraceful," and the sheriff did not want to take any chance with Kuok. The sheriff had little need to worry, as Kuok was a model prisoner. While he was offered special meals and Cuban cigars during his final days, he preferred regular jail food and his corncob pipe. He had no visitors and made no requests.

On the morning of his execution, Sheriff Furey gave him a new set of clothes. He also offered to cut off his queue, or ponytail, and send it to his brother, a custom that would let his family know he was dead. When Kuok asked to cut it off himself, Furey refused, fearing he would kill himself with the scissors. Kuok would die with his queue intact.

Around noon on September 18, Furey read Kuok the death warrant and then led him to a waiting buggy. They rode to Quigley Canyon northeast of Hailey to the site of a previous hanging. As a crowd of 200 looked on, Kuok climbed the steps of the gallows under his own power, his hands in his pockets. He surveyed the structure and the crowd as he took his place on the trap door. He faltered only once, and Sheriff Furey supported him as other deputies bound his hands and feet. The trap was sprung at 1:20 p.m., and Kuok fell to his death. Mr. Straingeway, the county undertaker, placed his body in a plain, black coffin and took it to Bellevue for burial.

Judge John T. Morgan

Following the execution, several local merchants sought reimbursement from the Alturas County Commissioners for services rendered in the case of Kuok. Thomas Bell, who constructed the scaffold, received forty dollars for his efforts, and L. Wertheimer, who provided Kuok with his new clothes for hanging, received twenty-six dollars for his goods and services. Dr. Brown, whose testimony convinced jurors that Kuok was sane, asked for twenty-five dollars in expert fees. The commissioners found this excessive and reduced it to fifteen.

Simeon Walters

Owyhee Stage Route, October 21, 1868
Idaho City, December 10, 1869

The best laid schemes of mice and men oft go awry.
—Robert Burns

When Simeon Walters came to Idaho in 1867, the young southerner did not travel to the mountains and mines like other young fortune seekers. Instead, he made his way to the Owyhee plains where cattle flourished on the abundant sage and bunchgrass that grew in abundance. He dreamed of owning his own ranch, and he made plans in the fall of 1868 to make that dream come true. Unfortunately, someone stood in his way.

In the spring of 1868, Walters met Joseph Bacon, a farmer who owned a place on Reynolds Creek, approximately twenty miles northeast of Silver City. The two formed a cooperative and throughout the summer worked the ranch for shares. Since Walters was interested in purchasing the ranch, he and Bacon entered into negotiations in August.

Where Walters would find the money was unclear. He was in his late twenties with no trade or means of support. He did not even own a horse. Born in Kentucky, his family moved to Missouri when he was a boy. He then made his way to Leavenworth, Kansas where he lived for some time before moving west. He worked in Montana before moving to Idaho. Although tall and handsome with a muscular build, some described him as a "bad man" who liked to pull his gun at the slightest provocation. If he had the money to purchase Bacon's ranch, he did not show it.

On October 19, 1868, Walters was in Silver City where he hired a buggy with two dark horses at the livery stable of A. C. Springer. He traveled toward Boise, spending the night at the ranch of Joseph Babington, eight miles from Silver City. The next morning, he continued his journey to Bacon's ranch. There he met B. McCleary, who was leasing the ranch from Bacon. McCleary told Walters that Bacon had gone to the ranch of William Richey, several miles down the road.

Walters continued toward Boise and came upon Bacon and John Bernard. They were driving a large herd of cattle to Bernard's place, Forest Grove, which was north of the Snake River, approximately one mile from Fruit's Ferry. Walters called on Bacon to leave Bernard and travel with him

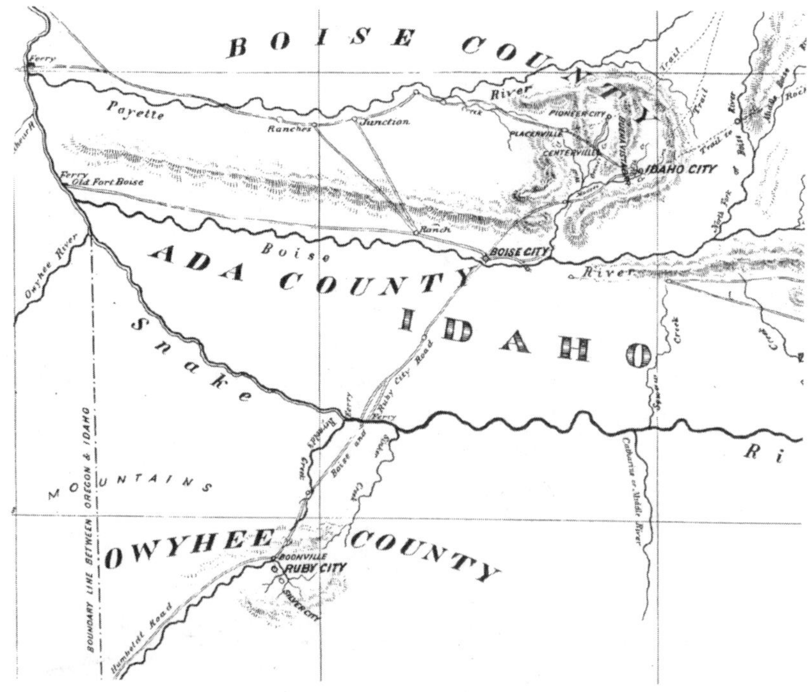

to Boise to finalize the sale of the ranch. Bernard objected, as he needed Bacon to help him with the herd. After some discussion, all agreed that Walters would go ahead to Bernard's ranch, taking Bernard's wife Anna with him. Bernard and Bacon would follow with the herd, and they would all spend the night at Bernard's place.

On the way, Walters took out his pistol and shot a crow. Whether or not he did this to impress Anna is unclear, but it is clear the events did not fit with the plan he was crafting to get the Bacon ranch.

After supper that evening, Walters continued to pester Bacon about the sale of the ranch. He wanted to continue to Boise that night to make the deal. But Bacon, with Bernard's support, refused. An argument ensued, with Bacon telling Walters that he would "give neither papers nor scratch of pen" until he had the money in hand. Eventually Walters let the matter rest and the group retired for the evening. In passing, right before he went to bed, Walters told Bernard he had done a "damned smart trick," forgetting his pistol in Silver City.

The next morning Bernard warned Bacon not to go with Walters to Boise, but Bacon was set on selling his property. He told Bernard that if he should make the sale to Walters, he would not return to the area. Bacon, who arrived in Idaho from Missouri in the mid-1860s, originally settled near present day Glenns Ferry, where he left his wife Eliza and two young sons, William and George. If the sale went through, he planned to return there to farm.

As Bacon and Walters prepared to leave, Bernard gave Walters some money and a list of supplies he needed. Walters agreed to purchase the supplies—tea, a box of candles, a box of nails, and ten pounds of coffee. He put the list and money in the pocket of his duster. With that, Bacon and Walters departed for Boise, leaving around 7 a.m.

Around 11 a.m., the pair passed J.H. Jackson who was on his way to Silver City. The three spoke briefly and Jackson noticed that Bacon was sitting in the driver's seat of the wagon, the right side, but was not driving. This struck him as odd, but he did not say anything and continued on his way.

About an hour later, approximately one mile north of Dry Creek (Five Mile Creek), a black buggy pulled by two dark horses passed Thomas Kifer who was driving an ox team toward Boise. Only one man, Walters, was in the buggy. A short time later, Kifer met Walters on the road, this time coming towards him. Walters asked Kifer if he had seen a six-shooter along the road; Walters explained he had stopped along to the way to shoot something and apparently lost it off the buggy. Kifer had not seen it, and Walters decided the search was futile as the road was too dusty. He turned around and headed toward Boise, arriving there between 1 and 2 p.m.

Walters had stopped to shoot something—Bacon. As the two men passed Dry Creek, Walters pulled out his pistol and shot Bacon in the head just below his left ear. Bacon, who wore a brown glass eye in his left socket, never saw it coming. The strange seating arrangement Jackson noticed had all been part of Walters' plan to kill Bacon without a struggle.

Dry Creek ran dry in the late fall. After the shooting, Walters turned the buggy off the road and followed the creek bed to a small mound of dirt and rocks covered with high grass in the middle of the bed. He deposited the body behind the mound, then turned back to the road toward Boise.

Once in Boise, Walters drove to the livery stable of J. D. Agnew. He asked Agnew to look after the horses, indicating he would need them again that evening. Walters then began to clean the dust off the buggy. When Agnew offered to wash the buggy for him, Walters declined, stating he did not want to hurt the paint.

Walters left the stables for a short time and then returned, retrieving a pistol, belt, and scabbard from the buggy. Agnew noticed the belt, as it had an unusual cap box attached to it. Walters told Agnew the items belonged to a man who had ridden in with him and whom he had dropped off at the edge of the city.

Walters took the gun to Lewis Heyd, a gunsmith, who bought the gun, belt, and scabbard for twelve dollars. Walters also presented his gun with two empty chambers, which Heyd reloaded. From there, he went to Daniel Roth's store where he purchased the items for Bernard. Coming up short, he charged the candles to Bernard's account. He told Roth he would be back later in the day to pick up the supplies and a receipt.

After supper, Walters picked up his buggy and drove to the home of Sylvester Polk. There he obtained an old wooden trunk belonging to Bacon that contained the deed and other papers relating to the property on Reynolds Creek. Walters took the papers and returned to Roth's store with the trunk. He left the trunk in care of Roth, loaded the supplies he had purchased for Bernard, and left Boise.

Everything had gone according to plan until Walters traveled south out of Boise. He drove back to Dry Creek and retrieved Bacon's body, wrapping it in a blanket he had borrowed from Bernard. With the body loaded, he turned the buggy back toward the road, only to catch a wheel on some sagebrush, nearly tipping the wagon on its side. Walters righted the cart but was unaware that the coffee he had purchased for Bernard had fallen out of the buggy.

Back on the stage route, Walters drove to an old ferry site on the north bank of the Snake River. There he threw the body into the river along with the blanket and his bloodstained duster and overalls. Then he drove north to Bernard's ranch, arriving around 7 a.m.

As Walters unloaded the supplies from the wagon, Bernard questioned him about Bacon and the sale of the ranch. Walters claimed he left Bacon in Boise after paying him $1200 in cash. He produced all the deeds to the property save the one that belonged to Sarah Bacon, a daughter from Bacon's first marriage. Bacon had promised to deliver it the next time he was in the area.

Bernard had no reason to doubt Walters' story but still he was suspicious. Walters arrived without his duster or overalls. He did not have the blanket Bernard had loaned him. His eyes were bloodshot; his face stained with dirt and sweat. His horses were completely worn out. When

Walters asked to borrow a horse to ride to Record's Stage Station, Bernard refused, but did offer him a place to rest. Walters slept for about an hour, cleaned himself up, then saddled one of horses from the buggy and rode north.

Perhaps sensing Bernard's distrust, Walters spent the next four days making sure he covered his tracks. After he left Bernard's, he rode to Record's Station, reaching there about noon. He spent the rest of the day in the vicinity of Dry Creek where he seen by several travelers on the stage road.

By dark he was back at Bernard's where he spent the night. The next morning he took his buggy and drove to the old ferry site on the Snake River. He then made his way downstream to a ranch operated by Thomas Price and P. Meyers. There he picked up a horse belonging to Bacon and traveled toward Silver City, stopping for the night at the Richey ranch. The next day he returned the buggy and horses to Silver City, then left on foot toward the ranch on Reynolds Creek, the place he now claimed as his own. He arrived there on October 25, showed McCleary the deeds, and demanded possession of the property. But McCleary refused, saying he would not turn over the ranch without specific orders from Bacon.

The next morning, Walters traveled north, and once again visited the ranch of Price and Meyers. He asked if he could borrow a skiff and a rifle, for he had seen a deer on an island up river and wanted to shoot it. Meyers refused and Walters moved on. However, he spent the better part of the day searching the banks of the river, making sure the body of Bacon had not washed up on shore. He may have even swum to the island to make sure Bacon's body had not surfaced there.

Finally, on October 27, Walters' plan completely unraveled. He arrived at Bernard's in the morning and complained that McCleary refused to give up the ranch. By that time, Bernard had discovered that the coffee was missing from his order and confronted Walters. Walters denied ever purchasing the coffee, even though the receipt indicated he had. He offered no logical explanation for the missing coffee.

Bernard now suspected that Walters had killed Bacon. He left for Boise that morning and on the way overtook Babington who was taking a team to Boise. The two discussed Walter's behavior, and they decided to search along the stage road for any signs of foul play. By nightfall they had reached Record's Station but had found nothing.

The next morning they resumed their search. Upon reaching Dry Creek, Babington found buggy tracks leading off the road. He followed them a short way and found a hat stuffed in a badger hole. Bernard identified it as Bacon's hat. They found blood on the underside of the hat, along with what appeared to be a bullet hole along the rim.

They continued their search following the tracks to the mound of dirt in the creek. They found footsteps, the imprint of something heavy, and blood stained soil. Bernard gathered samples of the soil along with the hat and made his way to Boise. There he gave his evidence to Deputy Sheriff Forsyth and swore out a warrant for Walters' arrest.

The next morning, Bernard and Forsyth rode to Bernard's ranch where they found Walters. Forsyth placed him under arrest and took him to Boise where he was confined to the Ada County jail.

For the next two days, Bacon's friends continued to search for his body, along with evidence that might convict Walters. They found the coffee Walters had spilled and discovered Bacon's boots nearby. At the ferry landing, they found the tracks of a light buggy and drag marks leading to the river. In searching the riverbank for the body, they found a necktie and collar belonging to Walters. Back in Boise, the gunsmith came forward with the gun, belt, and scabbard he had purchased from Walters. They were identified as belonging to Bacon.

On November 3, Walters made his first appearance in court where Probate Judge Augustus Flournoy found probable cause to keep Walters in jail until a grand jury could be convened.

Attorney Edward J. Curtis was selected to build a murder charge against Walters. He knew that without a body, he would have a difficult time showing a murder had even occurred. But on November 24, he stood before a grand jury and laid out his case. When he was finished, the grand jury indicted Walters for murder. As for the method of murder, the indictment listed that Bacon may have met his death by knife, hammer, six-shooting pistol, hands and feet, or "by some manner or some means to the jurors unknown."

Following the indictment, Walters was arraigned before Judge Thomas Bowers of the Second Judicial District. Walters asked for a continuance, telling the judge he wished to procure funds from family so he could hire a good lawyer. Bowers agreed and set the trial date for December 19.

The delay was a big mistake for Walters. On December 1, a body was found on the north bank of the Snake River, twenty-five miles below Fruit's

Ferry. The remains, along with a brown glass eye, were collected and taken to Boise where Ada County Coroner Joseph Forsythe and Dr. E. Bishop positively identified the body as Bacon's. They also determined his death was caused by a single gunshot wound to the head, the bullet entering the skull just below the left ear and exiting above the right eye.

On December 19, Walters was back in court. As he had not received any money from family to hire a lawyer, Judge Bowers appointed George C. Hough and H. E. Prickett to defend him. Two days later, Hough and Prickett asked the judge to set aside the indictment. They believed the grand jury had erred in its proceedings, and listed the ambiguous causes of death as one of their reasons. Judge Bowers, however, denied the motion.

The next day, Walters stood before the judge and pleaded not guilty to the murder charge. Knowing that public sentiment was against their client, his lawyers requested a change of venue to Boise County. Judge Bower granted their request and ordered Sheriff L. B. Lindsey to deliver Walters to the sheriff in Idaho City where he was to be confined in the territorial prison until a court could be convened.

He would wait two months. Finally on March 10, 1869, Walters appeared before Judge Bowers to once again hear the charges. He had two new attorneys—Powhatan E. Edmonson and A. O. Bowen—who asked for a continuance in order to find witnesses essential to their defense. Bowers denied the motion. The trial would begin the next day.

Two southerners, Romilly E. Foote and Samuel A Merritt, would direct the prosecution. For two days, their witnesses detailed Walters' movements before and after the murder. Their testimony built a strong, circumstantial case against Walters.

Defense attorney Edmonson had little hope. While he called several witnesses, none could exonerate his client. One claimed the area around Dry Creek was so flat it would have been impossible to commit a crime without being seen. Another testified that he had seen Springer's buggy with two men aboard arrive in Boise on the afternoon of October 21. But he could not identify Walters and he did not know Bacon, so he did little to help Walter's cause.

In a desperate effort to save himself, Walters took the stand where he tried to explain away the accusations against him. He swore that he and Bacon arrived in Boise together. When they had passed Kifer on the road, Bacon had been in the back of the buggy sleeping; that is why Kifer did not see him. He sold Bacon's gun at his request. He also gave Bacon $1300 for

Walters was confined to the territorial prison in Idaho City.

the ranch. As for the trunk, Bacon told him to leave it at Roth's. He would pick it up at a later date. But prosecutor Merritt hounded Walters on the details and the inconsistencies in his story. Walters could not explain the spilled coffee or how his tie and collar came to rest on the north bank of the Snake River. He could not account for Bernard's missing blanket or his actions on the night of October 21. By the time Merritt was finished with his cross-examination, Walters' treacherous scheme lay exposed, his story all a lie.

Closing arguments were presented on March 16. That evening, Judge Bowers gave the jurors their instructions and at midnight they began their deliberations. They argued throughout the night. At 10 a.m. they were back in court and told Judge Bowers they were unable to make a decision. Bowers gave them further instructions, and once again they retired to find a verdict. That afternoon, after seventeen hours of deliberation, they finally decided Walters was guilty.

Throughout the trial, Walters had remained stoic. But at hearing the verdict, his knees buckled, the blood drained from his face. Although the jury had recommended mercy, Walters knew the punishment for murder was death.

Walters' attorneys immediately moved for a retrial. Judge Bowers would hear the motion on March 24. He also planned to pass sentence on that day.

On March 24, Walters and his lawyers appeared before Judge Bowers. They asked for a new trial, once again claiming numerous errors by the grand jury. Bowers denied the motion, and instead sentenced Walters to hang, setting the execution for May 12, 1869. Following the sentence, Walters faced the judge and in a faltering voice told him, "The sentence has been passed, but I am innocent. I know I am, and God knows I am."

After the sentence, Walters' attorneys filed an appeal with the territory's supreme court. The justices heard the case in May but refused to intervene. Instead, they ordered the case back to the district court at Idaho City and directed the judge to reset the day of execution. Walters would not be called to court until October 15, 1869. On that day, Judge David Noggle told him he would hang on December 10 at precisely 2 p.m. Attorneys Edmonson, Bowers, and Prickett made one last attempt to save their young client, asking Judge Noggle to reduce Walters' sentence to life in prison. Arguing that the jury did not authorize a death sentence, they felt justice would be better served if Walters were imprisoned, not hanged. But Noggle refused and ordered Sheriff Frank Britton to carry out the execution.

As his execution approached, Walters sought solace in the Catholic faith and was attended by two priests, Father Toussait Mesplie and Father A. Z. Poulin. Mesplie traveled to Boise and pleaded with Territorial Governor David Ballard to commute Walters' sentence, but public sentiment against the murderer was clear. There would be no executive interference in the sentence.

Although he granted an interview with a reporter from the *Idaho World*, Walters revealed little about himself and steadfastly claimed his innocence. Instead, he said he knew the true killers, but had no proof to support his suspicions, so preferred to remain quiet. However, he believed he had probably done something to deserve the punishment, but he did not know what it was. He claimed that he did not fear death, for he had made his peace with God.

On the morning of his execution, Walters gave the reporter a letter and asked that it be published after his death. In it, he thanked his jailers and the people of Boise County who had supported him in his final days. With his death upon him, he had no reason to conceal the truth and the truth was that he was innocent. Nor did he write the letter to change people's opinions of him. Instead, he said, "If no one has done wrong, all will be well in time."

At 1:45, Sheriff Britton and Under Sheriff Henry Sayrs escorted Walters from his cell. He wore a black broadcloth suit, with a white hat and white gloves. Although he looked pale and haggard, he walked to the scaffold in the prison yard unassisted and with firm steps mounted the scaffold. The two priests steadied him on the trap door, and Sayrs read the death warrant. Sheriff Britton asked Walters if he wished to say anything, but Walters declined.

Britton stood with his watch in hand. As two o'clock approached, he shook hands with Walters. Then he and his deputy placed the noose around his neck, secured the leather straps on his arms and feet, and drew the white cap over his face. There was no sound. Then Britton turned to go down the scaffold steps. As he did, he pushed the lever, the trap opened, and Walters fell to his death.

Britton did not stop. He continued down the steps, walked out of the jail yard, and went home. He could not bear to see what he had done.

Walters was then cut down and placed in a wooden coffin. Fearful that he would be buried alive, he had requested that he be laid out for one day before he was buried. That request was granted, and his sealed coffin was carried into the visitor's room of the prison, where it remained for the night. The next day, Fathers Poulin and Mesplie led a procession to Idaho City's cemetery where Walters was buried in an unmarked grave.

Ernest Walrath
Troy Powell

Boise, May 8, 1950
Boise, April 13, 1951

They were very young men, one still in his teens. One was brash and brooding, brilliant and arrogant, even in the face of death. The other was a wanna-be tough guy, easily led, a little boy in a big man's body, worried about money and how to support his family. Together they would commit a heinous crime and together they would hang, the youngest criminals to face the gallows in Idaho.

In 1950, approximately 34,000 people lived in Boise. One of those was sixty-five-year-old widower Newton Wilson, who owned a corner grocery store at 1401 E. State Street. Established in Boise since 1934, Wilson had his living quarters in the back of the store.

On the evening of May 8, 1950, two young men, Ernest L. Walrath, Jr. and Troy D. Powell, called on Wilson under the pretense of using his phone. When they left, Wilson was dead, and the people of Boise would be outraged.

Ernest L. Walrath, Jr. was born February 25, 1931 in Bend, Oregon. His parents, Ernest and Mary, originally from Colorado, moved to Bend in the late 1920s. They bought a forty-acre farm three miles east of town. Ernest, Sr. also supplemented his income working in a sawmill. There were three other Walrath children besides little Ernest, all girls: Evelyn, Leonora, and Delphine. They attended Bend schools, Ernie starting when he was just five. He excelled in school and was set to graduate in the spring of 1948. By then, he had grown into a slender young man, 5'10", 150 pounds, with light brown hair and brown eyes. His eyesight was bad, and most of the time he wore wire-rimmed glasses.

Court records mention that as early as age sixteen, Ernie was involved in several car burglaries and other minor crimes. Ernest Sr. reported that his wife prevented him from punishing his son when he broke home rules, and eventually they lost all control over him. Mary admitted to the police that although they tried, they were "unable to control proper jurisdiction over the boy." Ernie was finally sentenced to the Boys' Training School in Woodburn, Oregon. Whether he actually spent time there is unclear, but

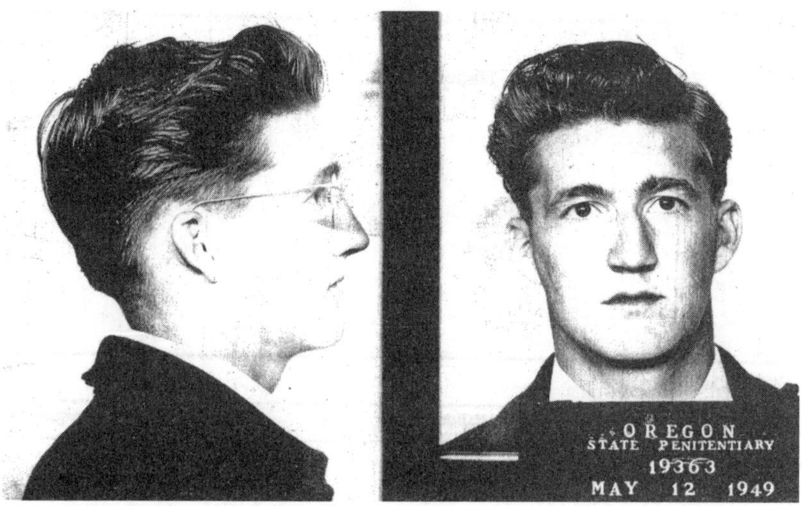

Ernest Walrath on the day of his release from the Oregon State Penitentiary

in December 1947, he was on parole. Just after Christmas, Ernie, his sister Delphine, and two other young men drove to Redmond, Oregon. There, they broke into several cars and pilfered what they could. They also broke into two service stations.

Eventually they were caught. Of the four, Ernie was charged with burglary and held in the Deschutes County Jail. He appeared before Judge Ralph Hamilton on February 19, 1948 where he pleaded guilty to the charges. District Attorney A. J. Moore informed the court of Ernie's prior criminal behavior and Deputy Sheriff Harry Johnson stated that he had "considerable trouble" with the defendant in the past. While his lawyer asked the judge for leniency, Ernie said nothing in the courtroom. After hearing all the testimony, Hamilton sentenced Ernie to two years in the Oregon State Penitentiary.

Later, Hamilton would say it was a mistake to send Walrath to the state prison. According to Hamilton, he was sick on the day of the trial but had been pressured by Moore to sit in on the case. Looking back, he said, "Had I been feeling myself, I would have never heard the case and never sent him to the state pen." He felt this was especially true since he later learned that none of the accomplices were even charged.

But the sentence was passed, and on February 23, Ernie became prisoner #19363. Acknowledging his age—he would turn seventeen on February 25—he was placed in the juvenile section of the prison where he was assigned to the yard crew. His mother wrote him copiously, nine letters in March alone, and Ernie responded with frequent letters of his own. There were no letters from his father.

Ernie spent five months in the juvenile facility of the prison. He received no disciplinary referrals and all records indicate that he stayed out of trouble. Because he had served his time well, he was paroled on August 11, 1948. In addition to the usual parole conditions, two stipulations were placed on him: he was to re-enter high school in September and complete his schooling, and he was to write a letter to the parole board at the end of the first semester, telling members of his progress.

He never got the chance. Ernest, Sr. would later say that his son had been mistreated by his parole officer. The parole officer "had it in for Ernie," and had used "Gestapo tactics" to revoke his son's parole. Although Ernie never had a hearing in the matter, both he and his family surmised his parole was revoked because he had missed a few days of school. Whatever the cause, he was picked up on October 28, 1948, and sent back to the state penitentiary. This time he was placed in the general population.

According to Ernest, Sr. this move was disastrous. Influenced by older, more vicious felons, Ernie began smoking marijuana, talking back to guards, and causing trouble at every turn. Because of his attitude, the guards beat him and eventually put him in solitary confinement. Ernie responded by laughing at the guards, which only caused him more grief. He continued to correspond with his mother, where he relayed his plight. As a result, his parents began regular visits to the prison. So angered by the conditions, Ernest, Sr. began a crusade to free his son.

He started with Governor John Hall, asking for a full and complete pardon. The governor referred him to the state parole board. On March 10, 1949, Ernest, Sr. wrote to H. M. Randall, director of the Oregon State Board of Parole and Probation. In the letter he criticized the handling of his son not only at the prison but also in the courts and by "specialized officials." He wrote, "Criminals are made by ruthless officers and prison environments. Never has there been a loyal subject made by brutal force."

Among other things, Walrath wanted an apology from everyone involved. He questioned in his letter, "how deep in the ocean I would have to go to kiss the buttocks of adult men who are so immune…not to be able to admit to a boy…that they are sorry."

In the end, he challenged the parole board to pardon his son. "If the parole board…can approach this boy in a 'not holier than thou' attitude, and explain that this has been an unfortunate experience…which you all deeply regret and that you are interested in him and his future, then prove it. You will not have cause to regret it."

For good measure, Ernest Sr. enlisted the aid of Dellmore Lessard, once a state senator from Portland. Lessard contacted Governor Hall, the parole board, and Judge Hamilton. His efforts were successful. On May 6, Ernie went before the parole board and was granted his release. He was freed on May 12, 1949. As required, he reported to the parole office in Salem. He later stated that he was ordered to leave Oregon immediately. On May 16, Ernie and his mother, along with his sister Delphine, moved to Boise.

Ernie's future accomplice, Troy Powell, was born January 5, 1930, in Endicott, Nebraska. The Depression dug deep in the heartland, and his parents Harvey and Beulah Powell could not make a living. When Troy was four, they moved to Emmett, Idaho, where Harvey found work as a farm hand. He also worked at the local sawmill as a sawyer but was often laid off. According to Beulah, the family struggled, especially in the winter.

Troy Powell

Troy attended Emmett schools and made it through his first semester of high school. He quit school because he "just got tired of going," but his mother said he never quite fit in. According to Beulah, Troy endured much teasing over the family's Pentecostal faith. While he refused to attend Sunday school, he did attend regular services with his parents. However, this did not keep him out of trouble.

While Powell would state that his parents always gave him his way, they did not agree to the "spare the rod, spoil the child" principle. His father called Troy "headstrong" and admitted to whipping his only son to keep him in line. His mother claimed that Troy "never seemed to have enough money," and to alleviate that, over his parents' objections, he began spending time with Don Sheppard. A habitual criminal, Sheppard was involved in a variety of minor crimes in both Idaho and Oregon. According to Beulah, Sheppard had tremendous influence over Troy. Eventually, Troy would be implicated in several minor crimes in the Emmett area, but no charges were filed against him.

With little education, no job prospects, and only trouble seemingly ahead of him, Troy enlisted in the army. He entered at Fort Douglas, Utah on October 28, 1946 at age sixteen. He made it through basic training and was given the rank of private, but on July 1, 1947, he was honorably discharged for being "underage."

Troy returned to Emmett where he found work pruning fruit trees for four months. He then hired on with Morrison-Knudson as an equipment operator on Anderson Dam for eighteen months. When that job ended, Powell's troubles began. He traveled to Oregon, hoping to find work and renew his friendship with Don Sheppard. But Sheppard had troubles of his own; he was incarcerated in Grant County in September 1948.

In John Day, Oregon, Troy met Matt Baldwin, an acquaintance of Sheppard's. With no work prospects and his mentor behind bars, Troy quickly lost interest in Oregon. He also missed his girlfriend. On impulse, he stole a car and drove to Boise with Baldwin. They stayed three days, and on the fourth day returned to Grant County and abandoned the car near where they had stolen it. They were apprehended shortly after.

Troy confessed to the crime and pleaded guilty, waiving his right to an attorney. On November 15, 1948, he stood before Judge M.A. Biggs of the Grant County Circuit Court and heard his sentence: two years in the Oregon State Penitentiary. Before passing sentence, Biggs warned Powell of the dangers of the state pen, claiming "...you are going to be thrown with men who have committed crimes before who probably are going to attempt to educate you in the way to commit other crimes and still not get caught; but remember one thing...the one that is trying to teach you also made a mistake someplace himself, or he would not be in the penitentiary. Don't be misled by those."

On December 1, he officially became prisoner #19800 in the state pen in Salem. Although just eighteen, Troy's size belied his age. At 6'2" and 179 pounds, he fit in with the general population of the prison, right down to his tattoos. His left upper arm featured his initials "TDP," while his left forearm was decorated with a five-point star. On his right forearm, he displayed a bathing girl on a dagger blade, with the words "my kind of love." In his prison mug shot he looked squarely into the camera, his dark eyes staring through the lens.

His parents kept in close contact with him, writing thirty-seven letters to him during his first eight months of incarceration. Audrey Urban, his girlfriend and the woman he intended to marry, was less enthusiastic. She wrote only three times, her last letter reaching Troy in March 1949. Troy also corresponded with a Boise woman named Marlena Whaley. Their relationship is unclear, but she wrote him once a month and he, in turn, replied to each letter.

Prison records do not reveal any problems Troy may have had, but prison life could not have been easy for the young man. Oregon's penitentiary was old, built in the 1860s; the facility was cold, and prisoners reported not having enough blankets. In the general prison population, Troy was exposed to the worst of Oregon's criminals. He would later say that he was greatly influenced by the vicious men he met there. To survive, he made alliances, renewed his friendship with Don Sheppard and struck up a new one with young Ernie Walrath.

Learning quickly to do what he was told, Troy assimilated well into the prison work system. Upon his arrival he was assigned to the sawdust crew and later the yard crew. Over the next nine months, he worked in various areas of the prison, receiving commendations from the prison staff. One staff evaluation made in June 1949 indicated Troy had kept out of trouble and had done his work well. It noted that both his industry and conduct were good. During his entire stay, he received no write-ups for misconduct.

His good behavior led to an appearance before the State Board of Parole and Probation. After good reports from the prison staff, the board paroled Troy. His parents picked him up on September 3, 1949, and together they returned to Boise. He wasted little time in getting on with his life. By the end of the month, he had married Irma Anne Givens and became stepfather to her twin girls. But the marriage was short lived; after just six weeks, Irma left him. According to Beulah, the breakup was a huge blow to Troy who "always seemed to have the need for a girl."

That need was soon satisfied. In November he met Delphine Walrath, sister of Ernie, his friend from prison and now in Boise. In March 1950, they would become brothers by marriage. They would also become partners in crime.

As ex-cons and with little work experience, both Powell and Walrath had trouble finding jobs. Walrath, who lived with his mother, had the support of his family. He eventually got a job at the Boise Car Corral.

Later his mother would tell officials that her son was despondent and drank heavily after his release from prison. Powell did not find a job in Boise until April 1950, when he went to work for Beall Pipe and Tank. Until then, he had been supported by Delphine who worked as a telephone operator. Her $34 a week paycheck did not cover their expenses, and when she became pregnant and quit her job, Powell became desperate. At the end of April, he estimated that he was $3500 in debt.

Powell told his mother that he had learned enough in prison that "he wouldn't ever have to do without money again." Walrath, who had demonstrated his propensity for thievery before prison, had no qualms about getting back into the business. Before long, the two partners had committed a series of robberies in Boise. They burglarized a filling station, the Collister Store twice, and the Black Diamond Tavern, where in addition to cash, they took a gun. Still, it didn't seem to be enough for either.

The Powells lived at 1407 E. State Street, two houses away from Newt Wilson's grocery store. Both Delphine and Troy frequented the store, and in May 1950, owed Wilson approximately thirty dollars. Wilson gave the Powells credit because he liked Troy. On several occasions, Troy had run off bullies who were causing trouble at Wilson's store.

After work on May 8, Powell drove to Walrath's home and used his shower, a regular occurrence as his house did not have one. Afterward, the two men picked up Walrath's girlfriend, Barbara Cooper, then drove to Powell's home, where they picked up Delphine to go for a ride. According to Cooper, during the ride the boys stopped the car to pick up some rocks, which they stuffed into a sock creating a weapon called a "sap." Then they returned to the Powell home.

At some point, the conversation turned to money and Wilson's store. Powell believed Wilson had a lot of money stashed in his home because he had lived through the Depression, and people like him did not "really trust the banks anymore." Walrath concurred. They were both broke, especially Troy, and the two needed to find something to rob. The old man seemed the perfect target.

Walrath and Powell walked to Wilson's store. It was closed. Walrath, his head wrapped in a white scarf, went to the back door and knocked. The plan was for Walrath to enter the house, pull out the gun obtained in the previous robbery, and force Wilson to face the wall. Powell would then enter and search the house and store for money. Once they found what they wanted, they would leave.

For whatever reason, they did not carry out their plan. When Walrath knocked, Wilson opened the door, but did not unlatch the screen. In a pretext to get inside, Walrath asked to use the phone, and once inside, he did not turn on Wilson. Instead, he used the phone to call the girls back at the Powell home. He made small talk with Cooper, asking, "When are you coming to pick me up?" After the phone call, he left Wilson and returned to the house with Powell.

Safe at the Powell home, the two laughed about their stunt, Walrath commenting that he had "fouled up." At some point, there was a challenge to try again. Cooper would say it was Powell who asked Walrath whether he had the guts to do it, to which Walrath responded, "I have the guts if you do." However, Powell denied making the statement, and both Walrath and Delphine said it was Cooper who teased the two men, stating, "you don't have the nerve to rob Wilson." Whoever said it, the challenge was made and accepted.

Powell put on some brown cotton gloves and armed himself with the sap. Walrath found some green women's gloves and once again took the handgun. Together, they walked back to Wilson's, and together, they knocked on the door. When Wilson answered, Walrath once again asked to use the phone. Wilson opened the door, and both Walrath and Powell entered. According to Powell, their plan was to knock Wilson out, search the place and take whatever they could find. At no time, he said, did they ever discuss killing him.

Once inside, Walrath again called Cooper, asking when she was coming to pick them up. As he made his call, Wilson sat down in a chair where he looked over the newspaper and listened to a baseball game on the radio. After Walrath hung up the phone, he approached Wilson, called his attention to an article in the newspaper, and then hit him in the head with the pistol. As Wilson struggled to his feet, Powell hit him once, perhaps twice, in the head with the sap, after which the rocks came out of the sap. Walrath hit him again with the gun, then dropped it on the floor. As Wilson was still on his feet, Walrath began pummeling him with his fists until Wilson fell to the floor unconscious.

Powell later testified he was frozen in disbelief as Walrath beat Wilson. As soon as Wilson hit the floor, however, Powell took Wilson's billfold and emptied it. He then went into the store and began searching for money. He found little: twelve dollars and a few rolls of change. Walrath searched the house, including the kitchen. As he went through the drawers of the kitchen, he found a large knife. He would later say it was at that moment he realized Wilson had to die. "It just hit me all at once," he testified. "Then I was right beside him and in the act of stabbing him."

Powell entered the living room and saw Walrath stab Wilson for the last time, leaving the knife in his back. He felt sick to his stomach and ran from the building. According to Cooper, Powell arrived first at his house, looking like he was going to cry. Walrath followed and told Cooper they had just killed Wilson, giving her all the details. Then both men

Walrath and Powell on the day of their arrest for the murder of Newt Wilson

washed and changed their clothes. Together with the women, they got in Powell's car and took a ride.

According to Powell, the rest of the night was "kind of a blur." They stopped to get gas for the car, then stopped again to get beer. At some point in time, they realized they needed to destroy the evidence, so they drove toward Horseshoe Bend, turning onto Cartright Road. After driving about fifteen miles, they threw the clothes into a ravine. They drove a bit further and did the same with the rolls of change.

Cooper, who would be the state's key witness, recalled the boys tried to act happy. They made several attempts at singing. Walrath also bragged about how calm he was and how normal he felt. But she also noted that at times the car was eerily quiet, almost depressing. Powell, especially, was subdued and told Cooper she was not to say anything to anyone. They concocted a story Cooper was supposed to tell if anyone ever asked: they picked her up that evening, stopped to buy Budweiser and Miller High Life, and then went for a ride.

Back in Boise, Powell dropped off his passengers, first Cooper, then Walrath. He and Delphine drove back to their home and went to bed, two houses down from where Newt Wilson lay dead. According to Delphine, neither one of them could sleep.

118

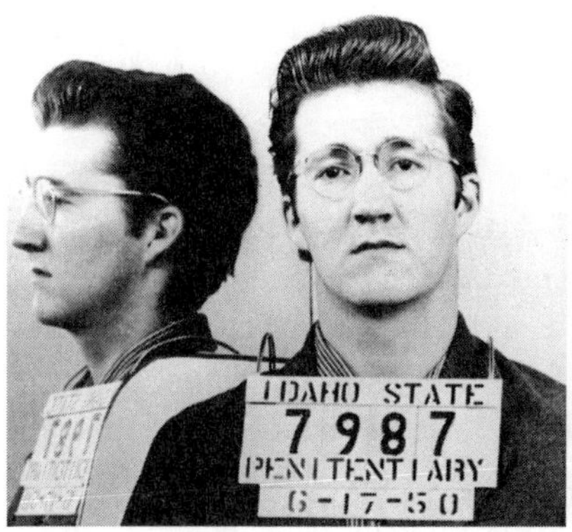

Ernie Walrath

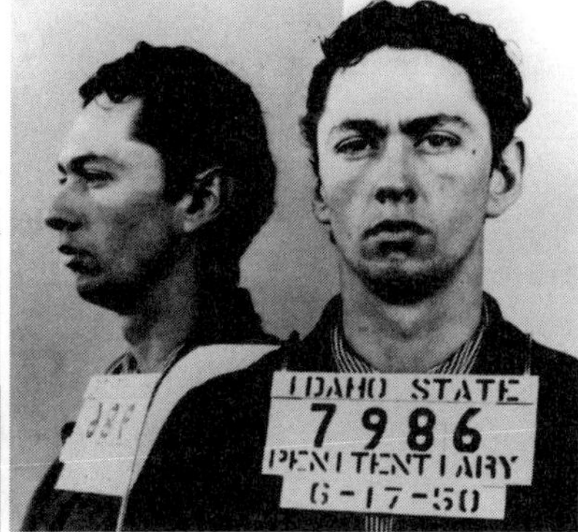

Troy Powell

The next morning, Loretta Jacobsen, a clerk at Wilson's store, reported for work as usual. Waiting for her was a Mrs. MacDonald, a regular customer. Both women tried the front door and called for Wilson. Eventually, MacDonald called the police. James Brandon, captain of the Boise Police Department detectives, arrived. He entered the house through a bedroom window and found Wilson's body, the knife still in his back, the radio playing softly.

At the same time, Barbara Cooper's conscience got the best of her; she notified the police of the previous night's events and told them where they could find both Powell and Walrath. Late Tuesday afternoon, the police arrested Walrath at work. They found Powell at his parents' home in Garden City. Both were taken to the Boise Police Station and interrogated.

Powell was first to make a formal confession, telling police stenographer Maxine McGee the entire story. He gave her the details on the robbery and admitted he had hit Wilson with the sap, although he could not remember how many times. He denied stabbing Wilson, laying the blame directly on Walrath.

Walrath was then brought before McGee, but prior to making his statement, he was allowed to read Powell's confession. Seeing that his partner in crime had laid the murder on him, Walrath stated that both of them stabbed Wilson, adding that it was Powell's idea. Later at his sentencing hearing, he would recant and admit he stabbed Wilson on his own.

Legal maneuvers began on May 11 and various hearing and court appearances followed. Boise defense attorneys Jess Hawley, Jr. and Claude Marcus guided Powell and Walrath through the proceedings, while Ada

County Prosecuting Attorney James Blaine presented the case for the state. Early on, Blaine made the decision to try the boys together and to seek the death penalty.

On June 1, Walrath and Powell stood before Third District Court Judge Charles E. Winstead and pleaded guilty to the charges. Blaine asked the court to reject the pleas, as he wanted further time to present his case to the court. But Winstead overruled, and set June 15 for a pre-sentence hearing. Then, he would listen to evidence to help him determine sentences. At the time he seemed amenable to both prosecution and defense alike.

On that day, a full courtroom hung on every word as prosecutor Blaine laid out his case. Pushing for the ultimate penalty, he submitted physical evidence for the judge, including seventy-four colored photos and the bloody clothes and gloves worn by Walrath and Powell on the night of the murder. He produced the gun with a broken handle and the bloody sock used for the sap. He painted a horrific scene, one created by two young career criminals turned ruthless killers.

Blaine relied heavily on Barbara Cooper and Dr. Joseph Beeman, who performed the autopsy. Under oath, Cooper recalled the events of the night and her fear of Walrath. She wondered out loud if "she should stop going out with him." She also testified it was Walrath who stabbed Wilson, as he admitted it to her shortly after the crime.

Beeman's testimony both gripped and outraged the crowd. Every detail he gave illustrated the savagery of the crime. Wilson had a broken nose, a broken jaw, and a fractured skull. His false teeth had been found on the floor in the living room, broken into several pieces. He had seven stab wounds in his back. Beeman was unable to say exactly which blow caused Wilson's death, concluding Wilson died from the "inhalation of blood" from a combination of all the wounds. Blaine was building his case against both men; Powell may not have stabbed Wilson, but the blows from his sap contributed to Wilson's death.

By the time Blaine finished, the judge had little sympathy for the defendants; as the day wore on, he gave the defense attorneys little leeway. Hawley and Marcus would have a difficult time presenting their clients as anything but cold-blooded killers.

The entire Powell family—Troy, Harvey, Beulah, and Delphine—made for sympathetic witnesses, but did little to help Troy's cause. They were all subdued on the stand, regretful for what had happened. Delphine sobbed through her testimony. Troy was firm; they never intended to kill Wilson, just rob him. He explained the gun they used didn't even have a firing pin. He denied stabbing Wilson, saying instead that when he saw Ernie over Wilson with the knife, he felt sick to his stomach. He remembered hitting Wilson once with the sap, maybe twice, but that was all.

For all the courtesy and regret the Powells showed on the stand, the Walraths countered with hostility and insolence. At times, Ernie, Jr. refused to answer questions or was evasive. Under cross-examination by Blaine, he was especially hostile. When Blaine asked him if Wilson was dead when he went to the floor, Ernie replied, "I am not a doctor; I would not know."

Ernie also admitted that he alone stabbed Wilson. Blaine pushed him on this issue, mockingly asking, "The reason you said both of you stabbed Mr. Wilson was you were just mad at Powell for squealing?" At first Ernie refused to answer, but eventually admitted it was true.

Also, according to Ernie, Cooper was not the innocent witness she pretended to be. It was Cooper who teased them after the first botched attempt at robbing Wilson. It was Cooper who made up some of the alibi. Cooper was also mistaken about the sap; he and Powell had actually made the sap a week prior to the murder to use in a different robbery.

Ernie's full disdain for the law and the courts came in his final exchange with Blaine. Blaine believed Wilson was killed because he could identify his attackers. But Ernie said he never worried about Wilson. "The faults of eye-witnesses are probably well-known to you," he said directly to Blaine. "With just one eye-witness, it would be rather difficult, in my opinion, to secure a conviction."

In an effort to give reason for Walrath's antagonism, Hawley tried to introduce his mistreatment by the Oregon justice system as a mitigating circumstance in the case. He called Delmore Lessard, who had helped secure Walrath's release from the Oregon State Penitentiary. But when Hawley began questioning Lessard concerning Walrath's troubles in Oregon, the judge intervened.

"What's the purpose of the testimony?" Judge Winstead asked.

"I believe I can present information on what goes into a boy's life as part of mitigating circumstance," Hawley replied.

Not satisfied, the judge continued, "How long will it take to finish the case?" When Hawley answered it might take several hours, the judge was terse, "I am not going to give that much time," he told Hawley.

He did allow Lessard to give background into Ernie's Oregon conviction and parole revocation, but midway through the testimony, the judge stopped him.

"I am confused," Winstead said. "Was he guilty of the original charge?" he asked Lessard. Lessard confirmed that he was.

"Then I don't want to hear anymore," at which time Lessard was excused.

Walrath, Sr. took the stand and tried to explain how the Oregon justice system corrupted his son, claiming after just six months in prison, he was an "entirely different young man." When he tried to explain that Ernie's parole officer "had it in for him" and returned him to prison for no reason, the judge stopped him.

"I don't care about that part of it," Winstead said. "What did he do to get his parole revoked?"

"We never learned. I can quote the exact conditions."

"I don't want the conditions," Winstead admonished. "I want to know, because they never revoke a parole without cause, and I want to know what the reason was."

"He said he didn't need any reason," Walrath said of the parole officer. And with that, Walrath was excused.

By the end of Thursday, Winstead had heard enough, but Hawley and Marcus had one key witness they still wished to call. Reluctantly, the judge continued the hearing until the next morning.

The defense attorneys called on expert witness Dr. M. M. Campbell, a psychiatrist from Seattle, who began his testimony by explaining his qualifications. Prosecutor Blaine told the court he was willing to forego the doctor stating his credentials, but was overruled by the judge, who wanted to hear them. Campbell then laid them out, an extensive list of degrees and experience. The judge was skeptical, questioning whether Campbell could accomplish all he claimed. Campbell assured the judge he had both the experience and the knowledge to evaluate the defendants.

Campbell, along with another doctor, spent over three hours with each defendant, in addition to interviewing family members and acquaintances of each. His conclusion was that Powell had an under-developed character, which caused him to be easily manipulated. He was impulsive and child-like, and because of that, he was easily attracted to dominating personalities. But, according to the doctor, he was not sick or perverted. Campbell believed he could be salvaged given appropriate discipline, training, and

Judge Charles Winstead had no sympathy for Walrath or Powell.

opportunity. He called his chances for rehabilitation favorable.

Walrath, Jr., on the other hand, was highly egocentric and selfish. Campbell described him as a psychopath, an individual who was "incapable of conducting himself with decency and propriety in the business of life." Campbell stated that Walrath, Jr. totally disregarded the rights of others and "always had to make himself superior." Campbell's analysis was that he was abnormal; he could be rehabilitated, but "the problem would be more difficult."

At the conclusion of Campbell's testimony, the judge seemed unimpressed.

"Now, Doctor," the judge chided Campbell, "stripped of the verbiage, you do not say either of these men is insane?"

"No," Campbell responded. "Neither is insane in the legal sense."

Following Campbell, Hawley asked the judge for a day to submit a written argument, but Winstead would hear nothing of it.

"If you want to present an argument, Mr. Hawley, I want it today," the judge said. "I have other matters to dispose of."

Hawley could see little value in continuing and rested his case. Judge Winstead recessed for lunch. He would render his decision that afternoon.

That afternoon, Walrath and Powell stood before the judge. A standing-room only crowd heard the judge tell the defendants he could find no mitigating circumstances surrounding the crime. Instead, the two had committed a cold-blooded, heinous, premeditated murder for which they had to pay the ultimate penalty. Handcuffed together, they rose to hear the judge sentence them to death. Their hanging was set for August 2, 1950.

Walrath and Powell were taken to the Idaho State Penitentiary, placed in solitary confinement, and put on suicide watch. Their lawyers launched an immediate appeal with the Idaho Supreme Court.

They remained in solitary throughout the appeal. Powell missed the birth of his son. While Delphine came to visit him often, it is unclear whether he ever saw his boy. Walrath, who had visits from his sisters, took to writing poetry. Filled with anger and contempt, the poems show an unrepentant young man, who blamed the courts and prison system for his woes. In a four-page poem titled "Youth" he chides America for failing its children, especially in the areas of justice.

> *"…Shall we each go cut off a finger?*
> *To learn that it does not pay?*
> *Or take up abode in a dungeon*
> *To learn the most modern way?*
> *Or club and beat down our children?*
> *Break their hearts and their spirits too?*
> *While he herald our national freedom*
> *And define it as privilege for you…*
> *To punish a child in a dungeon*
> *Or to wreck a boys life in the pen*
> *Can never be mentioned with 'justice'*
> *Nor said of the civilized men.*
> *He who will rule with a vengeance*
> *Over lads who have fell by the way*
> *Smells of the stench of a caveman*
> *And falls short of manhood today…"*

At the supreme court hearing, Hawley and Marcus took aim at Judge Winstead. Citing the judge's actions as "arbitrary and impatient," Hawley and Marcus claimed Winstead limited their presentation of mitigating circumstances, adding that the judge was "prejudiced" after viewing the numerous crime scene photos. The defense team also appealed to the court to consider that "no one as young as these defendants has ever been executed in Idaho." Finally, they believed the testimony of the psychiatrist, who called both boys "abnormal," should have been taken into consideration by the judge.

Attorney General Robert Smylie represented the state. Although he was personally against the death penalty and believed the legislature should abolish it, he did his job. He argued forcefully and clearly that the defendants were career criminals and that the focus of the trial was not their age, but the brutal crime itself. As for the psychiatrist's testimony, the doctor readily admitted that Powell and Walrath knew right from wrong, and in Idaho, that was the test of accountability. As such, according to Smylie, the judge did not abuse his discretion when he sentenced the men the death.

On February 1, 1951 the court issued its decision: the judgment was affirmed. Hawley and Marcus asked for a rehearing but were denied. Powell and Walrath went back to Third District Court where Judge Winstead set their execution for Friday, April 13. Unless the board of pardons or Governor C. A. Robins intervened, Walrath and Powell would hang.

On the Monday before their execution, the condemned men pleaded for their lives in front of the Idaho State Board of Pardons. Appearing separately, they detailed their crime. Walrath took responsibility for the murder, telling the board that "Troy ought to pay for robbery and as an accessory. He wasn't even in the room." Powell agreed, stating, "I have never killed anyone, nor have I had the urge to kill anyone. I don't think I should hang for a murder I did not commit."

Powell was repentant but also defensive. He blamed a bill collector, a Mr. Hill, for pressuring him into the robberies. He explained how Barbara Cooper teased them after they returned from Wilson's the first time without any money, how she had urged them to go back. He also did not believe he had a fair trial, claiming the prosecutor glossed over his non-involvement in the killing of Wilson. He begged the board to spare his life, claiming, "my wife's and son's future are at stake. I know I can become a useful citizen if given a chance."

Walrath did not apologize and was more philosophical in his answers. He too blamed Cooper. He also felt the court had been unfair, that he had been misled into the guilty plea as he "was under the impression that a life sentence would be automatic." He also alluded to his troubles with the entire justice system, telling the board "society makes its own deviates from its code, but not willfully." He argued against execution in general, stating that capital punishment "will not gain anyone anything. If you lay it aside, society will gain." Although he admitted he had done little good in his life, he added, "I can learn. I can study. I can make a contribution to society. That would be the first thing I have ever done, but I'd like the chance to try."

Of the two, Walrath was afraid to die. "It's just not knowing," he said. "It's the stepping off into infinity…the blank spot."

The board heard testimony from both the Powell and Walrath families, their lawyers, and their clergymen. Rev. Hartzell Cobb spoke on behalf of Walrath, and Rev. Martin Sumner, Jr., pleaded for the life

Attorney General Robert Smylie argued the case for the state before the supreme court.

of Powell. They also listened to comments from several people who were against the death penalty, particularly in a case where the guilty were so young.

In fact, the board of pardons, Governor Robins and Prison Warden Lou Clapp were inundated with letters, the majority supporting a commutation of the sentences to life in prison for both men. Many of them were based on religious grounds, "God gives no man the right to take the life of any person," but others, like Rev. E. H. Edwards of Boise noted, "There are other men still alive whose crime is just as great as that of these young men."

But it was Idaho Secretary of State Ira Masters who had the last say before the board. "The courts have decreed that these two men shall die for the crimes they have committed against society," he said. "I do not consider it reasonable that the state legislature of Idaho created the State Board of Corrections to overrule the opinions of the courts of our state."

For good measure, Masters added, "Since we are forcing so many of our upstanding young soldiers to die in Korea to preserve democracy from communism, isn't it fair that those at home who so flagrantly violate our laws pay the supreme penalty?"

On April 11, after deliberating all day, the board of pardons announced its decision. The board could find no good reason for setting aside the laws of the state and upheld the decision of the court. On the following day, Hawley and Marcus made one more appeal before the supreme court, but again they were denied.

On the afternoon of April 12, Powell and Walrath met for the last time with their families. According to prison guards, there were no tears, the boys telling their families they were "ready to go." Warden Clapp visited in the early afternoon and asked the boys if they had special requests for their final meals. They seemed surprised at the notion, and told the warden they would have whatever the other prisoners were having. As the afternoon turned to evening, they sat with the ministers Cobb and Sumner and awaited their fate.

Powell's headstone at Morris Hill Cemetery

A portable scaffold had been moved into place outside the prison yard, out of the view of all inmates. Clapp, concerned the double execution would disturb the prison population, tried to keep the affair as low key as possible. Although he had many requests from outsiders to view the executions, he denied them all. Only the warden, a member of the board of corrections, a few prison guards, three doctors, and coroner Clyde Summers and his aides bore witness. He also set the executions for just after midnight on April 13. He wanted them done and all evidence gone by the time the sun came up. Executioner Thomas J. Hubbard obliged, doing his work quickly and quietly in the shadows of the prison.

Walrath was first to leave his cell. Accompanied by Rev. Cobb, he walked unassisted from his cell to the scaffold, his arms tied to his sides. As he stood on the scaffold, he looked down at Cobb and said, "I'll be seeing you," to which Cobb, his voice raised, yelled back, "I'll be seeing you." The warden placed a black hood over Walrath's head and then stepped back. In his last words, Walrath offered a prayer, "Lord, Jesus, receive my spirit." He was pronounced dead at 12:22 a.m.

While Walrath's body was loaded into a hearse parked out of sight, the scaffold was readied for Powell. All visible signs of Walrath's execution were gone when Powell made his appearance. He, too, walked to the gallows unassisted, accompanied by guards and Rev. Sumner. He had told Sumner earlier that "there's no blood on my hands," and that when he faced his death, he would "go like a man," without fear. As he stood on the scaffold, hood in place, rope around his neck, he told the darkness, "I know I'm right with God." He was pronounced dead at 12:50 a.m.

The bodies were taken to Summer's Funeral Home. On Saturday, April 14, they were buried side by side at Morris Hill Cemetery. Rev. Cobb led a graveside service for the families. Following the ceremony, funeral workers placed temporary markers on the graves, which were stolen immediately. Inmates made additional markers for each grave, one of granite, the other of wood, but these, too, were stolen. At least six markers were placed on each grave, and each time, they disappeared. Today, Powell rests under a bronze military plaque, while Walrath lies unmarked, their short lives remembered in headlines and heartbreak.

> *Any fool will face a day of judgment.*
> *As he has done to others is the rule.*
> *Upon his soul may the God of Hosts have mercy*
> *Poor fool, who in his lifetime, played the fool*
> *—ELW*

James Romain
David Renton
Christopher Lower

Nez Perce Trail, October 11, 1863
Lewiston, March 4, 1864

Idaho Territory was a scant six months old when the murder of Lloyd Magruder and his traveling companions rocked the west. The subsequent capture of his killers, along with their trial and execution have become a western legend as fact and fiction mingled to create one of the strangest tales in Idaho history.

Idaho played little role in the early development of the Pacific Northwest. Originally part of Oregon Territory, it became part of Washington Territory in 1859 when Oregon became a state. Even then, Idaho was considered hostile country, filled with mountains, fast-flowing rivers, and high deserts that tortured travelers on their way to the more hospitable regions of Washington and Oregon. That changed when gold was discovered in 1860 near present-day Pierce, and thousands of fortune-seekers flocked to the area. At the time, no government agencies existed to control the influx of people. To help maintain order, Washington's territorial legislature established Shoshone and Nez Perce counties, which covered all of present-day northern Idaho. But the power center of Washington Territory was too far removed from the gold fields of Idaho. In 1862, when gold was discovered in Florence and the Boise Basin, the need for a new territory to encompass Idaho's mining communities was clear.

While politicians haggled over the boundaries of the new territory, resourceful businessmen made their way to newly established communities. One such entrepreneur was Lloyd Magruder, who saw fortune in the gold fields of Idaho. Born in Maryland to a wealthy plantation owner, Magruder's early life was one of privilege. However, both his parents died by the time he was eleven, and he was left to rely on his sisters and their husbands who provided for him until he was old enough to go out on his own. At age 20, he joined a brother in Arkansas, where he worked as a surveyor and studied law. After a stint with the U.S. army in the Mexican War, he married and

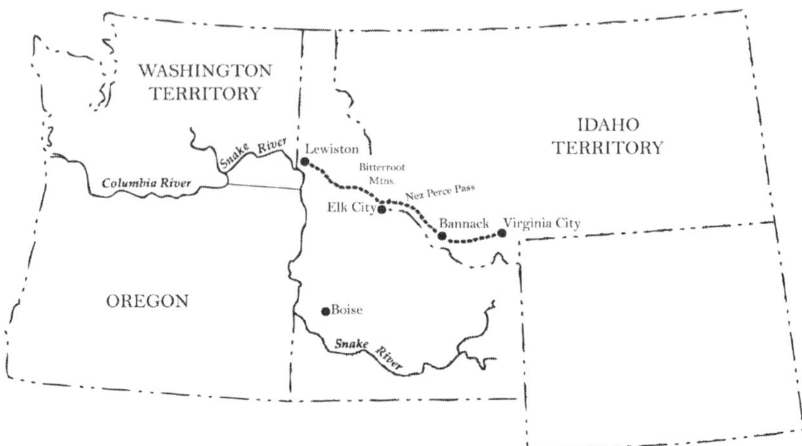

traveled with his new bride to California. They eventually settled in St. Louis, a small mining town where he opened a general store.

He found success in St. Louis until a fire wiped out the town. From there he moved to Marysville, California, where he dabbled in politics and practiced law. A Democrat who supported slavery and the union, he served as a state legislator until the Civil War. Then he fell out of favor with party leaders who favored secession. Eventually, Magruder was forced out of office. With his political aspirations dashed and his finances depleted, he decided Idaho offered brighter prospects. In April 1862, he and several others started toward Lewiston, Idaho. They arrived in July and stayed at the Luna House, a hotel owned and operated by Hill Beachy (Beachey).

Beachy was also from Marysville. He had arrived in Lewiston in 1860 at the height of the Pierce gold rush. Whether he encouraged Magruder's resettlement in Idaho is unclear, but the two were good friends. Beachy would be instrumental in bringing Magruder's killers to justice.

After visiting with Beachy in Lewiston, Magruder realized there was money to be made driving pack trains from the port city to the mining areas of the Salmon River. He would load up with supplies in Lewiston, travel to Florence, Elk City, and Dixie to sell his goods, then return to Lewiston for more. The work was dangerous; highwaymen haunted the supply routes, and packers were frequently robbed of both merchandise and gold. But Magruder avoided trouble and found great success. He eventually sent for his family in Marysville and put them up in a modest home in Lewiston. He did well enough to start a small general store in Elk City, which was becoming a thriving community on the Nez Perce Trail, a route that linked Idaho to present-day Montana.

While Magruder was building his business, Idaho became a territory. Created on March 4, 1863, Idaho territory was huge, even by western standards, encompassing all of present-day Idaho, Montana, and most of Wyoming. As a new territory, a new government would have to be established, but its sheer size created problems for the organizers. Idaho's first governor William Wallace named Lewiston as the temporary capitol and called for Idaho's first legislative session, which began on December 7, 1863. But Wallace resigned the day before the session started leaving territorial secretary William Daniels to oversee the proceedings, which lasted until February 4, 1864. During the session, delegates managed to establish the rules of law and organize the supreme court, but little else would be accomplished. In fact, the territory would not become officially organized until July 10, 1864. By that time, Idaho had been reduced in size, as Montana became its own territory and Wyoming was attached to Dakota Territory.

Magruder had hopes of being a leader in the new Idaho Territory. In August 1863, he had been asked to run as a representative of Idaho Territory on the Democratic ticket. He accepted the challenge as a chance to get back into politics. But he still had a business to run and was especially interested in the gold strikes near Bannack and Virginia City, part of the new Idaho territory, now part of Montana. Miners in these isolated towns would pay dearly for the materials he could provide.

In early August, Magruder was in Lewiston purchasing supplies, outfitting his pack train for the grueling trip across the Bitterroot Mountains to Bannack. He would take the southern Nez Perce Trail, which traveled southeast out of Lewiston, passed Elk City, climbed over the Bitterroots and Nez Perce Pass, and continued on to Bannack. As Magruder purchased additional mules for his train and hired more packers, his enterprise did not go unnoticed. Magruder's friend, Hill Beachy, was concerned.

Beachy worried that highwaymen would see Magruder as an easy mark. A string of loaded mules, not heavily guarded on an isolated trail, would be an easy target for someone intent on robbery. Legend also has it that Beachy had a dream in which he saw his good friend murdered with an axe. Beachy was alarmed enough to loan Magruder a gun for the trip, and he warned his friend to be careful.

Magruder, Louis O. Holt, Charles Allen, and several packers left Lewiston in mid-August. By August 20, they were in Elk City and on August 22, they made their final push toward Bannack. Because of their heavy load, they were able to make only ten to fifteen miles a day. They reached Bannack around September 10. On or near their arrival, Magruder's party met four men—David Renton, (aka Doc Howard and William Renton), James P. Romain (Romaine), David Christopher Lower (Lowery), and William "Billy" Page.

Over the years, this meeting has been the focus of much conjecture. Some historians claim that Renton, Romain, and Lower had been in Lewiston on the day Magruder left with his pack train. Seeing opportunity, the unscrupulous trio planned to intercept him on the route to Bannack with the intention of robbing him. Others believe that Renton, Romain, and Lower simply came upon the pack train as they traveled south toward Bannack from the Mullan Road, an alternative route across the mountains. In the story told by Billy Page, he met the trio along the Mullan Road and traveled with them to Bannack where they had a chance encounter with Magruder. Whatever the case, the meeting would lead to disaster for Magruder.

Not much is known about Renton, Romain, or Lower except they were shady characters, all with criminal records. Renton and Romain, originally from New York, met in New Orleans and eventually made their way to Marysville, California. Romain ran a plastering business and worked on the building that housed the *California Express*, Marysville's newspaper. Magruder worked for the newspaper a short time, and it is possible the two met. Romain, who was also a gambler, was well spoken, well mannered and handsome. Renton, who went by the name of Doc Howard while in Marysville, ran a stable where he was known for his work with sick horses. He may have been involved in a bank robbery in St. Louis, and in Marysville he was suspected of several robberies, but no charges were ever filed against him. Renton was also articulate and gave the impression that he was well educated. Both he and Romain did not act like murderous criminals.

Lower, on the other hand, was a foul-mouthed, uncouth criminal. Heavy set, with blond hair and a light complexion, he was quarrelsome and taunting to anyone who disagreed with him. He also revealed nothing about his background. No records exist to explain where he was from or what he did. The only mention of his past came from Sheriff James Fisk of Lewiston, who reported that Lower spent time in San Quentin.

It is unclear when the three men met. Renton and Romain left Marysville together and spent some time in John Day, Oregon before traveling to Lewiston. Lower was already in Idaho when they arrived,

Lewiston, around 1863

having traveled the Nez Perce and Mullan trails. He knew Billy Page prior to their meeting on the Mullan Road in September.

Billy Page was a jack-of-all-trades, a simple man who did what he could to survive. Born in England, he arrived in the United States in 1848 and made his way west. He spent much of his time around Walla Walla before heading to Lapwai with a herd of cattle, which he sold on the reservation. He also worked as a trapper and miner, and because he was good with stock, he was often hired to work on pack trains. At some point, he met Lower, and the two traveled together to Bannack prior to the fall of 1863. Page would survive the Magruder massacre, and his story would doom Romain, Renton, and Lower.

When Magruder reached Bannack with his pack train of supplies, he was disappointed to find that much of the excitement had moved east to Virginia City with a new gold strike on Alder Creek. Magruder, along with his new companions, went ahead of the pack train to Virginia City to check out his prospects. They arrived there on September 15 and set up a tent that would serve as a general store. When Charles Allen arrived with the pack train on September 22, Magruder was in business.

While most of Magruder's help left once he arrived in Virginia City, Page, Renton, and Romain stayed on to help with the store. They were busy, and by the end of the month, they had sold all of the supplies, earning

133

Magruder anywhere from $15,000 to $30,000 in gold. As for Lower, he occupied his time at the gambling halls of the new mining town.

With his supplies sold and winter approaching, Magruder made plans to return to Lewiston. Allen agreed to lead the pack train over the mountains, but Magruder would need additional men to help with the stock. When Page and his friends offered their services, he accepted, even though he had been warned that Romain, Renton, and Lower were "tough characters." An acquaintance of Romain's from Marysville, William Phillips, also hired on, although Romain did his best to dissuade him. Two other men, Robert and Horace Chalmers, also joined the party. The two brothers from Missouri had done well in Virginia City, earning well over $2000. They were ready to move on.

Sometime between September 29 and October 3, the party, minus Allen and Lower, left Virginia City and traveled toward Bannack. The first night they stayed on the Beaverhead River where Allen joined them. The next day, Lower joined them as they made their way to Bannack. Along the way and in Bannack, Magruder purchased more mules. They stayed in Bannack at least two days and then Magruder's party with nine men, six horses, and forty mules left Bannack enroute to Lewiston.

It is unknown how long Romain, Renton, and Lower planned the robbery and murder of Magruder. Romain's advice to his friend Phillips to stay in Virginia City indicates the scheme was in place before they left. According to Page, they were seven days into the trip before Renton spoke to him about a plan to steal Magruder's gold. With Lower and Romain standing by, Renton told Page not to be afraid, that they would take care of all of the dirty work. His job was to put his bedroll next to Phillips. He was not to respond to any commotion, but if Phillips woke up, he was to shoot him. Page would claim he was confused and frightened, but also curious about this sudden turn of events. He agreed to go along with the plan, especially when Lower told him that if Page "valued his life," he would keep quiet and do what he was told.

Why the trio chose Page and not Phillips to be their accomplice will never be known. Perhaps they needed Page's knowledge of the Nez Perce Trail to get them out of the mountains. Page was also good with stock, and a pack train of forty mules, even unloaded, needed an experienced handler. Page was also an old man, somewhat gullible and not too bright. Maybe they believed he could be bullied into silence. Whatever the case, Page would be the only person left alive after the carnage who was willing to tell the story.

On the night of October 11, Lower left camp to check on the stock, which were in a meadow above the camp. He returned, retrieved an axe, and told the group he was going back up to make a better fence. Magruder offered to go with him, and Lower agreed, stating they could build a fire and spend the night there. For some reason, Magruder took his gun, and the two walked up the hill. The rest of the men went to bed.

At some point, Renton took an axe and made his way up the hill. Together, he and Lower attacked Magruder, using the axes to strike mortal blows. The assault was so unexpected, Magruder did not have time to use his weapon.

With Magruder dead, Lower and Renton returned to camp. They lay down next to Romain for a few minutes and then Renton and Romain, axes in hand, crept to the tent of the Chalmers brothers where they killed the two young Missourians.

Renton and Romain were not finished. They returned to Lower's bedroll and Renton removed a shotgun. He then made his way to Allen's tent while Romain with his axe approached Phillips. When Renton fired, Romain struck Phillips with the axe. Phillips rose up to defend himself, and Romain swore at him, telling him he had warned him not to come. Romain continued the attack until Phillips was dead.

There was no rest for the wicked. Page was sent up the hill to check on the stock. There he found Magruder dead, and the campfire spreading in the dry grass. He put out the fire and returned to the main camp to find the bodies of Allen and Phillips already wrapped and tied in blankets. Page helped do the same with the Chalmers brothers. Then they carried the four bodies away from the camp to the edge of an incline. They rolled the bodies down the hill where they could not be seen. As for the body of Magruder, they left him where he fell.

Page was ordered to pack camp, taking only the supplies they would need. He was to burn everything else. Page did as he was told. He collected the items that would not burn, stuffed them in a cloth sack, and hid them behind a large log. The other three men gathered the guns. They decided to take only the pistols, leaving behind two shotguns and a rifle, the one Beachy had given Magruder before he left Lewiston.

In the morning, they sorted and took only the horses and mules they wanted. Among them was Magruder's favorite saddle mule complete with

Hill Beachy

his saddle. Then they left camp, leaving the remaining mules untethered. To their surprise, the mules followed. Renton tried to frighten them off by shooting several of them, but to no avail. Knowing the large pack train would be recognized as Magruder's, the men were desperate. When they reached a small clearing, they drove the mules off the trail and shot them.

The group continued toward Elk City. As the town came into view, they met two men on the trail. One of them knew Renton. The meeting so spooked Renton, he discarded a watch and compass he had taken from Magruder. Concerned their appearance in Elk City would raise suspicions, they by-passed the little town and continued on to Lewiston. Once out of the mountains, they stayed off the main trails for fear they would be recognized.

On October 17, they reached the outskirts of Lewiston where they stopped at the stockyard of James Hays. Here Page remained with the stock while the three others went in search of a boat they could take down the Snake River. But no boat could be found, so they came up with another plan. They would spend the night in Lewiston and then take the stage to Walla Walla. Once there, they could catch a steamer down the Columbia and eventually to California.

Concealing their faces, they made their way to the Hotel de France where they would spend the night. Page, however, still had to take care of the horses. He went in search of Bishop Goodrich, a Lewiston rancher and former employer. Together they gathered the horses and mules and took them to a corral on the edge of town. Page paid for their care in advance and told Goodrich he would be back in the spring to collect the stock.

While Page took care of the animals, Lower went to the stage office located at the Luna House. There he purchased four tickets to Walla Walla using the names William Johnson, G. Clark, D. Smith, and F. Perkins.

He told the clerk, Chester Coburn, to have the stage pick them up at the French hotel.

Beachy, who was sitting by the stove in the ticket office, watched the transaction. Although he did not recognize Lower, he was suspicious; Lower was trying to hide his face, and he seemed to stumble over the names he gave for the tickets. He was concerned that Lower might be planning to rob the stage. The next morning Beachy was at the French hotel where he watched Lower and the others board the stage. Some accounts claim Beachy recognized the group as the same men who had followed Magruder out of Lewiston. Others relate that Beachy was simply wary of the men and their actions. Whatever the case, Beachy decided to find out more about the mysterious men.

First, Beachy knew that two pack trains were due back in the area— one belonged to A.P. Ankeny, the other to Magruder. Shortly after the stage left, he sent riders to search for both groups. Then, three packers who had left Bannack after Magruder arrived in Lewiston. They had not passed Magruder on the trail. At that point, Beachy knew trouble had found his friend. He and Coburn went in search of the horses ridden by the four mysterious men. Goodrich came forward with the stock, and Beachy recognized Magruder's mule and saddle. His worst fears were confirmed; Magruder had been murdered, and those responsible were getting away.

Beachy was well aware that law enforcement was almost non-existent in Lewiston. Nez Perce County did not even exist as part of Idaho Territory since the new territorial government had yet to establish its own counties. But Beachy was determined to bring Magruder's killers to justice even though he had no real proof that Magruder was dead. He also had no idea who may have been killed with Magruder, but he assumed that Charles Allen, Magruder's chief packer, was among those murdered. As he pursued his arrest warrant, he listed both of their names as victims.

Beachy was anxious to get underway to apprehend the suspects, although he had no official capacity to do so. This was solved when Sheriff Fisk deputized both Beachy and Thomas Farrell (aka Thomas Pike) to go in pursuit. But the suspects were no longer in Idaho Territory. Beachy would need the proper paperwork from Idaho's territorial leaders to enlist the help of other states or territories.

On October 23, Wesley Wickersham, Magruder's partner in the Elk City general store, appeared before William B. Daniels, acting governor of Idaho Territory. Wickersham presented an affidavit accusing William

Johnson, G. Clark, D. Smith, and F. Perkins of the robbery and murder of Magruder and Allen. He asked for Daniels' help in apprehending the murderers. After careful consideration, Daniels agreed, and wrote letters to the governors of California and British Columbia, asking their cooperation in the capture and return of the fugitives to Idaho Territory. Now with the blessing of the territory, Beachy could seek justice for Magruder.

Beachy planned his journey and telegraphed ahead, warning law enforcement in Oregon, Washington Territory, and California of the murderous gang. Then he and Pike set out to find them.

Tracking them turned out to be relatively easy. From Walla Walla, they traveled to the Columbia River where they booked passage on a steamer to Portland. There they stayed for several days drinking and gambling heavily. Beachy and Farrell were hot on their trail, arriving in Portland just two hours after they had left on a ship to San Francisco. An attempt to intercept the ship before it reached the open waters of the Pacific failed.

Undaunted, Beachy and Farrell took the stage toward San Francisco. They stopped briefly in Yreka, California where Beachy sent a telegram to the chief of police in San Francisco. In the wire he described the fugitives in detail and gave the chief the name of the boat on which they would arrive, the *Sierra Nevada*. Beachy added that the suspects would be carrying a large amount of gold.

While Beachy hurried on to San Francisco, the chief of detectives there, Isaiah Lees, went to investigate. He found the *Sierra Nevada* already docked and empty, but with inquiry he learned of four men who had recently exchanged thousands of dollars in gold dust for coin at the U.S. mint. The men fit the description of the fugitives. He eventually tracked them to the gambling halls of San Francisco where they were busy spending their new-found wealth. Lees arrested them and took them to jail.

Beachy could not believe his good fortune; the murderers of his good friend were behind bars. But they would not give up without a fight. After denying any involvement in Magruder's murder, they hired a lawyer and asked for a writ of habeas corpus. Because all of the evidence against them was circumstantial, Beachy worried a judge would release them. With an impassioned plea for justice, Beachy laid out his case against the four men. The judge agreed and ordered the prisoners released to Beachy with the stipulation that they were to get a fair trial. Beachy promised they would.

Beachy, along with Farrell and Lees, left immediately for Idaho with their prisoners. Along the way, they picked up an escort of U.S. soldiers who accompanied them to Lewiston. When they arrived, sometime during the first week of December, an angry mob greeted them, ropes at the ready. But Beachy told them of his promise to the California judge. Calling on the citizens of Lewiston to allow justice to run its course, Beachy, with the help of the soldiers, diffused the crowd.

The capture of the prisoners brought relief to Beachy and Sheriff Fisk but also created problems: Lewiston had no jail. After conferring with his deputies, Fisk determined the safest place to house the prisoners would be the Luna House. Beachy would continue to be in charge of the prisoners.

On December 4, the four appeared before Nez Perce county probate judge John Berry. By this time, their identities had been established—James Romain, David Renton, Christopher Lower, and William Page. Berry read the complaint charging them with murder and ordered them held until their case could be heard in a court of law.

The court of law was a problem. When Idaho Territory was created in the spring of 1863, no rules of law were established. It would be up to the first territorial legislature to create these rules. On January 4, 1864, the first legislative assembly of Idaho Territory adopted the common law of England. The district court now had the authority to hear murder charges.

While the territorial legislature haggled over the laws of the land, Beachy and Fisk realized they did not have the evidence to convict their prisoners. Since snows had closed the Nez Perce Trail, no search had been made for a crime scene or Magruder's body. All their evidence was circumstantial. Their only hope was to get a confession.

Of the four men, only Page had no criminal record. Older and uneducated, he also was not like his companions. So Fisk began to work on Page. He separated him from the others and offered him his freedom on the condition that he tell what happened to Magruder.

At first, Page resisted. Lower and Renton had threatened him on many occasions, and he was afraid if he talked he would end up like Magruder. But Fisk was persistent and eventually Page told the story. On January 11, 1864, Page became the state's witness before a grand jury, and Romain, Renton, and Lower were indicted for the murder of Magruder, Allen, and Phillips. As for the Chalmers brothers, they were simply listed in the indictment as "two others" because Page could not remember their names.

The first criminal court case in Idaho Territory would be heard by Judge Samuel Parks, associate justice of the territorial supreme court. On the first day of the trial, defense lawyers William Thayer and J. W. Anderson filed a motion to overturn the indictment. They argued that the clerk of Nez Perce County had filed the original charge, but Nez Perce County had been established by Washington Territory. Since Nez Perce County was no longer a part of Washington, and Idaho Territory had yet to organize, no authority existed to bring charges. While their argument had literal merit, Judge Parks denied their motion. The trial would go on.

The case would hinge on Page. Prosecuting attorney Enos Grey led Page carefully through his testimony, and whenever he could, produced additional witnesses who could support Page's story. Louis Holt, who had been with Magruder on the trip to Virginia City, identified Romain, Renton and Lower as the men who left with Magruder on the return trip to Lewiston. Holt also claimed the mules left with Goodrich belonged to Magruder. Another witness, Charles Frush, had retrieved packsaddles and ropes abandoned by the murderers at Cottonwood Creek. Page had directed him to the spot. Grey used this testimony to show that Page's account of the murders was accurate.

Defense attorneys attacked Page at every turn, questioning his motives, his memory, his integrity. But Page stuck to his story. While he admitted he should have done something to stop the murders, he claimed he was too afraid. Lower and Renton constantly threatened him to go along with the plan and keep his mouth shut. Fearing he would end up like Magruder, Page chose to do just that.

On January 23, the jury rendered its verdict. They found all three guilty of murder and recommended the punishment of death.

The defense immediately asked the court to arrest the judgment. They again argued that the court had no jurisdiction because of territorial issues. They also claimed trial testimony did not prove anyone had been killed, and in the case of the Chalmers brothers, there was no proof of their existence. Judge Parks, however, refused the request and on January 26, sentenced the men to death. He set their execution for March 4. They would file no appeal.

The prisoners remained jailed at the Luna House. On several occasions they stated they were ready to confess, but they were never serious. Lower, especially, taunted reporters with his behavior. All three claimed their innocence, calling Page the mastermind of the robbery and subsequent murders. Only Romain was willing to admit he was present at the massacre, but he denied any part in the killings.

On the day of the executions, Sheriff Fisk took the prisoners by wagon to the waiting gallows, which had been constructed at the foot of Poe Grade on the outskirts of Lewiston. He was accompanied by federal troops from Fort Lapwai who were charged with controlling the crowd, which Fisk estimated at several thousand and included Magruder's five-year-old son, James. As they approached the scaffold, the condemned men saw three chairs, one beneath each noose. Once on the platform, they took their seats, bowed their heads, and listened while a minister prayed for their souls.

For the most part, they were unrepentant. Following the prayer, Renton rose and reached for the noose that would soon be around his neck, claiming that it would "strangle an innocent man." Lower claimed he knew the guilty parties, but was unable to reveal their names. Instead he apologized to Renton and Romain, claiming to the crowd they were innocent. In a quiet voice he turned to Romain and said, "Forgive me, Jimmy."

Romain struggled to gain his composure, crying much of the time. Finally he found his voice and spoke directly to Beachy, who was in the crowd. "You know that I am innocent," he said. "What I have told you, Beachy, is true. I die an innocent man."

At 12:28 p.m., Sheriff Fisk released the trap door and the condemned men dropped to their deaths. Their bodies remained suspended for thirty minutes before they were cut down and placed in individual coffins. They were buried in a common grave near the gallows.

In May, after the snow had left the Nez Perce Trail, Page led a group of men, including Beachy, to the massacre site. There they discovered the bodies of Allen, Phillips, and the Chalmers brothers at the bottom of an incline, just as Page had described at the trial. They found the gunnysack of cooking utensils Page had hidden behind a log. In the meadow above the campsite they found Magruder, his body beside the remnants of an old campfire. Beachy's gun, the one he gave to Magruder before the ill-fated trip, lay nearby.

Before he left the site, Beachy removed Magruder's skull. He delivered it to Magruder's widow Caroline, who kept it the rest of her life. When she died in 1900, the skull was buried with her. Beachy also managed to recover some of Magruder's stolen gold, reported to be as much as $12,000, which he gave to Caroline. For all of his efforts to catch the killers, the territorial legislature gave Beachy $6,240.

Page remained in Lewiston where Beachy helped him find a job. Although some questioned his truthfulness at the trial, most believed he was not a murderer, just a simple man who got caught up in a tragic, brutal crime. Still, they could not forgive him for failing to stop the massacre, and no one seemed concerned when he, too, met a violent death. On December 25, 1866, Page stopped to visit his favorite prostitute, Eliza Wilson. Instead, he found Wilson engaged with Albert Igo. Page went into a jealous rage and went after Igo, who grabbed a shotgun and fired, killing Page instantly. Although a coroner's jury concluded that Igo should be charged with murder, no trial was ever held. Most saw it as a fitting end to Page.

3. For Honor

ALEX WOODS

POCATELLO, MAY 5, 1887
BLACKFOOT, AUGUST 17, 1888

Alex Woods, a barber at the Pacific Hotel in Pocatello, had a strange habit. At least once a day he would leave his shop, climb the stairs to the second floor of the hotel, and gaze out the hallway window that faced west. From there he could see the street where he lived, and the front door to his house. Most importantly, he could see the comings and goings of his wife Sarah. Woods had reason to worry about Sarah's faithfulness. She had raised her skirt for other men in the past, and Woods vowed she would not do it again. On May 5, 1887, he made good on his promise. In a jealous frenzy, he beat and then shot his wife to death.

Woods was a mulatto, born a slave in Springfield, Missouri in 1858. As a young boy, he was quickly caught up in the turmoil of the Civil War. Missouri was especially volatile, and as soon as the war began and their freedom secured, Woods and his family fled to Lawrence, Kansas. Here in 1863 they would witness the Lawrence Massacre, the slaughter of over 150 citizens by a Confederate gang led by William Quantrill.

When the war ended, his family moved east, settling in Indianapolis. In his late teens, he struck out on his own, moving to Auburn, Illinois where he met his wife Sarah, a young mulatto divorcee. The two remained in Auburn for two years, until Woods became concerned about Sarah's faithfulness. Thinking a change would do their marriage good, he packed their belongings and moved back to Kansas. He worked in a saloon for a short time, then traveled to Texas where he worked on a cattle drive. At some point he learned the barber trade. After brief stops in Colorado Springs and Ogden, Utah, they settled in Pocatello in 1874 where Woods set up a successful shop in the Pacific Hotel, part of the Union Pacific train station.

The moves did not help the relationship. Both of them demanded much of each other. Woods wanted his meals served on time and Sarah home whenever he was. Sarah enjoyed going out and spent much of her time visiting with neighbors. If Woods refused to go with her, she went by herself. To earn extra cash she worked in a laundry, but Woods thought she

1906 postcard of the Pacific Hotel

flirted too much with the customers and made her quit. To spite him, she continued to take in laundry, specifically for single men.

Sarah was overly concerned with money. Although Woods was a good provider, Sarah was never happy. She wanted to know where Woods spent every penny. Eventually, she demanded to be in charge of the family finances, and Woods relented. He later regretted this, as Sarah was so tight that he sometimes had to borrow money from friends for a drink. Around town, people knew that Sarah held the money in the family. She kept a large sum of it in a leather pouch around her neck.

In the fall of 1886, Woods hired Emmanuel Ramirez to take care of his horses and perform chores around the house. Ramirez boarded with the couple and he and Sarah became friendly, a little too friendly for Woods, who fired Ramirez.

In December 1886, Sarah took the train to visit relatives in Payette. From there she continued on to Portland. When she hadn't returned home by January 7, Woods decided to go and get her. He told his friend Albert Fisher that if she refused to return home with him, he would kill her. "If I can't have her," Woods told Fisher, "no other man shall have her." Apparently Woods was convincing. On January 11, he sent Fisher a telegram that simply said "Ok." Two days later, Woods and Sarah were back in Pocatello.

The quarrels continued, as did Woods' suspicions. When Sarah was not at home, he would look for her, checking with all the neighbors. One evening in mid-April, Woods tracked her to the home of Mr. and Mrs.

145

Gus Atchison. He confronted Sarah, wanting to know why she could not stay home, why his supper was not ready. Fearing violence, the Atchisons escorted them home. On the way walking along the railroad tracks, Alex picked up a large hitch pin. He told Gus Atchison, "she makes me so damn mad, I have a good notion to kill her."

At the beginning of May, Woods became convinced Sarah was involved with a handsome Spanish cowboy named Carmen Asevedo, a friend of Ramirez. The two saw each other often, as Asevedo kept horses at a stable near the Woods' home, and Sarah did his laundry. On the afternoon of May 4, Asevedo went to the Woods' home to pick up his laundry. It was not done, and Sarah told him to return the next day. What happened over the course of the next day is disputed, but when the day was done, Sarah was dead.

On Thursday morning, May 5, Sarah and Alex were both in town at the Keeney House and Saloon. Asevedo, who roomed at the hotel, was also there. According to Woods, he overheard Sarah tell the cowboy, "I will meet you where I met you before." While Asevedo would later testify that he saw Sarah that morning, he denied ever hearing the directions.

Woods fumed, then acted. First, he went to the local druggist where he requested ten cents of strychnine. The druggist, A. W. Cook, would recall that Woods was "quite excited and in a hurry." He refused to sell him the poison. Woods would later claim that he wanted the strychnine so he could kill himself.

After being turned down at the drug store, Woods went to visit Neils Neilson, the constable of Pocatello. Neilson had borrowed Woods' gun, a short .41 Colt. Woods asked for the gun, telling the constable he would need it for a week or so. Neilson gave him the gun.

Then Woods went to work at his barbershop. He was in and out of the shop all day. Sometimes he would be on the second floor looking out the window. At one point, he went to the Keeney House to have a drink. According to Charles Napper, the bartender, Woods drank whisky that afternoon and evening, which was out of character. He usually drank beer.

In the late afternoon, Woods went home and confronted Sarah. Bessie Croshaw, Woods' hired girl, saw the two of them in conversation in their bedroom. She then saw Woods leave and walk towards his barbershop. He would be seen in and around the hotel until about 8 p.m. Most noticed he was constantly watching his house.

Sarah left the house just before dark, walking to the home of Bertha Sells, a quarter mile away. Sarah, who usually visited for an hour, told Bertha she couldn't stay. Bertha would testify that Sarah acted strange—both excited and nervous—and that she kept looking out the window toward the river. After a few minutes she left, telling Bertha she was going for a walk.

Woods, who had been watching her all day, followed her. He found her just 400 yards west of their home on the east bank of the Portneuf River. There he killed her.

Then he went to his home, gathered some clothes, and returned to his barbershop where he collected his tools and took all of the money out of the safe. He left town, traveling south by horseback. Near Inkom, he met an Indian who guided him over the mountains to McCammon. From there another Indian took him to Odgen. His plan was to continue south.

Woods and Sarah's disappearance did not cause immediate alarm. Bessie informed authorities that she had last seen Sarah on Thursday night walking toward the river. Another man claimed he had seen the two together at the river. After a search of the riverbank turned up a woman's slipper but nothing else, the sheriff suspected foul play. He offered a $500 reward for the capture of Woods and set out to find Sarah's body. As the sheriff and his crew dragged the river, local citizens conducted a thorough search of the bushes lining the riverbank. On Tuesday, May 10, they discovered her body. On the same day, Woods was captured in Corrine, Utah.

Sheriff Taylor left the body in the hands of Bingham County Coroner George Davis, who examined the already decomposing body in a hasty inquest. He concluded that Sarah died from a fractured skull, the front of her head bashed in with a blunt object. He then ordered the body buried in the local cemetery.

While Davis was determining a murder had been committed, Sheriff Taylor traveled by passenger train to Corrine to pick up his prisoner. On his return he received a telegram telling him that over 200 men were waiting on the train platform at the Pocatello station, ready to take justice into their own hands. The sheriff contacted the railroad and arranged for a freight train to pull out of the Pocatello station at the same time he and his prisoner were pulling in. The sheriff managed to get Woods on to the caboose of the freight train, and as the lynch mob waited, the sheriff and Woods traveled the rails to Blackfoot where Woods was incarcerated in the Bingham County Jail.

As Bingham County Prosecutor H.M. Bennett gathered evidence against Woods, stories circulated about the coroner's less than thorough examination of Sarah's body. Bennett also spoke to witnesses who had heard a single gunshot near the river that night. Not wanting any surprises, Bennett demanded another autopsy. Davis enlisted the aid of an enthusiastic young doctor, J. C. Blickensderfer, who had been practicing medicine for only one month. Together they exhumed Sarah's body. Blickensderfer wanted to examine the body to see if Sarah was pregnant, but Davis stopped him. Instead, they removed her head and returned to Pocatello. After closer scrutiny of her skull, they determined Sarah had been shot in the right temple, the bullet lodging in the skull behind her left ear. They turned the bullet over to Prosecutor Bennett. Bennett had enough evidence to get an indictment from the grand jury so on May 19, Woods was arraigned before Judge J. B. Hays in the Third District Court of Bingham County where he pleaded not guilty on two charges: assault and murder.

On May 25, Woods was back in court for the start of his trial. His lawyer, H. W. Smith asked for a continuance, but Judge Hays denied the request. By the end of the day, the jury was in place.

Bennett had a solid case. He had the threats Woods had made against Sarah, his mysterious behavior on the day of the murder, and his flight from Pocatello. Bennett had testimony about Woods' gun and expert witnesses who claimed the bullet found in Sarah's skull came from a short .41 Colt. He also had testimony from Carmen Asevedo who denied any relationship with Sarah.

Smith, who teamed with former territorial Supreme Court Justice John T. Morgan to defend Woods, went after Asevedo. Under cross-examination, he caught the Spaniard in a lie. On the day of the murder, Sarah sent him a note. Asevedo at first denied receiving it, but eventually admitted that early in the evening he had been given the note and then destroyed it. When Smith asked him what it said, the prosecution objected and the objection was upheld. Asevedo did not have to reveal its content. The defense also brought out that Asevedo owned a short .44 Colt. Expert witnesses for the defense believed the bullet could have come from either a .44 or .41 caliber gun.

For his part, Woods took the stand and denied killing his wife. On the night of the murder, he claimed he saw Asevedo walking toward the river. When he went home and found that Sarah was not home, he headed toward the river and stumbled upon the couple "lying down together."

Woods said he felt so disgraced he had no other option than to leave town and start over. His wife would embarrass him no more.

In his closing argument, Smith told the jury there was no direct evidence to prove Woods killed his wife, and even if he did, any murder committed out of passion or jealousy should be considered manslaughter. Sarah had given him ample reason to be jealous, and if Woods did find her with Asevedo, the murder was not excusable, but at least understandable. But the jury didn't buy any of the argument, and after two days of testimony, it had little trouble finding Woods guilty of first-degree murder. A week later, Judge Hays declared Woods should hang, setting the execution for July 22, 1887.

Woods' lawyers planned an appeal, but Woods apparently had little faith in the justice system. On June 22, he made a mad dash for freedom, along with every prisoner in the Bingham County Jail,

The escape was orchestrated by Lum Nickerson, who was serving time for horse rustling. Nickerson's wife and children visited him every Sunday, and on the day of the escape, she brought him a revolver, wrapped in his baby's blanket. As they sat in the jailor's office, a guard nearby, Nickerson held the baby on his lap and gripped the gun. When the guard turned to spit a wad of tobacco juice into a spittoon, Nickerson pulled the gun and aimed it squarely at the guard's head. He then locked the guard in a cell and proceeded to release all the other prisoners, including Woods and Frank Williams, also sentenced to hang on July 22.

As the day wore on, the prisoners remained in the jail, locking up anyone who happened by. No one seemed to notice. Then at 7 p.m. they made their break. Four of the prisoners, including Williams, went north. Woods and one other man went east, toward the Blackfoot River. They were seen by Rev. T. M. Stewart who recognized Woods and sounded the alarm. Woods was captured within the hour. The others remained at large until morning when they were caught trying to cross the Snake River. All were returned to the Blackfoot jail and preparations for the hanging of Woods and Williams began.

On July 11, defense attorneys Smith and Morgan notified the district court of their plan to appeal Woods' sentence. This action postponed the execution. The supreme court then set January 3, 1888 for the hearing. Woods would have six months in jail before learning his fate.

Woods' case before the supreme court was over before it started. For whatever reason, his attorneys filed no briefs in the case. They did not appear before the court. Attorney Richard Johnson represented the territory, but he really had nothing to say. The justices looked over the trial transcript, saw no errors in the indictment or the trial, and affirmed the judgment. Woods would hang. He appeared before District Court Judge Broderick who reset his execution for July 21, 1888. Williams, who also had his appeal denied, was sentenced to hang the same day.

Woods was a model prisoner. He was gentle, appreciative of the guards, giving them no trouble. But he also knew he was going to hang, so on July 8, 1888, when Williams unlocked his cell in another daring escape attempt, Woods used the opportunity to get away. He dressed himself in Indian leggings and wrapped himself in a red blanket. While officials were frantically searching for the armed Williams, Woods quietly made his way out of the jail to freedom. His disguise was so good, no one even saw him leave.

Williams was captured in ten hours, but Woods seemingly vanished. As the day of his execution approached and he remained at large, Sheriff Taylor contacted Governor Edward Stevenson and requested that Woods' execution be rescheduled for August 17. The governor granted the stay. The authorities did not want to have to wait until the next term of court to re-sentence Woods; the execution had been delayed long enough.

He remained at large for two weeks. While reports put him in Utah and Colorado, he was really in Montana. Disguised as an Indian, he had taken a passenger train to Butte and then walked to Bozeman. There he was captured and escorted back to Blackfoot to await his execution.

His supporters mounted a frantic effort to save his life. They wrote letters to Governor Stevenson, asking for clemency and a life sentence. Even Prosecutor Bennett asked the governor to spare Woods' life. But the governor refused to intervene.

In his final days, Woods finally confessed to the murder of his wife. He apologized for lying to the court, claiming he did so under the direction of his lawyers. He had no recollection of the murder, only that he was "wild with rage." He insisted that he loved his wife and was devoted to her but was unable to control his jealousy. If his wife actually was with Carmen Asevedo that night, he never said.

On the day of his execution, Woods awoke early and asked for a drink of whisky. He remained in his cell, and those attending him were impressed with his calm. At 2 p.m. he was escorted to the gallows, where he mounted the steps without assistance. In his final words, he told the crowd he had no hard feelings towards anyone. "I forgive everybody," he said. "I hope to meet them in heaven."

With that, the trap was sprung and Woods fell to his death.

Woods' greatest ambition had been to be a successful, respected businessman. To his regret, his crime cost him not only his life but also his good name. His business, however, lived on. A barber from Blackfoot by the name of Murray took over Woods' barbershop at the Pacific Hotel. By all reports, the shop operated well into the 1900s.

GEORGE PIERSON

VIENNA, AUGUST 25, 1882
HAILEY, AUGUST 1, 1884

The tale of George Pierson reads more like fiction than fact. Filled with colorful, ill-fated characters, it easily could have sprung from the imaginations of writers like Mark Twain or Bret Hart. But Pierson was real, and his story, both humorous and tragic, played out in the rugged hills southwest of Sawtooth City in the early 1880s.

Pierson (also spelled Pearson) was born in Switzerland in 1840. He arrived in the mining town of Atlanta, Idaho in 1864 and stayed for six years before moving to Carson City and then Elko, Nevada. In 1879, he met Banjo Nell. From that time, he would be inexplicably tied to her.

What little we know of Banjo Nell comes from Pierson. She used the name Nellie Woodruff while in Elko and sometime during her time there married a man named Dinsmore. However, no public record supports that marriage. Nell would claim that Dinsmore died in 1879 leaving her destitute. To survive, she hired on as one of John T. Hall's girls.

Hall, also known as Johnny Behind the Rocks, was a colorful, if somewhat unscrupulous character. Always one step ahead of the law, he earned his nickname while in Nevada, where he escaped one of his enemies by hiding behind some rocks and shooting him when he passed by. To escape the consequences, he took Nell and fled to Oregon, then to Idaho, taking up residence in the various mining camps around Atlanta and Sawtooth City. The miners there were willing to pay for the services he provided—drugs, booze, and Banjo Nell.

When Pierson returned to Atlanta in early 1880, he became acquainted with Hall who proposed the two become partners in a saloon, where they could offer the miners spirits, gambling, and Nell. Pierson considered it, even going so far as procuring a building and fixing it into a workable gathering place. But when the time came to stock its shelves, Hall was unable to come up with his share. Instead, he encouraged Pierson to buy cigars and whiskey on credit, telling him the profit would easily cover the debt. But Pierson refused; he was not willing to go into debt on the scheme. He told Hall he could have the saloon to himself. However, due to Hall's reputation in Atlanta, he was unable to get credit, and the plan fell

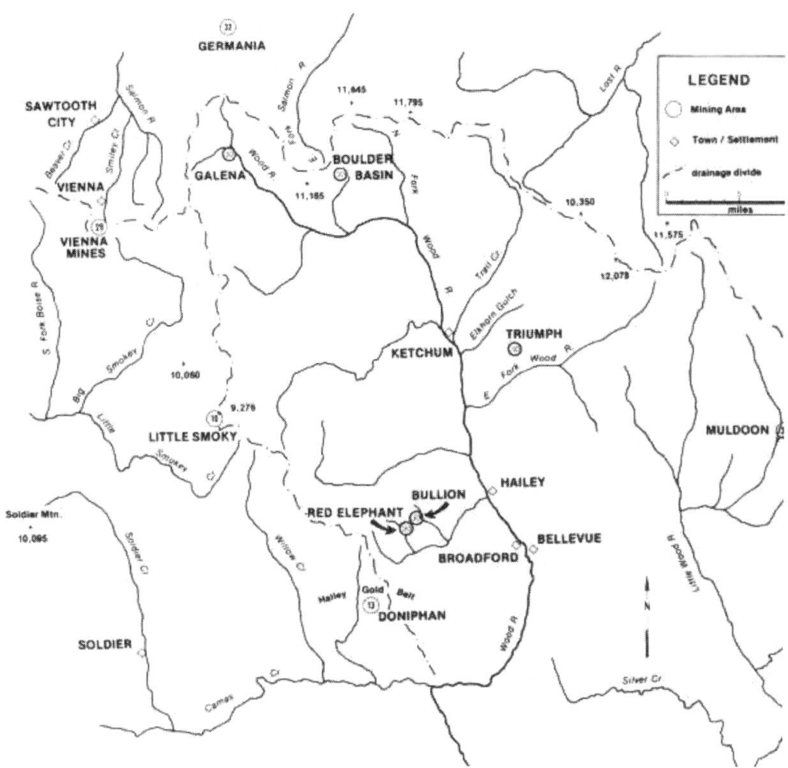

through. Hall blamed Pierson and swore one day he would get even. He left Atlanta, taking Nell with him.

Hall moved to Sawtooth City and built a cabin. The general consensus was that Nell, under the direction of Hall, ran a house of prostitution. Pierson, who knew Nell was with Hall, denied knowing her business and claimed he never visited her home. But on November 19, 1881, he and Nell happened to meet on the street in front of her cabin. Together they walked to a tavern owned by Billy Stevens, where eight or ten other men joined them. What came next was a practical joke of the grandest scale.

Pierson was a hard worker, and on this particular night, his pockets jingled with money. The other men in the tavern knew it, and soon Pierson was buying everyone drinks. According to T. S. Foulks, the bartender that night, his patrons were determined to spend all of Pierson's money. Although Pierson would claim, "seldom do you see me drunk," this night must have been an exception. By the time the night was over, everyone was drunk, Pierson was broke, and he and Banjo Nell were husband and wife.

Everyone in the bar was in on the ruse. They told Pierson that Nell would be a fine catch, and he should marry her on the spot. Someone produced a marriage license, and Thomas Mullaly, who claimed he was a justice of the peace from Lemhi County, offered to perform the ceremony. Foulks would commend Mullaly for his work, stating he performed the ceremony "just like they talk it in books." Pierson paid him seven dollars for his trouble, and everyone involved had a great time.

The next day Pierson and Nell traveled to Galena. When they returned to Sawtooth City, Pierson began to have doubts about the legitimacy of the marriage. He gave Bob Gordon, a former justice of the peace of Sawtooth City, the details, and Gordon advised him that the union probably would not "amount to much." Pierson then sent two of his friends to question George McCallister, who at the time was justice of the peace of Sawtooth City. Pierson wanted the judge's opinion on the status of the marriage. The friends returned and told Pierson the ceremony was official. He was legally wed to Banjo Nell.

But he wasn't. Mullaly was really a carpenter from Rocky Bar, who later bragged he had married Pierson and Nell. And Pierson's two friends who were supposed to talk to Judge McCallister never did; they just continued the joke.

Although Pierson would later tell people he believed he was married, he and Nell went their separate ways within one week of the ceremony. He returned to Atlanta to work in the mines, and Nell went back to work for Hall. They would not see each other again until the spring of 1882. Pierson would eventually settle in Vienna, another mining town in the area, and Nell would end up in trouble.

Sawtooth City was a small community; only three women lived there in the winter of 1881, and one of them was Nell. The other two were respectable ladies, married to merchants in the town. They found Nell so "disgusting" and her behavior so immoral, they threatened to leave if McCallister didn't do something. When they lodged an official complaint against her, McCallister issued a warrant for her arrest, charging her with disturbing the peace. He filed the same charge against Hall. Nell was arrested and taken to Rocky Bar where she was jailed. For his part, Hall skipped town before he could be caught.

Hall visited Nell in jail, and according to Winfield Tatro, the mail carrier for the mining areas, the sheriff turned a blind eye to the activities that took place there. Eventually, Nell was released and went to live in a cabin near Rocky Bar. Hall let it be known that Nell was "ill" and asked the men of the community to drop in on her from time to time and keep her supplied with "medicine." They were more than happy to oblige.

What caused this arrangement to come to a disagreeable end is unknown, but in the spring of 1882, Nell showed up at Pierson's door in Vienna. She was through with Hall. According to Pierson, she asked if she could be his wife. He agreed, but only if she promised to conduct herself properly and take care of his place and him. A deal was struck, and she moved in. Whenever Pierson came down from the mines, he stayed with her.

Whether this was just a cover-up for a business venture between Nell and Pierson is not known. Nell certainly had a reputation in the area for being a prostitute, but no one ever accused Pierson of being involved. William Reinhart, who lived near Pierson's cabin in Vienna, believed she ran a house of "ill-fame," and described Nell as "profane," trolling the taverns looking for business whenever Pierson was gone. Deputy Sheriff Anthony Ethier also suspected Nell may have been a "woman of pleasure," but he never saw anyone in Vienna frequent Pierson and Nell's cabin, except Hall, who showed up in late June and immediately began causing trouble.

Nell had been Hall's meal ticket, perhaps even his lover, and he was unable to let her go without a fight. On June 26, he arrived at Pierson's cabin. Pierson was gone, but Nell was there. She refused to let him in, so he kicked in the door and proceeded to ransack the cabin. He beat up Nell and then left. Pierson returned home the next day, surveyed the situation, and tracked down Hall. Pierson claimed that Hall apologized, blamed the outburst on opium and whiskey, and promised to never do it again.

He was good to his word until August 15. That evening, Hall walked into Pierson's cabin like he owned it, put his feet up on the stove, and pulled a pistol for good measure. Pointing the gun at Nell, he told her, "I have put the grand fuck in you once and I am going to do it again, you God-damned whore." Pierson told Nell to run and get the sheriff, and a fight ensued between Pierson and Hall. By the time Sheriff Ethier arrived, the fight was over. Ethier instructed Hall to stay away from Nell and then left. Hall left too, but not before threatening Pierson that he would return to "burn him up" before he left town.

Pierson left for the mines. When he returned on August 18, he once again found his door kicked in and Nell in bed with bruises on her face and torso. Pierson contacted Ethier, and this time the sheriff threatened Hall

Main Street, Vienna

with jail if he did not leave Nell alone. Hall kept his distance for the next several days, but on August 22, he told Pierson the quarrel was not over. He was going to Sawtooth and when he returned, the two of them could have it out.

He returned on August 25, and this time used his gun. He entered Pierson's cabin, kicked over the stove, fired two shots through the ceiling, and then beat Nell, leaving her lying on the floor. Pierson arrived soon after, as did Cliff Baldwin, a saloon owner in Vienna. Pierson helped an intoxicated and injured Nell into bed while Baldwin went to find the doctor. Pierson then went out to get the sheriff. The sheriff told Pierson to go home and stay put. He would be there shortly.

On the return trip to his cabin, Pierson ran into Hall, who would be described by others as "staggering drunk." According to Pierson, Hall confronted him, but Pierson passed without a response. When he reached his cabin, Dr. J. B. Patterson was there attending Nell. The doctor was concerned about who would pay his fee, and Pierson assured him that he "would pay for anything to help Banjo Nell." However, Patterson, who had only been in Vienna for two weeks, would not be compensated for what was about to happen, as he became the key witness to a murder.

According to Patterson, while he was working on Nell, someone approached the cabin. At the same time, he heard someone say, "You son of a bitch, I will fix you." He was not certain who made the statement, only that

156

it came from inside the cabin. Fearing he was in danger, Patterson left Nell and moved toward the door. He saw an unarmed Hall within a few feet of the cabin. At that point, Pierson picked up a revolver, aimed it at Hall, and shot. He missed and Hall turned tail and ran with Pierson in pursuit. The two men ran about twenty-five feet when Pierson fired a second time. Hall then darted behind a straw-covered cabin. Patterson heard one more shot, and Hall came reeling around the corner, a "shocked, bewildered" look on his face. He fell to the ground, mortally wounded; a bullet had entered his lower back and exited in the front at his hip. It severed his femoral artery, and he died in less than ten minutes.

Another witness to the shooting, William Paul, saw Hall reach for his back after the second shot. Following the third shot, he raced to Hall's side. Hall told him, "I am pretty badly hurt," to which he replied, "Johnny, I think you are gone." Then he went to Pierson who was standing in front of his cabin. He arrested him, took his gun, and waited for Ethier to arrive.

Ethier took Pierson into custody and organized an inquest. During the examination of Hall's body, Ethier removed a pistol from Hall's pants pocket. Two shots had been fired from the gun. This gun, Pierson's gun, and Pierson were taken to Sawtooth City and turned over to Hyrum Hunter, another deputy sheriff. There he had a preliminary hearing. The court found enough evidence to hold Pierson, and he was transferred to Hailey to await the findings of a grand jury.

On October 5, the grand jury indicted Pierson on first-degree murder charges, and he was arraigned the next day before Judge H. E. Prickett. Pierson pleaded not guilty and the judge set his trial date for October 20. Jury selection took three days and on October 23, District Attorney James H. Hawley and his assistant John Huston began presenting their case.

Huston gave the opening statement, which was more of an attack on Banjo Nell than Pierson. Calling Nell "one of those unfortunate specimens of feminine frailty," who had "marital monomania," he accused her of having a "matrimonial alliance with every man she laid up with," including Hall and Pierson. As for Hall, he was a "very inoffensive man," who like others, "when under the influence of liquor, would not behave with all the propriety he ought to." Huston claimed the prosecution would show that Hall's threats against Pierson were always made while he was in such a state of intoxication that everybody knew his threats "did not amount to anything." As such, Pierson was in no danger when Hall threatened him;

in fact, Hall was running away when Pierson shot him. It was a clear case of first-degree murder.

Huston also laid some of the blame on officials who allowed women like Nell to operate in the county. He argued the killing of Hall was "one of the unfortunate results which arise out of the bad state of society and the lax administration of the criminal law."

Judge Henry Prickett

Sixteen people were called to testify. Although each took an oath to tell the truth, many were less than forthcoming, especially about Banjo Nell. No matter how hard Hawley and Huston pressed, not one man admitted using Nell's services, although several acknowledged they did bring her medicine at Hall's request. Some denied knowing her occupation, stating that when Nell asked them to "spend a piece with her," they had no idea what she meant. Even officers of the court would not confirm Nell's occupation. Deputy Ethier could not state for a fact that Nell ran a house of prostitution, and officials from Sawtooth City testified they had heard rumors of Nell's prostitution, but they had never seen anything to support those accusations.

The prosecution had better luck in presenting its murder case against Pierson. Both Patterson and Paul testified they clearly saw Pierson fire three shots at Hall, and that one of those shots hit its mark. They also made it clear that Hall was running away when the fatal shot was fired.

For his defense, Pierson's attorneys George Ammond and Alanson Smith argued that Pierson was protecting his wife; thus the shooting of Hall was justified. But before they could do that, Judge Prickett ordered they must first prove that Pierson and Banjo Nell were married. When Pierson took the stand to explain how Judge Mullaly, a justice of the peace, had married them in Sawtooth, Prosecutor Huston could not resist poking fun. "I deny, sir, that he ever was a justice of the peace," Huston said, "but he may have been a judge of whiskey."

But Pierson stuck to his story, and several defense witnesses testified that Pierson truly believed he was married. Even Nell took the stand, and although her credibility was not the best, she swore she and Pierson had been living together as husband and wife. She also claimed that in the month before the shooting, Hall had been to their house four times, each time breaking in the door and beating her.

Besides maintaining he killed Hall to protect his wife, Pierson also claimed he had to shoot to protect himself. According to Pierson, Hall fired the first shot. As evidence, his attorneys presented the coat Pierson was wearing that day, a bullet hole through its side.

The pistol Ethier found in Hall's pocket with two spent shells further supported Pierson's story. Defense attorneys also presented five witnesses who heard Hall threaten to kill Pierson in the days preceding the shooting. One claimed that Hall planned to "kick the ribs out of that damned old whore and shoot the shit" out of Pierson.

Governor William Bunn refused to commute Pierson's sentence.

Yet for all of Pierson's justifiable reasons for shooting Hall, one clear fact remained. Pierson shot Hall in the back while he was running away. The jury could not overlook this and in the end found Pierson guilty of first-degree murder.

Judge Prickett scheduled the sentencing for October 31, but Pierson's lawyers asked for a postponement. They were back in court on November 4 to ask for a new trial but were denied. Instead Prickett unleashed the full fury of the law on Pierson.

"The facts showed by reason of a long course of immorality and vice in which you have indulged, your moral sense has become blunted," Prickett told Pierson. "Your presence here now under these circumstances is clearly attributable to the debasing character of your associations and your reprehensible course of life." Prickett went on to advise Pierson "to seek diligently and earnestly for that pardon which comes alone from God." Then he sentenced Pierson to death, setting December 29, 1882, as the date of execution.

Pierson's lawyers were quick to respond. On December 11 they filed an appeal of both the judgment and sentence with the Idaho Territory

Supreme Court. Prickett issued a stay of execution, and Pierson was left in jail to await his fate. While frontier justice was usually swift, in this case, he would wait over a year before the court heard his appeal.

As for Banjo Nell, no one wanted anything to do with her. For several weeks she lived on the streets in Hailey, stealing whatever she needed to survive. By the end of December, the merchants decided the best way to deal with Nell was to get rid of her. They took up a collection and raised forty-one dollars, enough to put her on the stage and send her to Salt Lake. She was never seen in the area again.

Pierson was housed in the Alturas County Jail. Designed to hold ten prisoners, the jail was a poorly built, wooden structure with no metal reinforcement. As the county's mining boom attracted many unscrupulous characters, the jail filled beyond capacity; by the end of June 1883, twenty-four prisoners crowded into its cells. For Pierson it was the perfect time to escape. He managed to remove a board from the wall of his cell and made his way to the front door. His plan was thwarted when Deputy John Campbell discovered him. Campbell put Pierson in leg irons and returned him to his cell.

Pierson was undeterred and on August 16 tried again. Using a hunting knife he secured from an unknown visitor, he cut through one of the boards of his cell, pried it loose, and slipped out. He then climbed through a window, escaping unseen and unheard.

The next day Sheriff Furey distributed handbills offering a $300 reward for the capture of Pierson, either dead or alive. Then he and his deputies began searching all the mining towns in the area—Galena, Sawtooth City, Vienna, Atlanta—but their efforts were thwarted by Pierson's friends and their own incompetence. At the mines they were given misinformation, sending the deputies in the wrong direction. Near Galena, Furey passed Pierson on the trail, but did not recognize him. For two days in Vienna, they staked out a cache left for him by a friend. While they waited, Pierson left the area. Because of all the missteps, the sheriff and his deputies became fodder for the *Wood River Times*, the local newspaper, which poked fun at their inability to catch Pierson.

For three weeks, Pierson eluded capture. He made his way through the rugged mountains west of Hailey and was on his way to Payette when the sheriff from Idaho City discovered him. Pierson told his captors he was "fagged-out and foot-sore," having walked over 300 miles in his bid for freedom. They took Pierson back to Hailey where he was locked in a cell with reinforced iron plating. Sheriff Furey paid the reward plus an extra $400 to cover additional expenses, and the county commissioners approved the construction of a new courthouse with a secure jail. It would eventually become Pierson's new home.

Pierson waited five more months before his case made it to the supreme court. He once again faced Judge Prickett, who as a district court judge also sat on the supreme court as an associate justice. Prickett heard the appeal along with Justices John T. Morgan and Norman Buck.

In the appeal, Pierson's lawyers argued that Judge Prickett had erred in the original trial by allowing testimony concerning Nell's reputation. They also felt Prickett's instructions to the jury did not allow room for justifiable homicide, and his refusal to allow testimony by Pierson concerning his conversations with Sheriff Ethier interfered with his defense. But after hearing the arguments, Prickett and Morgan believed Pierson had a fair trial and voted to uphold the judgment. Buck, however, dissented, claiming testimony relating to Pierson's state of mind before the shooting should have been admitted.

With the court's decision, Pierson was re-sentenced. On June 25, 1884, he appeared before Judge Case Broderick who scheduled his execution for August 1.

Pierson's friends rallied to his side. A petition with 149 names was sent to Governor William Bunn requesting he commute Pierson's sentence to life in prison. Calling Johnny Hall a "worthless character living off the earnings of a low prostitute," they asked that Pierson be spared because he was a hard-working, industrious miner who had received poor counsel at his trial. Names on the petition included John Gorman, the sheriff of Boise County who had arrested Pierson after his escape, and Judge M. B. Moore also of Boise County who believed Pierson should have been acquitted. Two Alturas County officials, Presley Bruner, who replaced Hawley as district attorney, and Probate Judge George M. Parsons, who would later become Idaho's Attorney General, also sent a letter to the governor asking for a commutation of the sentence.

Even Judge Prickett had a change of heart. In a letter to Governor Bunn, Prickett wrote, "If upon consideration of the evidence you find a commutation justified, I shall have no fault to find, or complaint to make of such action."

But Bunn was unmoved. Stating he was unable to find "sufficient reasons to warrant executive interference," he hoped Pierson would find "mercy in heaven." He went on to say that if the territory desired empty jails and unused scaffolds, it would come from "the behavior of the people and not by the pardoning power" given to the governor and his office.

With the governor's decision, Sheriff Furey prepared for the hanging. He found an isolated spot northeast of Hailey known as Emma Fair Gulch and erected a scaffold. He made sure Pierson was comfortable, providing him with a new black suit, a pint of whiskey, and an endless supply of cigars.

At 1:15 on August 1, Pierson left the jail accompanied by his lawyer Alanson Smith, Catholic Bishop Tuttle, and Furey, among others. A six-passenger buggy was waiting to take him on his last ride. Once at the site, Pierson, cigar in his mouth, walked unassisted to the scaffold and mounted its seven steps, pausing only once. The sheriff gave Pierson an opportunity to speak to the crowd of about 400 people, and he did, for twenty-three minutes. He recounted the entire altercation with Hall and defended his actions. When it came to Nell, he boldly stated, "she was my wife," and claimed, "no man with a heart in him can see a woman beaten without taking her part." He also took a shot at the legal system, saying he had bad legal advice and "no justice."

With that Pierson said he was "ready to swing." The sheriff gave him another drink of whiskey while deputies bound his hands and feet. Deputy Jack Campbell placed the hood upon his head and Pierson, his head high, yelled to the crowd, "Boys, an old timer is going to die. Revenge him if you can." With that, he was dropped to his death.

Pierson's body was removed by the undertaker and laid out in a room behind the German Beer Hall in Hailey where it remained for one day. He was then buried in the local cemetery.

Following Pierson's execution, Emma Fair Gulch became known as Deadman's Gulch, a name that remains to this day. It is located 2.1 miles northeast of Hailey on Quigley Drive.

John Jurko

Twin Falls, June 25, 1924
Boise, July 9, 1926

John Jurko never denied pulling the trigger and killing A. B. W. Vandenmark. He never tried to escape the law, turning himself in to the sheriff immediately after the shooting. But he firmly maintained up until the moment of his death that he was not guilty of murder because Vandenmark had it coming.

Jurko was born in Ohio sometime between 1878 and 1881. As a young boy he moved to Europe with his parents, both of Bohemian descent. He married in 1912 and in 1914 returned to the United States with his wife Theresa, making their way to Twin Falls, Idaho in 1916. The couple had only one child, a girl, who died in infancy.

A barber by trade, Jurko had light brown hair and blue eyes, stood 5'10," and weighed 162 pounds. His left leg had been amputated below the knee, but he was able to walk well with the use of a wooden prosthetic.

Jurko opened a barbershop in Twin Falls and became well respected around the town. He also staked several mining claims in the Rogerson area, but it is unclear how much he worked them or if they added to his income. He did at times travel to the mines in the evening and stay for several days at a time, leaving Theresa at home alone.

In May of 1923, Vandenmark entered Jurko's barbershop for a haircut and shave. Vandenmark first visited Twin Falls in the early 1900s when he was an agent for the U.S. Geological Survey. He was assigned to the Twin Falls Land and Water Company, which was developing the irrigation system for Twin Falls. Well-traveled, involved in numerous mining and oil leases around the country, Vandenmark returned to Twin Falls in the spring of 1923 to live. He was estimated to be between sixty and seventy years old.

Vandenmark became a regular at Jurko's establishment, and the two struck up a friendship and eventually a business partnership. In early November 1923, they opened The Cozy Billiard Parlor on 209 Main Avenue East where they also sold cigars and soft drinks. The operation started on a handshake; Vandenmark apparently supplied the start-up cash and the building, while Jurko ran the day-to-day operations. Vandenmark also worked the place whenever Jurko was gone.

Two apartments were located above The Cozy. When the pool hall opened, Jurko and Theresa moved into one of them, while Vandenmark occupied the other. Theresa, who was isolated from the community because of her poor English skills, cooked and cleaned for both her husband and Vandenmark. This arrangement would eventually lead to trouble.

According to Theresa, the couple had lived in their apartment for just two weeks when Vandenmark made unwelcome advances towards her. He often told her, "leave your husband," and offered her cash to run away with him. Theresa rejected Vandenmark's offers many times over the next six months. She also did not tell her husband of the proposals during this time, afraid of what Jurko might do.

Jurko was too busy to notice. Working the barbershop, checking his mining claims, and running the counter at The Cozy took all of his time. For six months, he struggled to make The Cozy a success, but his efforts did not meet the expectations of Vandenmark. In April of 1924 he told Jurko he wanted out of the business. Vandenmark offered to sell his share to Jurko, and Jurko agreed, if he could make payments. Three days later, though, Vandenmark changed his mind. Instead, he decided to raise the rent to $125 a month. An argument ensued leading Vandenmark to threaten Jurko with, "I have got a notion to blow your head off."

Time did not soothe the situation. A few nights after the first confrontation, Vandenmark returned to the pool hall, gun in hand, threatening to shoot up the place. He also told Jurko, "I'll get you some of these days." For his part, Jurko decided it was time to charge Vandenmark for all the cleaning and cooking Theresa did for the old man. When Theresa approached Vandenmark with a bill, Vandenmark refused to pay. He moved out of the apartment and into the Rogerson Hotel.

On June 3, Vandenmark filed papers with the district court to dissolve the partnership. In court documents he claimed he had ended the partnership, but Jurko had continued to operate the business over his objections. He also charged that Jurko was disposing of partnership assets and appropriating the sales for his own use. Vandenmark asked the judge to close The Cozy, stop Jurko from interfering with the property, and appoint a receiver to make a full accounting of the business, which the judge did. The Jurkos were forced to move from their apartment. The Cozy, which some referred to as "John's Place," was closed.

Charles A. Larsen was appointed receiver. On June 17, he reported to the judge that the partnership owed $500 to creditors and that merchandise in the business was deteriorating. He believed the best solution was to sell what was left and pay off the creditors. The judge agreed. Then on June 25, Vandenmark asked the court to dismiss the case permanently and at the plaintiff's costs. At that time, Vandenmark became sole proprietor of The Cozy, and it reopened for business that night.

The feud between Jurko and Vandenmark was well-known around Twin Falls. Throughout the month of June, Vandenmark made numerous threats against Jurko, but never to Jurko's face. He offered Jack Smith $500 to give Jurko a bottle of whiskey tainted with poison and offered similar sums to two other men to shoot Jurko. On two occasions, Vandenmark told T. E. Lucas that Jurko was a "dirty son of a bitch," and he was going to kill him. He told Martin Strandy, a barber, that Jurko was "good for nothing, crooked," and that Theresa Jurko "was worth thousands of dollars to any man."

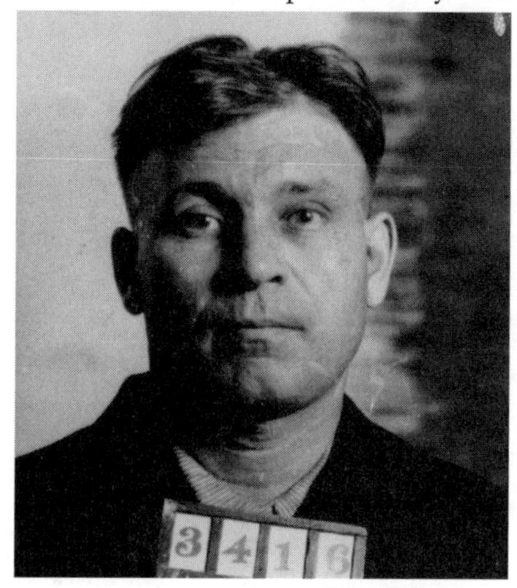

John Jurko

On June 25, on his way home after a long day at the barbershop, Jurko stopped at Frenchy's Garage to check on the status of his car. There William French told Jurko that Vandenmark had reopened the pool hall and was out to get him.

"What have you done to him?" French asked referring to Vandenmark. "He's pretty sore about you. He says he is going to take the barber shop and mine and everything."

"I ain't done nothing to him," Jurko responded. "We're split up now, that's all."

The Jurkos had moved to a house on Fifth Street, a few blocks from The Cozy. When John arrived home, he told Theresa about his conversation with Frenchy. Theresa then described her problems with Vandenmark, including a recent visit when he came into their house and asked if she "had changed her mind" about leaving her husband. Vandenmark told her that he "had plenty" and could show her a "lot better time" than her husband could.

The revelation, along with the embarrassment of losing The Cozy was too much for Jurko. For most of the evening, he stewed over Vandenmark and the trouble the old man had caused him. Jurko finally decided it was time to confront him. Grabbing a coat and his wife, he walked to the pool hall. The coat happened to have a small caliber handgun in the right pocket.

Jurko entered the pool hall with Theresa trailing. He saw Vandenmark sitting in the corner playing rummy with three other men. "Come here," he called to Vandenmark as he approached. "I came in here to make you take back what you said about my wife." Vandenmark stood, as did the other men at the card table. "I haven't said anything about your wife," he replied. "Go home."

Jurko removed his hat and placed it on the bar. "You've been telling my neighbors that you have been screwing my wife," he said.

Vandenmark, still holding his cards, gestured to Jurko to get out of the bar. At that point, Jurko pulled the gun and shot Vandenmark six times. Theresa screamed and ran from the building, as did several others.

Jurko surveyed the remaining crowd. "No man can say he has been fucking my wife and get away with it," he told them. Taking his hat from the bar, he left the pool hall and headed to the police station.

As soon as the shooting started, several men notified the police. Chief of Police P. O. Harriman was on his way to The Cozy when he met Jurko. The two walked to the police station, where Jurko turned over the gun he had carried in his pocket. He claimed he shot in self-defense. Jurko told Harriman that Vandenmark had thrown a glass at him and then reached out to grab him. Harriman let Jurko talk and then put him in a cell, pending an investigation.

Jurko hired W. P. Guthrie as his attorney and stood by his story that he had been provoked into the shooting. Witnesses, however, contradicted his version of events. As County Prosecutor J. W. Taylor collected evidence, he realized he had a murder on his hands. He filed first-degree murder charges against Jurko on June 30, and Jurko was bound over to the district court. His request to be released on bond was denied.

The trial began on September 16, 1924, in front of Judge William Babcock. Taylor would handle the prosecution, while Guthrie, along with Homer C. Mills, would defend Jurko. From the very beginning, Babcock made it clear that Jurko could not rely on the self-defense theory, although he did allow some witnesses to discuss that Vandenmark had indirectly threatened Jurko. However, he would not allow any testimony that discussed Jurko's mental state at the time of the shooting. Each time his defense attorneys tried to elicit information concerning how he looked or acted immediately prior to the shooting, the prosecution objected and the testimony was not allowed or stricken.

All the prosecution witnesses were clear: Vandenmark was not armed, nor did he attempt to attack Jurko just prior to the shooting. All agreed on the comments Jurko made concerning Vandenmark's advances on Theresa. Several witnesses stated that Jurko was angry but purposeful in his approach to Vandenmark, bolstering the prosecution's claim of a deliberate homicide.

The defense could do little to help Jurko. Mills called Theresa to the stand where she divulged she had been afraid to tell her husband about Vandenmark's advances. She testified that the first time she told her husband that the old man had been "bothering" her was the night of the shooting. She also claimed it was her idea to go to The Cozy and confront Vandenmark. But the prosecutor tore Theresa apart. Taking advantage of her poor command of English, he

Prosecutor John W. Taylor called Jurko a "Red," claiming he was anti-American.

crossed her up on dates and events, leading her to contradict herself and retract statements. Sometimes her answers did not fit the questions. Taylor reduced her testimony to a transparent attempt to help her husband.

Jurko took the stand in his own defense. He explained his business troubles with Vandenmark, the stories from friends that Vandenmark had a gun and was out to get him, the time the old man showed up at The Cozy, pulled a gun out of his pocket and threatened to shoot out the lights and him "one of these days."

As for the night of the shooting, Jurko testified he went to the billiard hall on the urging of Theresa, who wanted no more of Vandenmark's advances. All he wanted was an apology for Theresa. But the apology never came, and according to Jurko, he shot because he believed the old man was reaching into his right pocket to grab his own gun.

"He was threatening my life and coming between me and my wife," Jurko said. "I was afraid when he made so many threats on me and then he says he was going to fix me. I was afraid he would pull his gun and shoot me."

Jurko could remember nothing after firing the first shot, nor could he remember his discussion with the police after the shooting. He also could not explain how he happened to be wearing a coat with a gun in the pocket.

Following Jurko's testimony, the defense called several witnesses who confirmed that Vandenmark had been flashing a gun around town, claiming he was going to use it on Jurko. This testimony was allowed, as it affirmed Jurko's story. With Vandenmark's behavior revealed to the jury, the defense rested.

In his instructions to the jury, Judge Babcock carefully explained the differences between first-degree murder, second-degree murder, and manslaughter. He advised the jury it could find Jurko guilty of any of the three. When the defense asked for specific instructions concerning self-defense, Babcock refused. Instead, he told the jurors that, "in relation to the law of self-defense, one cannot claim its benefits after he has intentionally put himself where he knows or believes he has to invoke its aid…that if the defendant sought a meeting with the deceased for the purpose of provoking a difficulty with said deceased…then he would not be permitted to justify on the ground of self-defense."

The jury deliberated for six hours before finding Jurko guilty of first-degree murder. The jury also recommended that Jurko be hanged for his crime. The judge agreed and sentenced Jurko to hang on November 14, 1925, at the state prison.

Jurko was stunned, as were his attorneys. Guthrie was especially upset by the verdict. "I believe I made perhaps the best effort of my life in the way of defense," he said. "Naturally, the verdict comes as something of a shock."

For his part, Jurko said he was sorry, but was less than repentant. "My mind was blank during the time I am supposed to have killed Vandenmark," Jurko said. "At the trial, several of my main witnesses were not here to testify, and I do not think the jury gave me a square deal."

Jurko's lawyers immediately asked for a new trial and filed a motion to set aside the verdict. Their argument was based on several issues of self-defense, especially in the instructions, which Judge Babcock had given to the jury. They also claimed they had new evidence and witnesses that would support the self-defense theory. Babcock denied both requests. They appealed his ruling on a new trial and again were turned down. The next step was to appeal the judgment to the Idaho Supreme Court.

While all the legal maneuvering was taking place, Jurko was transferred to the Idaho State Prison. In gathering information about his new charge, Warden John Snook contacted John Taylor, who prosecuted Jurko's case. Although Jurko had never been in trouble in Twin Falls County prior to his arrest, Taylor was spiteful in his comments.

"He is a killer," Taylor wrote. "He is a criminal. He will kill for revenge, real or fancied." For good measure Taylor added, "He is a Red, in the habit of ridiculing American government and its institutions. His wife—a good woman—has expressed relief that she is no longer exposed to his brutality."

The communist connection interested Snook, so he contacted the FBI, requesting information on Jurko. J. Edgar Hoover replied, indicating the FBI had never heard of John Jurko.

As Jurko sat on death row, his appeal dragged on. Two brothers, Benton and Elbert Delana, joined his legal team and carried on his case before the supreme court. His case was heard on March 23, 1926, and while the court agreed Judge Babcock had made minor errors in his instructions, none were serious enough to reverse the judgment. The case was sent back to Babcock's court where he looked Jurko squarely in the eye and rescheduled his execution for July 9, 1926.

Jurko's last chance was before the state board of pardons. On July 7, his lawyers appeared before the board asking that Jurko's sentence be commuted to life in prison. While they reiterated that Jurko did not have a fair trial and had been provoked into the shooting, for the first time, they presented information on his sanity. They presented affidavits from physicians who claimed Jurko had been kicked in the head by a mule, and the injury left him excitable and "not in his right mind." According to one doctor, Jurko suffered from frequent headaches, and after the headaches, he suffered periods of "excitability" which affected his mental balance.

"The facts in this case strongly favor life imprisonment," Elbert Delana told the board. "This man was provoked, having been threatened

Jurko was buried at Morris Hill Cemetery.

by the deceased on more than one occasion. He was and is mentally unbalanced. The only fair and right thing to do in this case is commute his sentence."

The board of pardons appointed a "Sanity Board" to look into Jurko's claims. It took testimony from witnesses who heard Vandenmark threaten Jurko and listened to Rev. Alice Webb of Chicago decry the death penalty. But at the end of the two-day hearing, the board was unconvinced. The state doctors who examined Jurko found him to be sane. The witnesses who heard Vandenmark's threats never passed them on to Jurko, so he could not claim self-defense. The board denied his appeal, and an unrepentant Jurko prepared for his end.

"Tell the people never try to take a person's life," he told a group of reporters the night before the execution. "This crime I did was pushed on me. This man broke my heart. I lost my head and killed him. For this I must die."

At 12:05 a.m. on July 9, 1926, Jurko was led from his cell to the gallows in the prison yard. Claiming he had received "no mercy, no justice," he walked unassisted through the yard and climbed the scaffold steps alone to where Warden J. W. Wheeler and two guards were waiting. Before the noose was tightened around his neck, Jurko added one parting shot at the justice system.

"I am no criminal," he said in a calm, loud voice. "I ask the Lord to give me better justice in the next world."

With that, the trap was sprung, and Jurko was pronounced dead at 12:15 a.m.

At the request of Benton Delana, Jurko's body was autopsied. Doctors found evidence of a skull fracture and inflammation in the brain under the fracture, which they concurred could have caused irritability, forgetfulness, and lack of concentration.

As a last request, Jurko did not want to be buried in the prison cemetery. His lawyers and a group of clergymen arranged for private services, and he was buried in Morris Hill Cemetery in Boise.

Following the execution, Twins Falls District Attorney E. V. Larson was going through Vandenmark's effects. Many of the items he found were initialed "A. B. Baird." He also found correspondence to and from D. Meiklejohn, an attorney from Los Angeles. Larson contacted Meiklejohn, who traveled to Twin Falls. He confirmed the handwriting and possessions as those of A. B. Baird, a geologist who had disappeared from California in 1923.

4. In Desperation

Tambiago

Fort Hall, August 23, 1877
Boise, June 28, 1878

"That is always the Indian idea. A man for a man."

So wrote Alexander Toponce, an early pioneer of Utah and Idaho, who attempted to explain the murder of Alex Rhoden at the hands of Tambiago, a Bannock Indian. But Toponce, like many white settlers, refused to recognize the frustration and anger of Idaho's Native Americans. Tambiago's crime was not the result of some long-held Indian idea. He was simply tired of the white man ruining his way of life.

Although nomadic in their search for food, the Bannock lived primarily in southern Idaho, reaching as far north as the Lemhi Valley. They also migrated into southern Oregon and parts of Wyoming and Nevada. They were a small tribe, numbering less than 2000 in the 1850s. They were not overly aggressive, but when white settlers and the federal government threatened their existence in the 1870s, they were forced to react.

The Bannock's first encounter with white settlers encroaching on their homelands came in 1855, when Mormons established Fort Lemhi, south of present-day Salmon. At first the Indians welcomed the missionaries, but when more families moved into the area and the mission expanded outside the fort, the Indians became distrustful. In February 1858, Bannock and Shoshoni Indians raided the mission's livestock, driving off a large herd of cattle. A battle ensued and two Mormons were killed. Shortly after, Mormon leader Brigham Young ordered the mission closed.

During the 1860s, a steady stream of miners and emigrants passed through Idaho. They were subject to indiscriminate attacks by the various tribes, including the Bannock. In order to protect the travelers, the U.S. government proposed the Treaty of Soda Springs, promising the Bannocks $5,000 in goods each year if they would allow whites to pass through their homeland unharmed. The Bannocks agreed and for a short time all parties involved were content.

Eventually, instead of just passing through, the emigrants stayed in Idaho, laying out farms and claiming land for their own. Even though the Indians were peaceful, the settlers thought otherwise and called on Idaho Territorial Governor D. W. Ballard to establish a reservation. Ballard agreed

Bannock Indians at Fort Hall. The photo was taken in 1872.

and suggested the area around Fort Hall in southeastern Idaho was the perfect place. In 1868, the Treaty of Fort Bridger established the Fort Hall Indian Reservation for the Shoshoni tribe. The following year, President Ulysses S. Grant ordered the Bannock to join them.

The move proved disastrous. The land around Fort Hall could not sustain the 1200 inhabitants of the reservation. Early attempts at farming fell short of providing the food needed, largely because the Bannocks had little interest in farming. Even after farms were established, they were plagued by grasshopper invasions that wiped out crops. The federal agents in charge of the reservation made repeated requests for food, clothing, and blankets, but their requests were ignored by officials in Washington D.C. Fearing revolt, these agents allowed the Indians to continue traditional activities outside the reservation in order to provide for their people, much to the anger of the white population of the territory. For the next eight years, reservation life for the Bannock meant they spent most of their days hungry.

To make matters worse, white ranchers systematically destroyed Camas Prairie, where Bannocks had harvested camas roots for hundreds of years. The Treaty of Fort Bridger gave the tribe the right to use the prairie, but ironically, when the treaty was written, Camas Prairie was inadvertently written as Kansas Prairie. The mistake gave ranchers an excuse to take over the prairie, and their cattle and pigs devastated the camas fields.

In June 1877, the Nez Perce war erupted in central Idaho. Nez Perce warriors sought the help of both the Bannock and Shoshoni, but to the relief of government officials at Fort Hall, the tribes declined to get involved. Still, military leaders were afraid the conflict might spread, so troops began rounding up any wayward Bannocks and moving them to the reservation. The growing population brought more shortages. Hoping to quiet the increasing unrest over lack of food and other necessities, Fort Hall Agent W. H. Danilsen asked for more provisions, but these never arrived. Then, to alleviate the tensions growing among young Bannock braves, General Oliver Howard enlisted fifty of them to serve as scouts against the Nez Perce. With the warriors gone, the military hoped the reservation would remain quiet.

It did not. On August 8, 1877, a young Bannock named No Ho Wah attacked two freighters at Ross' Fork, near the Fort Hall agency. Other Bannocks, fearing retaliation, assured agency officials that this was a random act and offered to help catch No Ho Wah. But not all the Bannocks were in agreement, especially Tambiago.

The relationship between Tambiago and No Ho Wah is unclear. Some reports state they were brothers; others claim they were friends. Whatever the relationship, when No Ho Wah surrendered to Agent Danilsen on August 23, 1877, Tambiago responded in anger.

No Ho Wah was held at the suttler's store in Fort Hall awaiting the arrival of federal marshals who would deliver him to Malad for trial. Tambiago watched as the marshals led him away. Then, with rifle in hand, Tambiago walked towards a corral located behind the store. There he found Alex Rhoden, a Missourian, who had just delivered twenty-five head of cattle to the reservation. Without saying a word, Tambiago filed a single shot which struck Rhoden just above the left hip. He staggered forward about twenty feet and fell dead. Tambiago then fled.

Captain Augustus Bainbridge, commander of the troops at Fort Hall, sought the assistance of Bannock leaders to apprehend Tambiago. While they agreed to help, they used the search as a reason to leave the reservation. Other Bannocks threatened that if Tambiago were arrested, they would kill another white man. Nervous that an Indian uprising was at hand, Bainbridge requested more troops. Eventually an additional 100 soldiers arrived from Fort Douglas. On January 19, 1878, these soldiers captured Tambiago sixty miles north of Fort Hall.

Tambiago, along with his father and two brothers, was returned to Fort Hall where they were held in the stockade. On orders from Bainbridge, their hair was cut, and they were forced to wear military uniforms. Tambiago's father resisted, overpowering a guard and stealing his rifle, but he was quickly restrained. To defuse the situation, Bainbridge requested the father and brothers be sent to Fort Leavenworth, which was granted. Tambiago remained in custody at Fort Hall until May when he was transferred to Malad to stand trial.

Because the crime was committed on the reservation, the case required a special prosecutor. John Gray, serving as a special assistant to the United States attorney general was given the job. On May 20, 1878, Gray laid out his case before a grand jury, which indicted Tambiago on first-degree murder charges. He was bound over to the Third District Court of Idaho Territory.

Tambiago appeared before Judge H. E. Prickett on May 24 and pleaded not guilty. Prickett appointed lawyer B. F. White to defend him, but the young Bannock was distrustful of the entire proceedings. When the trial began on May 28, Tambiago refused to participate in his defense, and White presented no evidence or explanation on his behalf. He even waived his closing argument. The jury had little trouble finding Tambiago guilty. The next day, Judge Prickett sentenced Tambiago to death. He ordered Federal Marshall Joseph Pinkham to deliver the condemned man to the territorial prison in Boise and oversee his execution, which was to take place on June 28.

Canadian-born Pinkham was no stranger to Idaho. He had arrived in 1864 and operated a series of freight and stage lines throughout southern Idaho before President Grant made him a U.S. Marshall. Pinkham heard rumors that Bannock warriors planned to free Tambiago as he was transported to Boise. To avoid confrontation, Pinkham chose a route that took him south to Winnemucca, Nevada, then north to Silver City and Boise. He told the two men who accompanied him that in the event of an attack, they were to "kill the prisoner, then fight for their lives." But no attack came and on June 4, Pinkham arrived at the prison where Tambiago was placed in a cell next to No Ho Wah.

As he awaited his execution, Tambiago confided in Father Archambault, a Catholic priest, who spent time with the Bannock at Fort

Hall. He complained of the conditions on the reservation, the lack of food, the destruction of Camas Prairie, and the influence of James Dempsey, an interpreter at Fort Hall who had sold weapons to the Bannock in exchange for a woman. According to Tambiago, Dempsey encouraged the Bannock to go to war. Archambault offered to write a letter to the Commissioner of Indian Affairs on behalf of the Bannock, but Tambiago refused the suggestion, claiming, "chief at Washington no do anything for Indians."

A heavy rain greeted Tambiago on the morning of his execution. He watched as a crowd of approximately 250 gathered around the gallows in the prison yard to witness the event. He held out hope that his tribesmen would come to his rescue, telling Archambault that they must have confused their days. The priest could give him little solace.

Federal Marshall
Joseph Pinkham

Shortly before 1 p.m., Tambiago walked unassisted from his cell and up the scaffold steps. As he surveyed the crowd, a small, sad smile crossed his face. He said nothing and remained still until a guard attempted to place a black cap over his head. This he resisted. Whether the cap was ever in place is unclear. The trap door was sprung, and Tambiago dropped to his death. He was later buried in the prison cemetery.

While Tambiago's case made its way to its inevitable conclusion, the Bannock at Fort Hall reached their breaking point. On May 22, a group of warriors led by Buffalo Horn arrived on Camas Prairie to find cattle and hogs foraging on their much-needed camas. They confronted the ranchers and forced them and their animals off the prairie. Eight days later, two desperate young braves attacked three white ranchers, critically injuring two of them. Knowing there would be retaliation from U.S. troops, Buffalo Horn decided the Bannock would fight rather than surrender.

While some Bannock returned to the reservation for safety, approximately 200 warriors joined Buffalo Horn, who planned to lead his warriors to Oregon where they would join the Northern Paiute in a war against the whites. They gathered guns and ammunition, stole cattle and horses, and attacked whatever got in their way, including James Dempsey, whose body was left on Camas Prairie. When they reached the Snake River, they burned Glenn's Ferry and then traveled west before they were engaged by a group of volunteers from Silver City. Buffalo Horn was killed in the battle, but the Bannock continued to Oregon. Federal troops were soon on their trail and ensuing battles decimated the Indian fighters. On July 9, a battle in the Blue Mountains ended the uprising. To further ensure the Bannock were controlled, the military systematically hunted and killed peaceful Bannocks in Montana and Wyoming who had left the reservation in search of buffalo. In September, skirmishes at Clark's Ford and Dry Fork in Wyoming officially ended the Bannock War of 1878.

To explain the uprising, public officials laid the blame on the federal government and its treatment of the Bannock. Idaho Governor Mason Brayman called for the government to follow through on the Treaty of Fort Bridger and either give Camas Prairie to the Indians or adequately compensate them. Captain Bainbridge called for more food for the Bannocks, who in December 1878 were receiving only five pounds of meat each per week. In his evaluation of the war he told his superiors, "you can draw your own inferences as to the natural consequences of such starvation rations." But the harshest criticism came from General George Crook who was sent to Fort Hall to determine the causes of the war. His conclusion was made public in an interview he gave to the *Omaha Herald* on June 21, 1878. Blaming "hunger, nothing but hunger," Crook justified the actions of the Bannock, claiming the Indians had no choice but to go to war when "they see their wives and children starving." He added that sending Americans into battle to be killed by the Indians was hard, but it was harder "to be forced to kill the Indians when they are clearly in the right." He acknowledged with both anger and sorrow that, "Our treatment of the Indian is an outrage."

Seven days later, Tambiago swung from the gallows.

James Ellington

Boise, December 20, 1894
Boise, May 27, 1896

The case was filled with twists and turns, a mix of he said-she said, lost evidence, an incompetent juror, and a jailor and jury who asked for clemency. In the end it didn't matter. James Ellington killed Charles Briggs, and for that he had to hang.

Ellington and Briggs arrived together in Boise in September 1894. Briggs would claim that Ellington was a tramp he picked up along the way from California. Ellington admitted that for much of his life he had been a tramp. He left home—Barnsville, Georgia—in 1873 and wandered the country, eventually making his way to California in the late 1880s. Here he decided to settle down and took work as a roof painter. He claimed he met Briggs in the same line of work, and together they decided to travel to Idaho where they would start a roof painting business together.

On the way, they stopped in Burns, Oregon, working for one month before traveling on to Boise. An acquaintance there would later describe Ellington as a quiet, industrious man, quite the opposite of Briggs, who was ill-tempered and quarrelsome, especially when he had been drinking. The two men were also dissimilar in appearance. Ellington was forty-one, short and stocky with dark hair. He usually wore a full beard and had a "knocked about" appearance. Briggs was fifty-six and taller, clean cut with a stern countenance.

Once in Boise, they lived for a short time in a tent on the south side of the Boise River. Together they procured painting supplies and found work. Briggs eventually rented a home on 13th Street and was joined by his wife and a stepson. Ellington also moved into the home.

In November, the partnership began to disintegrate. John J. Abbott, another roof painter, overheard Ellington making disparaging remarks about Briggs, including threats that he would like to knock a ladder out from underneath his partner and "break his damned neck." Abbott passed these comments on to Briggs. Briggs also suspected that Ellington was undermining him in the business, taking jobs on the side and leaving him out of the picture. The tension eventually led to a confrontation, and on November 11, Briggs ordered Ellington out of the house. Although

Ellington resisted at first and threats were made by both men, Ellington eventually left after Briggs agreed to pay him for his share of the painting materials.

The two crossed paths in early December, and Ellington asked for his money. Briggs refused, calling Ellington a "God-damned tramp." Ellington would recall that Briggs pulled a knife on him. While no one witnessed this specific exchange, others would later testify that Briggs threatened several times to kill Ellington.

Out of the roof painting business, Ellington found employment cutting firewood for a gentleman who lived on 13th Street. On December 20, he was walking to work when he passed Briggs and the two exchanged civil greetings. Ellington should have kept walking but instead he turned to confront Briggs. What happened next became a focal point of the murder trial, viewed differently depending on who was telling the story. What is certain is that a fight ensued and three shots were fired; Briggs died five days later.

Briggs would tell anyone who would listen that Ellington shot him in the back after they passed on the street. Upon being struck by the bullet, Briggs claimed he turned and rushed toward Ellington to defend himself. Ellington demanded his money, and when Briggs refused, Ellington fired twice more and grabbed Briggs' watch, jerking it off its chain. Then Ellington ran away.

For his part, Ellington admitted he shot Briggs, but only in self-defense. After Ellington passed Briggs, he turned and asked Briggs for his money. Briggs responded by rushing him with a pocketknife, blade extended. To protect himself, Ellington fired one shot, hitting Briggs on the left side of the chest. They then wrestled, with Briggs falling to the ground on his back with Ellington on top of him. When Briggs offered his watch in exchange for the debt, Ellington let him up. But it was just a ruse, and as Ellington reached for Briggs' watch, Briggs lunged at him with the knife. Ellington shot twice, with one bullet hitting Briggs in the hand. Ellington then pulled the watch from its chain and ran as he saw an approaching policeman.

Three eyewitnesses who lived near the scene of the incident could not completely confirm either story. Nora Reber heard the two men arguing and then struggling with each other. She saw Ellington shoot Briggs twice before he ran off. Lanie Bowers also heard two shots and saw the two men fighting on the ground. She said she saw a pistol in Ellington's hand. She also saw something shiny that reflected light, but could not identify what it was or who was holding it. Her daughter, Lida Bowers, also saw the incident. After hearing two shots, she went to look and saw Ellington on top of Briggs. Then she heard another shot.

Briggs was transported to his home. He was fully alert and gave his version of the incident and a full description of Ellington to the police. A manhunt was on, and the next day Ellington was found

James Ellington

hiding under a bridge near Emmett. The gun and watch were still in his possession, and both were passed on to William Basil, the deputy sheriff of Ada County who transported Ellington to the Ada County Jail.

Briggs never believed he was going to die and at first refused to write or sign any dying declaration. However, his doctors insisted that he compose a statement identifying Ellington as the man who shot him. He wrote the statement on December 23 and died two days later. An inquest was held, and Ellington was bound over to the district court for first-degree murder.

From the very beginning lawyers Frank Martin and J. R. Wester believed Ellington acted in self-defense. On December 31, they filed a demurrer against the charge. On January 28, 1895, Judge J. H. Richards of the Third District Court of Ada County denied the demurrer and arraigned Ellington on the murder charge. He pleaded not guilty.

Jury selection took two days. Testimony began on February 6 with Dr. George Collister, who confirmed that Briggs had been shot in the back as Briggs had stated. However, when pressed by the defense attorneys, Collister could not say for certain that the bullet had entered through the back. Other witnesses spoke of Ellington's gun, which he obtained in trade for a tent, and the threats Ellington had made against Briggs. The prosecution also presented the three women eyewitnesses who heard the gunshots and saw Ellington with a gun.

The gun turned out to be a problem for the prosecution. The police could not produce the weapon; it had disappeared. The defense used the missing gun as a way to bolster its self-defense claim. As Lanie Bowers testified, she saw something shiny that reflected light. The prosecutor, C. M. Hays, argued the "shiny object" was the gun, but without the evidence, he couldn't prove it. Bowers also stated she "saw a weapon of some kind in the hand of the taller man." Ellington's lawyers asserted this was Briggs' knife. But the prosecutor presented testimony to show that no knife was found in the area or in Briggs' pockets after the assault. He also managed to make Bowers withdraw her comment about a weapon in Briggs' hand.

Attorney Frank Martin worked tirelessly to save Ellington

But Defense Attorney Martin was convinced there was a knife, and he would come back to the shiny object throughout the trial and beyond.

Ellington took the stand in his own defense. He admitted shooting Briggs, but only after Briggs attacked him with a knife. He testified that he never meant to kill Briggs; it was Briggs who instigated the fight. However, he had a difficult time explaining what he was doing on Briggs' street with a gun in his pocket.

Closing arguments were heard on Saturday, February 9. In the early afternoon, after receiving instructions, the jury retired to deliberate. At 10 p.m. the jury sent word to the judge that they were unable to reach an agreement. The judge, unmoved, told them to continue deliberations and come back with a verdict in accordance with his instructions. The night wore on. At 4:30 Sunday morning, the jury sent word to the judge. They had reached a verdict: guilty of murder in the first degree. The *Idaho Daily Statesman* would report that one man held out for a second-degree murder charge, but he eventually gave in to the others.

The next month would be filled with courtroom drama. Judge Richards set February 18 for sentencing, but Ellington's lawyers asked for a one-day postponement. Back in court on the February 19, they asked for an arrest of judgment. Judge Richards denied this motion and reset the sentencing for February 21. Back in court, Attorney Martin then asked for a thirty-day delay in order to file a motion for a new trial. This was granted.

Martin went to work to find the knife which would help him prove Ellington's self-defense claim. He first approached Nora Reber. Reber testified that Briggs did not have a knife, but under pressure from Martin, she admitted that it was possible that he did. At first she agreed to sign an affidavit to the fact, but changed her mind after a conversation with the prosecuting attorney. Martin had to settle for an affidavit by Justice of the Peace C.C. Siggins, who heard Reber tell Martin that Briggs "might have had a knife."

Martin also obtained a knife from Briggs' stepson, Jesse Tigard. Tigard had supposedly taken the knife from Briggs' pant pocket after the shooting. He turned it over to Martin when the lawyer confronted him at school. However, Tigard refused to make an affidavit concerning the knife and how it came into his possession. For her part, Mrs. Briggs claimed the knife Martin obtained could not have been in her husband's pocket at the time of the shooting. She alleged she had taken the knife to the home of George Montgomery on or around December 10 to peel apples and potatoes for his family, and she had left it there.

With the knife mystery and other legal issues, Martin hoped to obtain a new trial for Ellington. He returned to court on March 15, appealed the original judgment and asked for a new trial. The judge denied the motion and on March 25 sentenced Ellington to hang.

Still Martin was not finished. Immediately after the sentence was announced, he filed another motion for a new trial. He saw irregularities in the trial transcripts, the instructions given to the jury, the jury itself. The judge heard his arguments but found no reason for a new trial. Stating he was tired of the delays, he set Ellington's execution for May 17, 1895.

Ellington was never transported to the state penitentiary. Instead, he remained in the Ada County Jail where he agonized over his fate. His weight plummeted and he talked of suicide. His lawyers continued to work on his behalf, filing an appeal with Idaho State Supreme Court. They based their argument on faulty instructions to the jury and the inadmissibility of statements Ellington and Briggs made to police officers and others. Ellington was given a stay of execution until the court could hear the case.

Ellington made the most of his time in jail. He wrote to his family, he received visitors, and he made friends with the sheriff and his guards. In one incident he thwarted a breakout attempt by other prisoners. He sent a note to Deputy Sheriff Hugh Fulton to warn him. "Mr. Fulton," he wrote, "look out if you go inside. Thay have a gun an air going to kill you and escape. J. H. Ellington." Fulton searched the jail and found four razors, a butcher knife, and a loaded revolver. He credited Ellington with saving his life.

In December, the supreme court issued its ruling. The court praised Attorneys Martin and Wester for their efforts, claiming they presented Ellington's case with commendable zeal and persistency. However, they were "unable to find anything in the record that will justify us in disturbing the verdict and the judgment of the district court." There would be no new trial; the conviction and sentence would stand. The execution was reset for May 27, 1896.

Ellington had one last chance. He filed an application for the commutation of his sentence before the Idaho Board of Pardons. In a passionate letter he asked the board to spare his life and show him mercy. Affidavits were presented on his behalf, including one from Deputy Sheriff Fulton, explaining how Ellington had saved his life. Dr. W. D. Springer sent word that he had treated one of the jurors, A. Macklin, and in his opinion, Macklin was an imbecile, unable to form an opinion on his own. Still Macklin, along with eight other members of the jury, signed a letter asking that Ellington's sentence be commuted to life in prison. Even the Ada County sheriff thought it would be best if Ellington was sent to the state penitentiary rather than be executed.

But the strangest declaration came from Corrilla J. Robbins, a neighbor who had befriended Mrs. Briggs following the death of her husband. According to Robbins, Mrs. Briggs confided that she and her husband had separated two days before the shooting. While Briggs blamed Ellington for his marital problems, Mrs. Briggs left her husband because he abused her boy. Mrs. Briggs also admitted to Robbins that she found a knife on her husband after the shooting. She kept all of this information from the police, as it was her plan to leave Boise and go live with the Briggs family; she did not want to jeopardize her standing with them.

For her part, Mrs. Briggs presented an affidavit to the board of pardons claiming that everything Robbins said was "not true." However, she offered no opinion on whether Ellington should hang.

The board of pardons, led by Governor William McConnell, listened to the testimony, but in the end rejected Ellington's appeal. McConnell believed it was important to uphold the law of the land, and the law had deemed Ellington should hang. The execution would go on.

In his final days, Ellington struggled. Sometimes he babbled incoherently; other times he shook convulsively. He tried to find comfort in religion and welcomed various ministers. In the end, he became a Catholic and was baptized by Bishop Glorieux, the man responsible for building St. John's Cathedral in Boise. Glorieux stayed with Ellington throughout the entire ordeal giving him his last rights and overseeing his burial.

*Idaho Governor
William McConnell*

On the morning of the execution, Ellington awoke early to the reading of the death warrant. He ate a hardy breakfast and greeted the bishop, his lawyers, and several women from the Women's Christian Temperance Union. As he was led from his cell and out to the jail yard, his knees buckled. Deputy Sheriff Fulton caught him and quietly urged him to "Brace up, Jim." Fulton and the bishop led him to a small building in the corner of the jail yard where the gallows waited. Several times he stumbled; each time Fulton and the bishop steadied him.

On the scaffold stood his lawyers and Sheriff Moseley, among others. Ellington shook hands with Martin and handed him two letters, asking that they be released after his death. Martin then left. He could not bear to see Ellington hang.

Moseley asked Ellington if he had anything to say. The condemned man replied, "No, not a word," but while the straps were applied to his arms and legs, he called out to the crowd: "Goodbye, gentlemen...I thought I did right when I killed him. I had to fight for my life then, and I am not afraid to forfeit it now."

Fulton placed the black cap on Ellington's head and stepped back; Sheriff Moseley pulled the lever to release the trap. As Ellington dropped, the cap somehow came off his head. His face was uncovered as he endured his final throes of death. For fourteen minutes, Ellington hung before the crowd in what an *Idaho Daily Statesman* reporter called a "horrifying" spectacle.

Ellington's body was placed in a plain pine coffin and taken to the Glover Undertaking Parlor where a funeral was held. In a final twist of irony, he was buried in the Catholic section of Morris Hill cemetery, the same cemetery where Briggs was interred.

As directed, Martin released the two letters after Ellington's death. One, a general letter to his friends, was bitter and accusatory. He was especially harsh on Dr. Collister, who he felt lied concerning the course of the bullet. He also blamed the doctor for Briggs' death. "If Mr. Briggs had had competent medical attendance, he would have recovered, but how could he expect any medical aid from a doctor who could not trace the course of a bullet in a human body." In the end, Ellington contended, "it has been my life against his [Collister's] honor and reputation, and being a poor man…it is easy to see how he won and I lost." He also took aim at the board of pardons, which he claimed had "determined to make an example of me knowing that I was poor." After his death, he concluded, he would appeal his case to a higher court where "gold and power wield no power."

The second letter was a copy of one Ellington had previously sent to Judge Richards. In it he chastised the judge for failing to fulfill a promise. Ellington claimed that Richards agreed to address the board of pardons and ask for a commutation of his sentence. Instead, Richards refused to speak on his behalf, telling the governor that Ellington was guilty of "cold-blooded and willful murder." Ellington also claimed that leaders of the Republican party in Boise, of which Richards was a member, were using his execution to secure nomination and election to public office. The Republicans, according to Ellington, wanted to show the public they would be harsh on poor criminals.

It is unclear whether there was any backlash to Ellington's letters, both of which were published in the *Idaho Daily Statesman*. Republican Governor McConnell left office in 1897 and was succeeded by two Democrats, Frank Steunenberg and Frank Hunt. Judge Richards was elected the mayor of Boise in 1898. As for defense attorney Martin, a Democrat, he became Idaho's attorney general in 1901.

WILLIAM L. REYNOLDS
AKA FRANK WILLIAMS

SF SNAKE RIVER, DECEMBER 17, 1886
BLACKFOOT, JULY 21, 1888

In most places in 1886, forensic science was in its infancy. In Idaho territory, it was nonexistent. When a crime was committed, a prosecuting attorney had to rely on his power of observation and his instinct. He could call upon the opinions of local doctors, but many of them were ill-qualified to give expert testimony. If he was lucky, he could find an eyewitness or two, but most of the time, he was left to his own devices to decipher a crime scene and present enough evidence for a conviction. Such was the predicament of Bingham County Prosecutor H. M. Bennett when word of a double homicide reached him in the winter of 1886.

The crime took place near the South Fork of the Snake River, northeast of the Caribou Range, an isolated area in the southeast corner of Idaho. The area attracted miners and trappers, rugged men who learned to survive the harsh winters. Someone could get away with murder in such a remote place.

But Frank Williams, born William L. Reynolds, chose not to get away with murder. As far as he was concerned, no murder had been committed. From the moment his gun went off and killed Charles Reed to the moment he met his death, Williams stuck to his story: it was an accident.

Williams was born in South Portsmouth, Rhode Island in 1861. As a boy he intended to follow in father's footsteps as a sailor, but changed his mind and traveled west to Wyoming in the early 1880s. He worked for a time as a cowboy along the Platte River and eventually made his way to Utah. In October 1884 he used his real name to enlist in the U. S. Army at Fort Douglas. He was assigned to Company H of the Sixth Infantry. His enlistment card describes him as five feet, seven inches tall, with blue eyes, blond hair, and fair skin. Williams remained with his unit until April 10, 1886,when he deserted and headed to the mountains of Idaho.

Once in Idaho, he changed his name to Frank Williams. He worked throughout the spring and summer for the railroad near Market Lake, north of Idaho Falls. In the fall, he headed south, carrying his belongings on his back. He stopped one evening at the home of John Jones on Fall Creek,

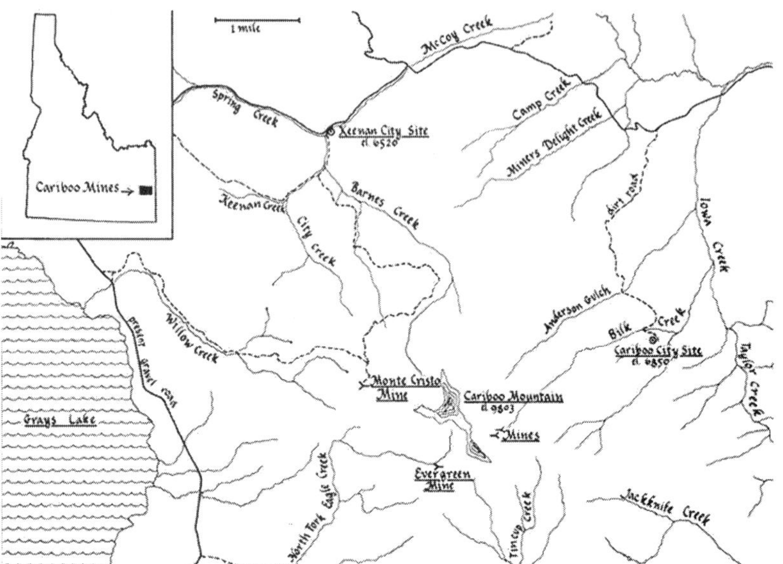

approximately fourteen miles from Eagle Rock near present day Idaho Falls. Jones offered him a meal and told Williams of the great opportunities to be found to the east on the South Fork of the Snake River.

For approximately three weeks, Williams stayed and worked for Jones. He collected supplies and information, and in mid-October, borrowed Jones' horse and traveled into the South Fork area. He took 100 pounds of flour, two sacks of salt, some blankets, and his rifle. He made his way to the mouth of McCoy Creek, where he found two cabins. One was unoccupied, so Williams claimed it for himself. At some point he returned the horse to Fall Creek, then traveled back to the South Fork where he planned to spend the winter.

Once settled, he began to explore the territory. One day while following the river, he met Charles Reed, who was fishing. Reed had spent several years trapping and mining in the area and was happy to share his knowledge with Williams. Reed lived three miles upstream from McCoy Creek, and he invited Williams to visit anytime. Williams accepted the offer and over the next several weeks, stopped to visit Reed at least twice. There he met the owner of the cabin and Reed's partner, Captain John Winn.

On November 11, Frank Glover and Matthew Johnson arrived at McCoy Creek. Glover had previously stayed at the cabin next to Williams', so he and Johnson took up residence there for the winter. They became acquainted with Williams, and although they were cordial and spent their evenings in friendly conversation, they did not share provisions or hunt together. Williams told his neighbors he had deserted from Fort Douglas; they didn't seem to mind. However, they did take note of his inexperience. Both agreed he was ill-prepared to survive the rugged winter that was to come.

Still, Williams was determined to succeed. Everyday he took his gun and went out hunting, and while most nights he came back empty-handed, he persisted. As usual, on the morning of December 17 he took his gun and his dog and set out through the snow to find some game. Unfortunately, all he found was trouble.

We have only Williams' story to explain the events of that day, and although the story is plausible, the people who heard him tell it, including a jury, did not believe him. We know for certain he left his cabin around 8 a.m. and walked up river. He was passing the Winn cabin when one of the men—either Reed or Winn—invited him in. Tired and cold, he was happy for the offer and took a seat by the fireplace. Within five minutes, he had warmed up sufficiently and moved to a chair in the middle of the room opposite Reed. Reed, who was sitting at a table mending a coat, pushed his work aside and asked to look at Williams' gun. Williams handed him the gun; Reed looked it over, then stood up to give the gun back to Williams, butt first. Williams reached for it, and as he did, the gun hit the corner of the chair and discharged, the bullet striking Reed in the head. Mortally wounded, he fell back into his chair. In the commotion that followed, he was struck in the head and fell to the floor.

Winn, who had been moving about the cabin, reacted immediately, grabbing an axe from near the door. He charged Williams, who fended off the blow with his gun. According to Williams he told Winn, "hold on Cap, let me explain," but Winn wouldn't listen. He struck at Williams again, breaking the stock of the gun. In retaliation, Williams hit Winn with the broken gun, knocking him down. As he fell, he lost control of the axe.

Williams picked up the axe and headed toward the door. Winn, back on his feet, threatened him, "I will kill you anyhow," and reached for his gun which hung above his bed. Williams then turned and struck Winn with the axe. The older man went down. He did not try to get up, but instead crawled into the corner of the room above the cellar where he died.

Williams could never completely explain what he did next. While he stated he wanted to lay the dead men on their beds, he was unable to lift them; instead he dragged them, placing one under each bed. He then took firewood and stacked it around the bodies along the bottoms of the bunks. According to Williams, he did this so passersby could not see them. He also wanted to keep animals from getting to them. With the bodies stashed, he straightened the room, placing a box under the table, the chairs against the walls of the cabin. He left, shutting the cabin door behind him, and returned to his cabin, arriving around 3 p.m.

Early that evening, Williams went next door to talk to Glover. At first he simply asked to borrow Glover's raft. He wanted to take the raft downriver to Eagle Rock and turn himself in to the marshal. Unaware of the events that had transpired, Glover thought Williams planned to give himself up because he was a deserter; he told Williams to reconsider. But then Williams told him he had run into some bad luck and explained the events of the day.

Glover, concerned that Reed and Winn could still be alive, decided to go check out Williams' story. Although it was near dark and snowing, Glover and Johnson, along with Williams, walked to Winn's cabin. Inside, they found the bodies well-cached under the beds. By candlelight they studied the scene, Williams again explaining what happened. Glover was especially attentive to the wounds on the victims and the condition of the cabin. Together they placed the bodies on the beds and covered them with blankets. Then they returned to Glover's cabin to plan a course of action.

Glover convinced Williams he should not turn himself in until the sheriff had been notified. To this end, he penned a letter to the Bingham County Sheriff explaining that a homicide had taken place near the mouth of McCoy Creek. The next day, Johnson set out for Caribou—a twenty-five mile journey—where he mailed the letter to Sheriff Samuel Taylor. He then returned to their cabin where the three men would await word from the authorities. In the meantime, Glover checked on the bodies almost each day. For his part, Williams continued to hunt, borrowing Johnson's gun. He also made occasional trips to the Winn cabin to make sure the bodies were not disturbed.

The letter reached the sheriff on December 20. The next day, he took the train to Pocatello and traveled on to Soda Springs where he procured a team of horses. Traveling was difficult, and by the time he reached Gray's Lake, the snow was too deep for him to continue. Instead, he stopped at the ranch of Simon Sibletts. Here he deputized Sibletts and Charles Nelson and instructed them to travel to McCoy Creek, arrest Williams, and return with him to the ranch.

Sibletts and Nelson reached Williams' cabin on the evening of December 27. The next morning, accompanied by Glover, they walked with Williams to the Winn cabin. Here they asked Williams to re-enact the crime, which he obligingly did. They also examined the bodies once more, as Sibletts and Nelson were to report their findings to Sheriff Taylor. From here, they made the eight-hour trek back to Sibletts' Ranch, turning over their prisoner to the sheriff. By January 3, 1887, Williams was sitting in the Bingham County Jail, where he would stay in legal uncertainty for the next four months.

Sheriff Taylor expected the county coroner George Davis to travel to McCoy Creek to secure the bodies and hold an inquest. When he failed to do so, the county commissioners ordered Dr. James H. Bean to the site. In April, Bean and Sheriff Taylor traveled on horseback from Idaho Falls west to the Conant Valley. From there they followed the Snake River to McCoy Creek then upriver to Winn's cabin where the badly decomposed bodies had remained throughout the winter and spring. After examining the bodies and the room, Bean removed Reed's skull and part of Winn's, leaving the bodies of the victims behind. He and Taylor then returned to Blackfoot with their evidence.

With Dr. Bean's report, Prosecutor Bennett convened a grand jury to hear evidence. He called Dr. Bean, Sheriff Taylor, Sibletts, and Glover. The grand jury found enough evidence to bring first-degree murder charges against Williams for the killing of Reed, but did not find cause to charge him for the death of Winn. On May 4, 1887, Williams appeared before Judge James B. Hays of the Third Judicial District where he pleaded not guilty. Hays set the trial date for May 9.

From the beginning, Bennett attacked Williams' version of the event. He relied heavily on the testimony of Glover, who described in detail the condition of the cabin and the bodies. Bennett introduced a map into evidence that showed the layout of the cabin and position of the furniture. Using the map, Glover explained where he saw bloodstains, what he saw in the room, and how he found the bodies hidden under the bunks.

Glover's testimony contained information that did not jibe with the story of Williams. According to Williams, Reed and Winn were killed just minutes apart. Yet Glover said the conditions of the two bodies were very different. When he and Johnson pulled Reed out from under the bed, he was limber, so limber they had a difficult time lifting him and placing him on his bunk. Winn, on the other hand, was stiff from the effects of rigor mortis. They had to work on straightening his legs before they could pull him out from under the bed. Once they did, the stiffness of the body made it easy for them to place him on his bunk. The condition of Reed's clothes also did not coincide with Williams' story. Reed's shirt and the top half of his overalls were wet and not from blood. However, from the waist down, Reed was completely dry. Based on what Grover saw, Bennett was informing the jury that Williams' story could not be true.

Another factor made Williams' story seem suspect. All four witnesses who had been at the scene—Glover, Johnson, Sibletts, and Nelson—described the large amount of fireplace ash covering the bodies and the blood spots on the floor of the cabin. Glover testified that Reed had so much ash on his face, he was almost unrecognizable. Nelson added that all the big blood spots on the floor had been covered with ash; only a few spatters were missed. Bennett's contention was that Williams went to a lot of trouble to cover up an accident.

But the biggest problem Williams faced was his original story. In his first account of the incident, Williams claimed Reed was sitting on a box at the table. As he stood to hand the gun back, it hit Williams' chair and went off. Williams told this story to both Glover and Johnson, and then re-enacted the scene for Sibletts and Nelson. But the four men testified they saw no blood on the table or the box where Reed had supposedly been sitting. Instead, they testified to seeing a large amount of blood on a chair and the floor in the corner where Winn had supposedly crawled to die. Their testimony directly contradicted Williams, who on the stand claimed that Reed had been sitting in a chair. This was the chair Williams had moved to the corner as he tried to put the place back in order.

Dr. Bean appeared as the prosecution's final witness. He presented Reed's skull as evidence, showing the extensive damage to the back right side of the head and a major fracture along the base of the skull running to the left temple. He testified the injuries could have been caused by a gunshot fired at close range. Although Bennett hinted that the bullet had entered from behind, Bean was certain the fatal shot had been fired from the front, the bullet entering Reed's right cheek and passing "straight through the head." The display of the skull and the massive destruction to the back of Reed's head certainly had an impact on the jury. When Bennett introduced the shattered remains of Winn's skull, which Bean described as "mashed all to pieces," the incident became much more than an accident.

Defense Attorney Willard Crawford did what he could to save Williams. He objected to much of the testimony involving the death of Winn, but was overruled each time. To explain the presence of rigor mortis in Winn but not Reed, he presented two doctors who testified that rigor mortis could set in any time from ten minutes to seven hours depending on conditions. Both agreed that a large loss of blood could also speed up the onset of rigor.

Mostly, Crawford relied on Williams' character as a defense. He presented two witnesses who testified to Williams' honesty, work ethic, and dependability, even though he was a deserter from the Army. He pressed Glover and Johnson, who admitted Williams never tried to run. Although he had access to a gun, snowshoes, and supplies, he chose to wait for the authorities to take him in. According to Crawford, Williams did not run because the story he told was true; it was an accident.

Williams took the stand to tell his story. It had remained unchanged from the beginning, with the exception of the chair on which Reed was sitting. He explained how the gun went off, how Winn attacked him, and how he had to kill Winn to protect himself. He explained why he covered the bodies and how he planned to turn himself in to the marshall. But Williams could not explain why he straightened the furniture or how the floor and bodies became covered in ash. He could only say that he knew he "was not to blame."

On May 11, Judge Hays gave the jurors their instructions. He gave them the option of finding Williams guilty of second-degree murder or manslaughter. But Bennett had done his job, and they took a short time to find Williams guilty of first-degree murder. On May 31, Williams was back in court with his lawyer, who filed a motion for a new trial. Judge Hays denied the motion and then sentenced Williams to die on July 22. Crawford immediately filed an appeal with the Idaho Territory Supreme Court.

Hays must have been in the hanging mood, because on June 3, Alex Woods, convicted of killing his wife, joined Williams in the Bingham County Jail. Sheriff Taylor was to prepare for a double hanging. However, Williams and Woods had other ideas, and on June 22, working with other inmates, they escaped. Woods was immediately recaptured, but Williams remained at large for a day before he was discovered hiding along the

Snake River. He went back to jail, where he learned he was given a stay of execution until the supreme court could hear his appeal.

On February 2, 1888, the court took up his case. Unfortunately, Crawford had filed no briefs on his behalf, and he did not appear to argue Williams' cause. The judges reviewed the court transcript and decided all was in order. Williams' appeal was denied. He was re-sentenced to hang on July 21.

Sensing his fate, Williams made one more attempt to escape. On July 8, he was taken from his cell to the dining room for dinner. In preparing the meal, one of the guards had absent-mindedly left a large butcher knife on a table, so Williams seized the moment and the knife. He threatened the guard, demanding the keys to the jail. At that moment, another guard arrived. Williams grabbed him and held the knife to him, once again demanding the keys. The two guards obliged and Williams locked both of them in a cell. Then before escaping, he freed Woods.

A $100 reward was offered for Williams' capture. Ten hours after his escape, he was back in jail. Woods, on the other hand, remained at large and would be on the run for two weeks. His execution would be delayed, but Willliams' hanging would go on as scheduled.

Sheriff Taylor did not want a public execution. To this end, he built a solid-fence jail yard behind his office, and instead of a scaffold, he constructed a suspension system with weights and pulleys. Williams would be standing on the ground and jerked upward to his death.

The night prior to his death, Williams spoke to a reporter. He admitted his true identity, but he stuck to his story that the deaths of Reed and Winn were accidents. He remained upbeat, telling the reporter that if there were a hereafter, he was "willing to take his chances."

His execution was set for 2 p.m. Dressed in a black suit, he walked confidently into the jail yard, a cigar hanging from his lips. In his final words, he once again denied his guilt, but accepted his fate, preferring to die rather than spend his life in prison. He thanked Sheriff Taylor for his kind treatment, calling him "a good man." Some reports state he put the noose around his own neck and claimed, "Let her go, gentlemen, all ready."

With those words, the life of Williams came to an end. He was buried in an unmarked grave in Blackfoot, the exact location, like those of his victims, now unknown.

THEODORE WARLICH

SF SALMON RIVER, JANUARY 28, 1886
MOUNT IDAHO, JUNE 9, 1886

When Theodore Warlich left his home in the Harz Mountains of Germany for a better life in America, he could not have imagined the trouble he would find. From Texas, to California, to Nevada, to Idaho, Warlich struggled wherever he turned. In America, he found only heartache, hard times, and the end of a hangman's rope.

It is difficult to trace Warlich's history, perhaps because the spelling of his name is inconsistent. Court documents list his name as Theodore Warlick and C. F. T. Wallich, as well as the most common, Theodore Warlich. What is known about the man came from Warlich himself during his trial.

Born in 1839, Warlich made his way to the United States in 1866. By 1869, he was in Texas, where he married Maren Emile Ohlsen. Why they married is unclear, as Warlich claimed that Maren never lived with him as his wife. Still, together they moved to California where in 1877, she divorced him. He then began moving northward, working for a time for the Northern Pacific Railroad. He landed in Walla Walla, Washington and in 1883, moved to the Camas Prairie in Idaho County.

For two years, Warlich struggled to make a living on the prairie. Although the area was filled with German immigrants, he struggled to fit in. His actions didn't help. He threatened to shoot people who came on his land, even though the land wasn't officially his. He was also seen arguing with himself, sometimes striking himself like a crazy man. As neighbor John Bryan would state, Warlich's mind was "not properly balanced." After someone ransacked his wagon and spread his belongings "all over the prairie," he decided to move to the mining country near Warren. He arrived there in the fall of 1885 and went to work at the Tramp Mine, eventually making his way to the South Fork of the Salmon River.

Home to miners and ranchers, the South Fork was wild and rugged. The men who lived along its banks worked small claims or mines, raised cattle and horses, and did whatever it took to survive. On almost every bar was a small cabin where someone had staked his claim. The closest community was Warren, and South Fork residents would take well-worn trails to the mining town to get supplies, make connections, and catch up on Idaho County news.

Henry C. Savage was one of those residents. Savage was born in Vermont and made his way west in the late 1860s. He arrived in Warren in 1869 and staked several claims, but mostly earned his living working for others. By 1885, he moved to the South Fork where he staked a claim and built a cabin on the east side of the river, approximately twenty-two miles from Warren.

Exactly how Warlich and Savage met is unclear, but Warlich claimed that Savage offered him a job doing trestlework for Frank Bricker, who had a hard rock mine near Warren. Warlich assumed that Savage was a partner in the mine, but when Warlich went to Warren to talk to Bricker, he found this was not true and there was no work. He returned to the South Fork and on the trail ran into Savage, who invited him to work on his claim. The two moved in together, and for most of November and December, they worked side by side, sharing tools and provisions, as well as any earnings they made.

From the beginning, the partnership was in trouble. Warlich liked to hunt, and rather than work on the claim, he spent his time roaming the hills of the South Fork drainage looking for game. He was good at it and provided not only for himself and Savage, but also sold his kills to others who lived on the river. This angered Savage who did not think Warlich did his fair share of work on the claim. But Warlich felt that he did do his share. Since all Savage wanted to do was work the claim, Warlich was left with all the domestic chores. According to Warlich, Savage was so wrapped up in mining, he would not even start a fire in the morning.

The trouble was apparent to Charles Peterson, another South Fork resident, who stopped to visit the pair in late November. He listened to the complaints of both men, but found Warlich especially disgruntled. According to Peterson, Warlich told him, "If it was not so hard to get out of the country, I would kill that Savage."

By mid-December, the two men realized they could not live together. They split their provisions and Savage began building a second cabin for himself on the bar. He completed the cabin in mid-January, but the new arrangement did not improve the relationship.

On January 10, 1886, Peterson stopped by to offer Warlich a job sawing lumber. Warlich accepted, but needed to borrow Savage's saw. When Peterson went to see about the saw, Savage would not let him borrow it.

He also told Peterson that since Warlich refused to work on the claim, he was going to reduce his portion of the earnings. When Peterson told this to Warlich, he had one response: "I will hunt him as I hunt a deer."

Warlich left the bar and went to Peterson's ranch where he worked until January 20. On his return to his cabin, he found that Savage had moved many of the belongings from the original cabin into the new one, including all the furniture, the only window, and all of the potatoes. When Warlich confronted him, Savage told him, "I will set my gun on anyone who comes near my house." Warlich said he had no choice but to back off.

About a week later, Warlich was out hunting and returned to find everything removed from his cabin save two items: an oven lid and Savage's gun. He was so angry he took the gun and threw it into the river.

Warlich was working in the blacksmith shop when Savage discovered his gun was gone. Angry, he confronted Warlich. When Warlich told him what he had done, Savage picked up an axe and went after him. Warlich, who had his Winchester close by, picked it up and aimed it at Savage, who then turned tail and ran.

Warlich chased him across the mine and through a gulch. As they approached another gulch, Warlich stopped, took aim, and shot Savage in the leg. He managed to get up, but Warlich fired another shot, this one striking Savage in the back near his heart. Savage went down, and Warlich fired one more shot, this one hitting the victim in the neck.

No one responded to the shots, and for several days Savage's body lay where it fell. Finally, Warlich realized the seriousness of his situation. He dragged the body into some brush underneath a steep hill and "scratched it in," covering it with about six inches of dirt. He covered it with brush and rubbish and did his best to cover his tracks. Then he made plans to leave the South Fork, deciding to go back to Camas Prairie.

Rather than take the established trail through Warren, down to the Salmon River at Shearer's Ferry, and then up to the prairie, Warlich tried to avoid detection by going over the mountains east of Warren. Four times he attempted to get through, but each time he was turned back by bad weather. The fourth time, after wandering for four days, he realized his escape was hopeless, and he returned to his cabin on the South Fork.

Savage's disappearance did not go unnoticed. In December, he had agreed to work for George Riebold in Warren, promising to show up in Warren before February. When he didn't arrive, Riebold went looking for him, spreading the word on the South Fork that Savage was missing.

The courthouse at Mount Idaho

On March 4, Frank Smith and William Kelly visited Warlich at his cabin. Smith informed Warlich that he was there to look for Savage; consensus in Warren was that Warlich had killed him. Although he denied killing Savage, he agreed he was in "a bad fix." When the group failed to find Savage's body, Smith decided to take Warlich to Warren and turn him over to the deputy sheriff. Warlich went peacefully.

The next day, Riebold pumped Warlich for information. Warlich was silent except to say that Savage was "the meanest man in the mountains" and had more mean tricks about him than anyone he had ever seen. Convinced that Warlich had killed Savage, Riebold, Sim Willey, J.R. Meeks, and Aaron "Pony" Smead went back to the South Fork to search the area around Savage's cabin. They found bullet casings and drag marks along the ground, but they were unable to find Savage. On March 8, they gave up and returned to Warren.

Back in Warren, Riebold once again spoke with Warlich, telling him it was not safe for him to return to the South Fork, as people there were sure he had killed Savage. Warlich remained adamant. "I did not kill Savage," he said, "but I wished I had."

On March 21, Riebold learned the body had been found. Two days later, he and fourteen others returned to the South Fork. They found the cache, removed the brush, and carefully scraped away the dirt to reveal Savage's body. The men then searched the area and found a blood-spattered rock, some drag marks, and a bullet. The next day, the Idaho County Coroner arrived to hold an inquest. With the help of Riebold and Smith, he removed the body from the shallow grave and examined it. He determined that Savage had been shot three times, most likely by Warlich, and forwarded this information to James Edwards, justice of the peace in Warren. Savage's body was then re-interred on the bar.

Warlich appeared before Edwards on March 27 to answer questions concerning the murder. Whether he admitted his involvement is unknown, but Edwards had enough information to send him to Mount Idaho to face a grand jury. On the way, he confessed the details of the crime to his escorts, Smith and Bobby Mansfield, claiming that after what he did, he would "rather be dead that minute than alive."

Once Warlich reached Mount Idaho, justice was swift. On April 10, a grand jury brought first-degree murder charges against him, and he was arraigned before Judge Norman Buck. Warlich pleaded not guilty, and Buck set his trial for April 12.

Judge Buck was well known in northern Idaho for his iron-fisted rule in the courtroom. He followed the letter of the law and is best remembered for his decision that a jackass discovered the famed Bunker Hill Mine near Kellogg, which has become an Idaho legend. As the only judge for the entire First District of Idaho Territory and an associate judge of the Idaho Territory Supreme Court, he was a busy man. He was not one to waste time.

Prosecutor James H. Forney was up to the challenge. He called only three witnesses—Peterson, Riebold, and Smith—who gave credible accounts of what they had seen and heard. Defense attorneys James Poe and J. W. Parker could not dispute that Warlich had killed Savage. Instead, they tried to focus on mitigating circumstances—Savage's constant taunting and Warlich's erratic behavior. They presented witnesses who described Warlich as a "crazy man" who "did not have control of himself" and whose mind was "not properly balanced." Even the prosecution witnesses admitted that Warlich often became angry over nothing and that people on the South Fork called him crazy.

Warlich took the stand in his defense, telling how Savage made his life miserable. He testified that on several occasions, Savage had attacked him with an axe. He explained that he threw Savage's gun in the river not only because he was angry, but also because he thought Savage was going to shoot him. He related the troubles he had on his arrival in America, including head injuries that caused him to be excitable. Warlich regretted his actions, claiming, "I lose my temper easily. I don't know what to do."

Governor Edward Stevenson

Testimony and closing arguments took all day. Finally, at 9 p.m., Judge Buck gave the jury its instructions and the court adjourned. The jurors deliberated well into the night.

The next morning the jurors asked to be heard in court. They were unable to reach a verdict and asked to be discharged. Judge Buck refused. They then asked the judge to explain the differences in punishment for manslaughter and the various degrees of murder. Again, Judge Buck refused, ordering them back to deliberations. Two hours later, the jury still obviously conflicted, returned with a verdict: "We find that the defendant is guilty of first degree murder and strongly recommend him to the mercy of the court."

But Judge Buck, who followed the letter of the law, was bound by statute to give Warlich the ultimate punishment. He could show no mercy and sentenced Warlich to hang, setting the execution for June 9.

Six members of the jury were stunned by the decision. They contacted defense attorneys Parker and Poe and stated they never would have voted to convict Warlich of first-degree murder had they known he would hang. According to them, when the judge refused to discharge them, the jury had been hopelessly deadlocked, with six voting for second-degree murder and six voting for first-degree murder. Back in deliberations, these six were convinced by the others that a recommendation of mercy would allow Warlich to escape execution. Reluctantly, they had agreed to the first-degree murder charge.

Parker and Poe immediately sent a letter to Territorial Governor Edward A. Stevenson, asking him to commute Warlich's sentence to life in prison. They related the concerns of the six jurymen and offered to send sworn affidavits of each. They sent a transcript of the trial explaining that it would show a verdict of second-degree murder was warranted. They also admitted Warlich was no doubt a "crank," but had they more time to prepare for the trial, they would have been able to prove it, leading their client to a prison term and not death.

Stevenson refused to intervene, and Idaho County Sheriff Albert Talkington was charged with carrying out the execution. He built a scaffold in the jail yard of the Idaho County Courthouse at Mount Idaho and did his best to appease his surly prisoner. It was not easy. As the date approached, Warlich became more defiant, refusing religious counsel and spewing curses at Talkington and his deputies. When they gave him a new suit for the execution, he refused to wear it. But on the day of the execution, as Warlich faced the scaffold, his tough exterior cracked. Several times his legs buckled as he made his way, and he had to be supported as deputies placed the noose around his neck. He had no last words, but instead stood mute and dazed as the trap was sprung.

Warlich was buried in the Grangeville Cemetery, the exact location now lost. As for his victim Savage, the bar on which he was buried, a stream that runs nearby, and a mountain all bear his name.

5. The Demon Rum

JAMES CONNERS

BLACKFOOT, SEPTEMBER 25, 1904
BOISE, DECEMBER 14, 1904

Vigilante justice can be swift. Sworn deputies, a frantic manhunt, a mock trial, and a quick end—public security restored. While James Conners escaped the vigilantes, he was no match for Idaho's legal system. Conners' crime, trial, and execution spanned less than three short months.

Conners was a hobo, a tramp. By his own account, he had wandered the country for fifteen years, using the trains to make his way from one town to another. In the afternoon of September 25, 1904, he drifted into Blackfoot, Idaho. It would be his last free ride.

Conners and at least one other man, perhaps two, spent much of the afternoon drinking whatever they could find. Emboldened by whisky, hungry and broke, they made their way to a Japanese section house located just south of Blackfoot. Here, Japanese workers for the Oregon Short Line railroad had just finished their evening meal. At first, Conners attempted to barter with the men, offering to trade a knife in exchange for dinner or money, but he found no takers. Agitated, he asked for a cup of coffee; again he was turned down. At this point, Conners pulled a gun, and he and his accomplice(s) began rifling through the bunks of the workers, taking razors, watches, anything of value. With the thieves distracted, one of the section men escaped and enlisted the help of foreman William E. Fitzgerald.

Fitzgerald sent his nine-year-old daughter Lenora for backup. She found Deputy Sheriff Elbert P. Sweet, who joined Fitzgerald, and together they walked to the section house where Conners was waiting. He beckoned Sweet to enter, and as Sweet mounted the steps to the house, Conners raised his revolver and shot him once in the head. Sweet fell in the doorway, mortally wounded.

At the shooting, Fitzgerald ran for cover in an adjacent section house. Conners followed. Firing two shots, he broke down the door to the house and took aim at Fitzgerald, hitting him at least once. For good measure, he beat Fitzgerald about the head with the butt of the gun. Then he and his accomplice(s) fled along the railroad track toward Blackfoot.

Alerted by the gunfire, armed Blackfoot citizens hurried to the scene. Led by deputy sheriff James Kinney, they exchanged shots with Conners and at least one other man. Using boxcars for cover, they were able to pinpoint the outlaws' position. As the citizens kept up the fusillade, Kinney sneaked around the end of a boxcar and fired a load of buckshot into one of the rogues, who dropped his gun and went down.

Pandemonium reigned as members of Company F of the Idaho State Militia arrived and jumped into the fray. They had hurried to the scene from Blackfoot with the notion that the Japanese section men and Russian laborers had commenced a race riot at the rail yard. What they found was Conners unconscious and the other suspect(s) on the run. The militia then organized posses and began scouring the countryside in search of the other suspect(s). With Conners out of action and in custody, the crowd focused their attention on Sweet and Fitzgerald. Fitzgerald, while badly beaten, would survive, but Sweet died shortly after the capture of his assailant. Upon his death, the group turned on Conners, several calling for him to be lynched on the spot. Sensing his predicament, Conners played the dying outlaw. While he did suffer several gunshot wounds—besides the buckshot in his back, he had a bullet in his thigh and another in his neck below his left ear—none were serious enough to cause death. But he was bleeding profusely and remained unresponsive on the ground, convincing the crowd he would not last the night. He was loaded into the back of a wagon and carted to the Blackfoot jail. Only when he was safe behind bars did he sit up and respond to his captors.

With Conners in custody, the search for the other outlaw(s) began in earnest. Over the next two days, thirteen suspicious characters were jailed and questioned in connection with the holdup, but none turned out to be accomplices, and authorities abandoned their manhunt after two days. Conners would face the charges alone, if the sheriff could protect him from a lynch-crazed mob first.

Conners had his first court date on September 26, although it is unclear if he actually appeared before the judge. Probate court records of Bingham County show that Deputy Kinney filed a criminal complaint against Conners charging him with murder, and probate judge C.H. Bevans ordered him to be held without bond until the next term of the district court. Newspaper reports, however, indicate that on the morning of September 26, doctors operated on Conners to remove the bullet in his leg, so the court might have proceeded without him.

James Conners

When townspeople learned that Conners had survived his first night in jail, they decided to take matters into their own hands. Monday evening, angry and agitated, they gathered downtown. After several hours of milling in the streets, the mob garnered their courage and stormed the jail. Deputies, however, were ready and convinced the crowd to let the law run its course. The crowd dispersed, but not without threats against Conners. To be safe, the sheriff posted extra guards at the jail in anticipation of more trouble.

Wednesday, as the funeral procession for Deputy Sweet passed the railroad depot, a man appeared on the depot platform, rope in hand. As mourners continued toward the cemetery, a group of 100 men pulled away and silently made its way in the opposite direction, toward the county jail. Again, the vigilantes were met by armed deputies who quieted the crowd with news that Conners was on his death bed. The information had its desired effect, and while many in the crowd did not believe it, they once again dispersed. It would be their last attempt to take the law into their own hands.

For the next month, Conners remained confined to his cell, where he tormented his jailers. He said little to them, refusing to answer questions, spewing epithets at anyone who approached. According to the *Pocatello Tribune*, he wore a "brutal expression and had a course, vulgar mouth." Small in stature, he was approximately 5'5" tall and weighed 140 pounds with a full, dark head of hair and a sandy red mustache. His eyes were a steel blue. He had no visitors and revealed nothing about his past.

The fall term of the Sixth District Court began on October 21, 1904, with Judge James M. Stevens presiding. Conners, healed from his wounds, appeared alone, so the judge appointed J. Edward Smith of Idaho Falls to serve as his lawyer. The next day, Conners entered a plea of not guilty, and Stevens set November 1 as the opening date of the trial.

The United States Constitution guarantees a defendant the right to a speedy trial, a rule Judge Stevens certainly took to heart. Conners' trial spanned three short days.

There was no doubt Conners was guilty of killing Sweet. The eyewitnesses were in agreement that it was he who pulled the trigger. Defense attorney Smith's only hope was to show that Conners was so inebriated at the time of the shooting, he was unaware of his actions. Thus he was guilty of manslaughter, but not first-degree murder. Conners took the stand in own defense, explaining his afternoon of drinking, his history of drunkenness. Even one of the Japanese railroad workers, using an interpreter, testified to Conners' altered state. But the jury didn't buy it. Shortly after noon on the third day of the trial, the jury rendered its verdict, guilty of murder in the first degree. The following day, making sure that justice would be swift, Judge Stevens set December 14, 1904 as the date for Conners' execution. Conners responded by singing a bawdy tune and spitting on his escorts as he was led from the courtroom. No appeal to Idaho's Supreme Court would be filed on his behalf.

His defiant behavior continued at the state penitentiary where he arrived on November 5. He volunteered little information about his past, claiming only that he was born in San Francisco and was raised a Catholic. He refused to reveal the names of his parents or their backgrounds. He shouted at the guards, threw his meals across his cell, and ended up in solitary confinement, where he remained until the end of November. Eventually, he became resigned to his fate and treated his captors with a quiet respect during his last few days. He refused religious counseling and made no reference to the murder.

Warden D. W. Ackley supervised the construction of the gallows and set the time of the execution at 6:15 a.m. He wanted no surprises and limited the audience to law officials and those specifically chosen for the task. Conners awoke early on the cold Friday morning and declined to eat breakfast, instead steeling his reserves with a few draws on a pipe. When one of the guards asked him if he needed a drink, he refused.

"I was a pretty good fellow when I was sober," Conners told the guard. "Whisky brought me to where I am. I don't want any more of it." It was all he would ever say concerning the crime.

At 6 a.m, Conners walked from his cell into the prison yard. He was not shackled or handcuffed, a request he had made of the warden. He mounted the steps of the scaffold under his own power and took his place without being told. Father Fuchs, a Catholic priest called to administer last rights, asked Conners if he had anything to say, perhaps a message to his parents. He responded, "No, sir, I have nothing to say."

With those final words, the trap was sprung and Conners dropped to his death. His body was placed in a wooden coffin, and he was buried in the prison cemetery. The execution—from death march to grave—took less than thirty minutes.

That Conners was buried in an unmarked grave was not unusual, but in his case fitting. When he was arrested, he gave officials various names—Conners, Conroy, O'Conner—and admitted in court that Conners was not his true name, although he declined to reveal his real one. Following his death, Deputy Kinney told reporters that Conners was really Charles Lennon of Massachusetts, information he received from Conners' sister in Butte, Montana. While census records indicate two Charles Lennons born in Massachusetts in the 1860s, it is impossible to say if he was one of them. To the Idaho justice system, it really made no difference.

ANTHONY MCBRIDE

WEISER RIVER, AUGUST 11, 1867
BOISE, JANUARY 24, 1868

Somewhere on the banks of the Weiser River lies the unmarked grave of a man known only as John the Chinaman. Buried there in August of 1867, his murder would have gone unpunished had it not been for three strangers who believed the murder of any man, regardless of his race, was a crime.

On the moonlit night of August 11, Moses Roberts, James Worthington, John the Chinaman, and two other men were camped on the banks of the Weiser River. They were bound for Umatilla, Oregon with stock and a wagon owned by Roberts. It was a little after 9 p.m. when two of the men turned in for the night, making their beds on the side of the wagon. The Chinaman had also gone to bed, taking a spot approximately thirty feet in front of the wagon. Worthington had gathered some of the stock and led them downriver.

Roberts was mending rope on the opposite side of the wagon when he saw a young stranger, Anthony "Jimmy" McBride, walking toward the camp. He carried a pistol in one hand and bottle of whisky in the other. Although McBride was not staggering drunk, Roberts described him as a "little tight."

McBride approached the two men in the bedrolls, and Roberts paid little attention to the conversation, until McBride asked about the man sleeping in front of the wagon. He wanted to know if it was an Indian or a Chinaman. Both men told him it was a white man, but McBride did not believe them. "It's a Chinaman," McBride declared, "and I am going to shoot him." At that point, Roberts stepped out from behind the wagon and told McBride not to shoot. Incensed, McBride raised his gun to Roberts and said, "I don't want to hear another word out of you. Step back or I'll shoot you."

With the urging of the two men still in their bedrolls, Roberts backed away to the wagon to find his pistol. While he did so, McBride walked to within five feet of the Chinaman and fired, the bullet entering his left shoulder. He gave a quiet moan, but remained motionless after he was hit.

McBride returned to the wagon and asked Roberts and the other two men to help him drag the body to the river. Roberts refused, telling the killer he wanted nothing to do with the murder. He then left his camp and walked 200 yards downriver to the camp of William Myers.

Myers was a rancher on the lower Weiser River Valley. He and his crew had been cutting hay and had camped for the night along the Weiser. Along with Worthington, they heard the gunshot and were going to investigate when they heard a second shot. Shortly after, Roberts came into their camp and told them what happened. Myers grabbed his shotgun and together they returned to Robert's camp to confront McBride.

McBride, still holding his pistol, saw them coming. He approached Myers and asked him, "What do you want, hero?" Myers, trying to defuse the situation, told him he was looking for his stock. But McBride would not let up. "You wouldn't give a white man a show after killing a Chinaman?" he asked him. "You better help me to put a rope around his neck and throw him in the river."

Myers backed away, claiming he wanted no trouble. While he kept McBride occupied, Roberts came at McBride from behind, then moved up to his side and wrestled the pistol away. He knocked McBride to the ground and Myers put his foot on McBride's neck to hold him down. Together they tied him up. Once they had him subdued, Myers questioned McBride about the shooting. "I'll shoot any of them when I have the chance," McBride said of the Chinese. "They come here and work for three dollars a day. If it weren't for them, I could get five dollars a day."

The sound of gunfire caught the attention of David Bivens, who lived approximately one mile south of the campsite. Bivens, an early pioneer of the area, operated several ferries on the Payette River. He also owned a stage station and had recently employed McBride. When he heard the shots, he made his way to the camp to find McBride tied up, face down in the dirt. Bivens asked him, "In the name of God what are you doing here?" McBride told him he had "got into a little difficulty."

With McBride restrained, they turned their attention to the Chinaman. His breathing was labored; he made no attempt to move, and no one administered any aid. He died approximately forty minutes after the shooting. Worthington and Myers examined the body, turning it over to trace the bullet. They found the ball had entered the left shoulder and came out near the spine at the left hip. They searched the Chinaman's pockets and found $92 in gold dust, which Worthington took. They then changed his clothes. Roberts wanted to bury the victim, but Myers told him there would have to be an inquest in the morning. They covered the body with a blanket, and Bivens instructed one of his men to stay with it to keep the wolves away.

After some discussion, Worthington gave Myers the money with instructions. In the morning he was to take McBride to the nearest lawman, using the money to pay for the stage fare. Whatever remained he was to give to Roberts to distribute to John the Chinaman's friends. Bivens, Myers, and McBride then went to Bivens' establishment where they spent the night. Roberts and Worthington remained at the camp. They planned to leave at daybreak. They saw no need to stay for the inquest as Myers was a witness and had heard McBride's confession.

The next morning, Myers and McBride took the Overland stage toward Boise, while Bivens organized the neighbors to hold an inquest. Upon reaching the scene of the murder, Bivens found Roberts loading his wagon ready to move on. Bivens told him he needed to stay for the inquest, but Roberts refused. When he pulled out, Bivens sent word to surrounding neighbors that a possible suspect in a murder was leaving the area. He also sent three men to follow him.

While the drama with Roberts was unfolding, Bivens and eleven others held an inquest. While the actual report has been lost, they came to the conclusion that the Chinaman died as a result of a shot from a revolver. They did not claim that McBride fired the fatal shot. When the inquest was over, they buried the Chinaman.

Roberts made it as far as the Washoe Ferry, near present day Ontario, Oregon. Somehow he was persuaded to return to the scene of the crime and arrived at Bivens' place after dark and spent the night. The next day he left for the Payette Valley and eventually caught up with Myers. Whether Worthington and the others went on to Umatilla is unknown.

Early records and maps of the Payette River Valley show no organized communities, just ranches and stage stops on the Overland Road to Boise. Because of this, it is difficult to discern exactly where Myers left McBride. However, court documents show that Myers did leave McBride in the custody of Judge Lyons, and shortly after, McBride escaped. The judge ordered both Myers and Roberts detained while he ordered local citizens to recapture McBride. After three days, McBride was apprehended and turned over to Thomas Cahalan, a lawyer and founder of the Payette River Ranch, located approximately six miles west of present day Emmett.

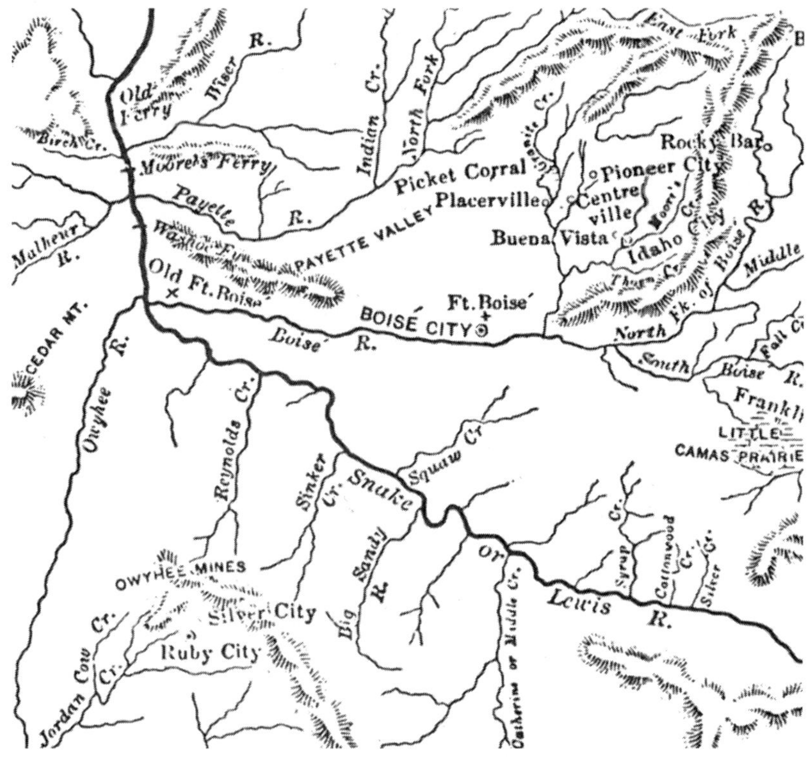

Cahalan informed both Myers and Roberts they would have to travel to Boise and file a complaint against McBride before he could be officially arrested. On August 16, Roberts stood before Justice of the Peace Robert L. Gillespie and made the complaint. At that time, Roberts either could not remember or did not know McBride's real name. Thus his complaint lists both the victim and the accused as "unknown." Later, Gillespie learned McBride's name and issued a warrant for his arrest.

On August 18, Cahalan, serving as a deputy sheriff, delivered McBride to Boise where he was arrested by Sheriff John Duvall and put in the county jail. In his first court appearance before Judge Gillespie, McBride admitted the shooting, but felt it was justified. "I shot him because I thought he was an Indian," McBride told the judge. "He would steal our stock and be likely to kill some of us."

Gillespie ordered McBride to remain in jail until a grand jury could be convened. He also ordered Roberts and Myers to post a $500 recognizance bond. The case hinged on their testimony, and he wanted to make sure they would show up for a trial.

On November 9, Ada County District Attorney E. J. Curtis presented his case before a grand jury. It indicted McBride for the murder of John the Chinaman. That afternoon McBride appeared before Judge John Cummins of the Third District Court and heard the indictment against him. Three days later he stood before Judge Cummins and pleaded not guilty. The trial was to start on November 18.

McBride must have realized his chances of acquittal were slim. He knew Roberts and Myers were going to testify against him, and he had confessed to Judge Gillespie. On the morning of November 17, he asked his jailor if he could get some fresh air. The jailor obliged, allowing him into the jail yard without leg irons or shackles. As he went out, the guard remained in the jail to lock an interior door. When he turned around, McBride was gone.

McBride made a mad dash to the Boise River where he hid for the remainder of the day. Sheriff Duvall called out all of his deputies and offered a $100 reward for the capture of McBride. In the cover of night McBride made his way to the newly built Fort Boise, where he asked to enlist. Instead, the soldiers detained him and turned him over to the sheriff. Judge Cummins reset the trial for November 20.

Jury selection took all of the first day. Finally on the afternoon of November 21, Prosecutor Theodore Burmester presented his case. He called only two witnesses—Roberts and Myers—who recounted the night of the murder and the behavior of McBride. While defense attorneys Albert Heed and Seth Weldy could not shake their stories, they did get both men to admit that McBride was under the influence of alcohol at the time of the shooting.

McBride did not take the stand. Instead, his defense relied on the testimony of Bivens, who had known "Jimmy" for approximately two months. Bivens called him a "quiet and peaceful" man, claiming that while McBride had lived at his establishment, he had never seen him drunk or out of control. But on the night of the murder, McBride was not himself. Bivens described him as "quite drunk," testifying that he seemed "wild and flighty." According to Bivens, McBride left the house that night with a bottle in his hand and the comment that he was going out "to have some fun."

Bivens also hinted that Roberts might have been the shooter. He explained how Roberts left early the morning after the murder, even though he was told to stay for the inquest. He also claimed there was talk along the river that Roberts had done the shooting.

Testimony closed on the afternoon of November 22. Judge Cummins gave his instructions, which included the various degrees of murder. He also explained "drunkenness will not excuse a crime." However, when it came to intent, the jury could consider drunkenness if the defendant was so drunk he was "incapable of forming a deliberate purpose or design." In that case, the jury could find the defendant guilty of second-degree murder.

The jury retired for its deliberations. That evening, they returned to the courtroom to ask Judge Cummins for additional instructions concerning drunkenness and the commission of a crime. Still they were unable to reach a verdict. Deliberations would continue the next day.

On November 23, the jurors were back in court, where they requested information on reasonable doubt. They also wanted to know if drunkenness could be the cause of a crime. With the clarification they were finally able to make a decision. That afternoon they found McBride guilty of first-degree murder.

McBride did not take the verdict well. Over the next several days, he proclaimed his innocence, arguing that he had been misled into killing the Chinaman, thinking he was an Indian. He also had harsh words for Roberts, claiming he should have killed him too.

As he stood before Judge Cummins on November 29 to hear his sentence, McBride was unrepentant. He claimed another man shot the Chinaman and then ran away. He took no responsibility for the crime. The judge listened to his rant and then sentenced him to hang. The execution would take place on January 24, 1868.

For the young McBride, it would be a bitter end to his short life. Although military records show he was born in Milford, Donegal County, Ireland in the early 1840s, he told the colorful story of being born at sea as his parents made their way to America from Liverpool. He claimed to have settled in Philadelphia where he supposedly married Elizabeth Tower, a widow with eight children.

McBride enlisted in the United States Army in 1862. He went on to fight in the Civil War with the 99th Pennsylvania Infantry, Company K that was soundly defeated in the Battle of Fredericksburg on December 13, 1862. McBride was shot in the right thigh during the fight and spent the next two months in a military hospital. He was discharged due to disability on February 13, 1863.

Healed from his wound, McBride re-enlisted with Company C of the 14th Infantry in August 1865. He was sent to Fort Lyon in Colorado where he deserted on April 17, 1866. He arrived in Idaho in the spring of 1867 and worked in the mines of the Boise Basin near Granite Creek before moving to the Payette River Valley to work as a laborer for various ranchers. It would be his last job.

During the days leading up to the execution, supporters of McBride petitioned Idaho Territorial Governor David W. Ballard to commute McBride's sentence to life in prison, but Ballard refused. They also asked Judge Cummins to hold a hearing to determine McBride's sanity. Instead, Cummins ordered three physicians to examine McBride. When they concluded that McBride was not deranged, the judge denied the request. Public sentiment also ran against McBride, as the *Idaho Tri-Weekly Statesman* reported that it was "quite time to put a stop to the reckless disregard for life which has reigned supreme in Idaho for the past four years."

On the morning of January 24, a crowd of 300 gathered at the mouth of Crane Gulch, two miles north of the city, to await the execution. At 1 p.m. Sheriff Lindsey and his deputies escorted McBride to the gallows. He was accompanied by Father F. P. Cazeau, a Catholic priest, who had been his constant companion in his final days. As McBride stood on the platform, he addressed the crowd and once again proclaimed his innocence, blaming everyone but himself. Deputies then tied his hands and feet, and as they placed the noose around his neck, McBride called to a soldier in the crowd, "By God, they got me now. Goodbye, Sergeant, we are not on the Truckee now." Sheriff Lindsey then pulled the trap, and McBride could say no more.

McBride was buried in the shadow of the gallows, his grave unmarked like that of his victim. The site is located east of Bogus Basin Road, northeast of the Highlands Elementary School.

Timothy O'Conner

Leesburg, February 3, 1880
Salmon, September 17, 1880

On February 3, 1880, a classic western duel played out in Leesburg, Idaho, as young, well-liked William Ludeman took on foul-mouthed Timothy O'Conner. When the smoke cleared, both shooters lay wounded. Both would eventually die, Ludeman from the bullet in his belly and O'Conner at the end of a rope.

In the spring of 1878, twenty-year-old Ludeman arrived in Salmon and made his way with a partner to the Yellow Jacket mining district. They went to work for Henry Van Horn, but wanting their own mine, soon struck out on their own. Inexperienced but persistent, they finally found what they thought was a promising claim and made their stake. But the search had taken its toll. Their meager bankroll depleted, they left the area for Moose Creek Basin where they went to work for David McNutt, a well-known mine owner in the area. They planned to return to their claim once they had earned enough to purchase supplies.

While at Moose Creek, they met Tim O'Conner (O'Conor). A Canadian, O'Conner was an alias for John McCullough, a thirty-seven-year-old drifter who arrived in Idaho in 1874. He befriended Ludeman, gained his confidence, and eventually learned of his claim. Ludeman had big dreams of establishing a mine and told O'Conner he was positive there was plenty of gold on his claim. O'Conner saw an easy mark and convinced the young German to let him in on the mine, which he did. The three then left Moose Creek and went back to Yellow Jacket to make their fortunes.

Unfortunately, the mine did not produce and neither did O'Conner. He became quarrelsome and impatient. Although Ludeman shared what little profit they found, it was not enough for O'Conner. He threatened Ludeman and demanded part of the claim in return for his work. The usually calm Ludeman told O'Conner that before he would let him have any ground, "either you or I will die." Knowing he was no longer welcome, O'Conner left, swearing he would get even.

Ludeman and his partner toiled for several more months before abandoning the claim. They went their separate ways, and Ludeman returned to Moose Creek where he went back to work for McNutt and became friends with many of the miners in the area. O'Conner eventually drifted back and the bad blood between the two became obvious.

The conflict erupted in the fall of 1879. O'Conner publicly accused Ludeman of cheating him out of the mining claim. Ludeman went one better: he spread the word that O'Conner was a thief, accusing him of stealing a pistol belonging to Augustus Atkins, one of his friends. He even wrote to Lemhi County Sheriff Samuel Young informing him of the theft. According to O'Conner, when he went to confront Ludeman about the accusation, Ludeman and several of his friends "mobbed" him, pulling their pistols and threatening to kill him.

But others in Moose Creek remember the incident differently. According to Michael Cullenan, a miner at Moose Creek, Ludeman and his friends did not threaten O'Conner with guns. Instead, hoping to end the conflict once and for all, Ludeman challenged O'Conner to a fistfight, but O'Conner refused. Instead, O'Conner began making threats, obsessed about getting even. He told everyone from Moose Creek to Yellow Jacket, Leesburg to Salmon City that he would like to "kill the damned Dutch son-of-a-bitch." He would soon get his chance.

On February 3, 1880, O'Conner was hauling a load of supplies to Robert McNicoll who owned an establishment in Leesburg. Because of heavy snows, he traveled on snowshoe, pulling a loaded toboggan behind him. About three-quarters of a mile from Leesburg, he met Ludeman on the trail. O'Conner would claim that as he attempted to pass Ludeman, the German pushed him off the trail and knocked him down. Ludeman denied the accusation, stating they simply passed each other on the trail. Whatever happened, Ludeman arrived in Leesburg in the afternoon about an hour ahead of O'Conner.

Upon his arrival, O'Conner stopped at the cabin of John Stover. He told Stover that Ludeman had tried to shove him off the trail, and if the "big Dutch son of a bitch looks crap at me again, I'll kill him."

After he left Stover's, he delivered the supplies to McNicoll's store. There he began drinking. He watched as Ludeman and others took part in friendly snowshoe races on the hill near the store and boasted to McNicoll that he could beat any of them, even pulling his toboggan. Then he told the shopkeeper that he was going "back up the mountain" and would return with more supplies the next day. He asked for his pistol, which McNicoll had been keeping for him, and the shopkeeper gave it to him. With gun in hand, he left the store and asked McNicoll to follow. Outside, he pointed

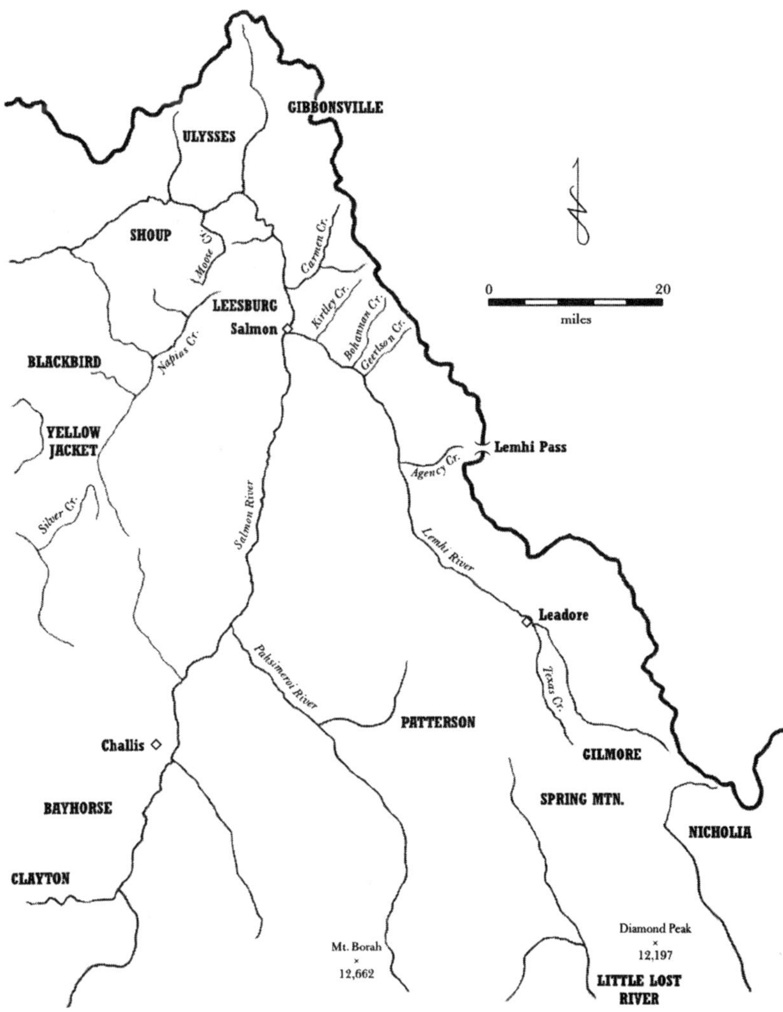

at Ludeman, "There is that damned Dutch son of a bitch," he said waving the gun. "I have something here I will shove into him."

McNicoll persuaded O'Conner back inside and tried to calm him. O'Conner then said he would leave if he could have two bottles of gin. McNicoll obliged, but O'Conner refused to go, instead continuing his tirade against Ludeman and his friends from Moose Creek. Calling them "prick-licking sons of bitches," he promised he would "fix" them. McNicoll, tired of the conversation, left the store.

Main Street, Leesburg

As the day wore into night, O'Conner continued to drink, the alcohol stoking his anger. By six o'clock others began to filter into the establishment, including Ludeman. He sat at the bar, away from O'Conner but could not help overhear the barrage of profanity aimed at the "damned Moose Creek fellows." When O'Conner mentioned Ludeman's friends, William Smith and Gus Atkins, Ludeman left.

He went to the cabin of John Stover where he had supper. While there, he took out his pistol, a five-shooter, and finding it was wet, he asked Stover if he could put it on the windowsill to dry. He then left, returning to McNicoll's store where he found a still ranting O'Conner. In fact, for two and a half hours O'Conner had been abusing the Moose Creek men, calling them "damned cock suckers" and "prick-eating sons of bitches." Ludeman listened for a few minutes, then left again, returning to Stover's cabin. He picked up his gun and put it in his pocket. If there was going to be a fight, he wanted to be ready.

Upon reentering McNicoll's, Ludeman sat down at the counter across the room from O'Conner. O'Conner, who was now seated at a table, watched him come in. Talking to no one in particular, he claimed there was a group of men on Moose Creek who had clubbed together and wanted to mob him. At that comment, Ludeman stood up and calmly approached O'Conner. As he came forward, he cocked the pistol in his pocket.

"Damn you, that's enough of this," Ludeman told O'Conner. "Dry up or you'll get hurt."

"You son of a bitch," O'Conner responded, "are you cocking that at me?"

They were only eight feet apart when they pulled their weapons and fired. O'Conner shot first, the bullet striking Ludeman in the thigh while Ludeman's grazed O'Conner's side. Ludeman retreated as both he and O'Conner fired a second time, and both were struck in their non-shooting hands. Ludeman staggered backward and tried to get off one more shot, but his gun misfired. He turned toward the door and O'Conner fired one more time. The shot would doom both of them.

Frank Limpach and George Clemow witnessed the first shots before dashing outside. Close behind was Ludeman. They watched as he staggered about twenty feet and then fell, calling "Oh, boys, I am shot through the bowels." As Clemow rushed to his side, O'Conner appeared in the doorway, gun raised. Clemow shouted at him to stop shooting, and Limpach went to get help. When he returned, they carried Ludeman into the store and laid him on the floor. They removed his shirt and pants, packed his wounds with bandages, and realized they needed a doctor. Michael Cullenan left for Salmon City to find Dr. George Kenney.

Despite his wounds, O'Conner continued his tirade against Ludeman. Eventually, McNicoll managed to get him into a bed in the back room of the store, but even then he continued to act like a "crazy man" claiming that if Ludeman "don't die now, I will fix him." O'Conner even asked McNicoll for a gun so he could "finish the Dutch son of a bitch." But as the night wore on and the effects of the liquor began to wane, O'Conner turned sullen. Thinking his wounds were fatal, he told McNicoll to write his father and tell him what happened. Then he added that it would be difficult for his father to hear that "his son John McCullough had been killed out here by a damned Dutchman." After this comment, he drifted off to sleep. When he awoke, he made no further comments about his identity or the shooting.

When Dr. Kenney arrived in Leesburg on February 5, he found Ludeman alert but suffering. He removed the bullets from Ludeman's thigh and hand, then turned his attention to the stomach wound. The bullet had torn through the stomach; he could do little to help Ludeman. When the doctor advised him the wound was probably fatal, Ludeman did not believe him, saying he was "not injured so much." But the next day, as the infection worsened, Ludeman realized he would not recover. He was resigned to his fate, but disappointed at his end, claiming, "My God, it is a hard thing to be shot down by such a wretch as he is."

On the morning of February 6, a still lucid Ludeman dictated a statement concerning the shootout to Dr. Kenney. Robert Stover and

William Martin served as witnesses. His dying declaration came just in time. By the afternoon, he was racked with fever and rational only at intervals. He died the next morning at 11 a.m.

Following Ludeman's death, Dr. Kenney examined the body. Calling it the "most perfect body" he had ever seen, he concluded that the fatal bullet had entered the left side of Ludeman's back approximately three inches from the spine. The bullet passed unimpeded into his stomach, perforating it and causing his death.

The next day, Dr. Kenney and the men of Leesburg escorted

James Hawley
prosecuted O'Conner.

O'Conner and Ludeman's body to Salmon. Here, O'Conner was jailed to await the findings of the coroner. On February 23, Lemhi County Coroner John Richardson held an inquest. He concluded that Ludeman died as the result of a gunshot fired by Timothy O'Conner. O'Connor then appeared before probate judge E. T. Beatty who found sufficient evidence to hold O'Connor without bail until a district court grand jury could be convened.

On July 13, a grand jury indicted O'Conner on first-degree murder charges. The same day, O'Conner made his first appearance in the Third District Court of Idaho Territory where he told Judge John T. Morgan that his true and full name was Timothy O'Connor. As he was without counsel, Morgan appointed John S. Fain and James L. Onderdonk to defend him. Although Morgan asked him to make his plea on that day, he deferred on the advice of counsel. The following day, he told the judge he was not guilty. Judge Morgan set July 19 as the opening day of the trial.

O'Conner and his attorneys appeared on July 19 and requested a continuance until the next term of court. According to O'Conner two men—Garley (Gorley) and Tracy—were material witnesses who would state that Ludeman had made numerous death threats against him. O'Conner asked that the trial be delayed until they could be found. Morgan thought otherwise and denied the continuance. The trial commenced with jury selection and Prosecutor James Hawley's opening statement. When court adjourned for the day, Morgan ordered the jury members sequestered for the duration of the trial. He appointed deputy James Fuller to look after them.

Over the course of the next two days, Hawley built his case. McNicoll and Stover testified about O'Conner's behavior and threats toward Ludeman on the day of the shooting. Over the objections of the defense, he produced six other witnesses who also heard O'Conner make threats against Ludeman in the days and months leading up to the shooting. He led Limpach and Clemow through their eyewitness testimony, and introduced the statement Ludeman had dictated from his deathbed. But Hawley still had a problem. Neither Limpach nor Clemow actually saw O'Conner fire the shot that killed Ludeman. By the time that shot was fired, they were both outside. For that, Hawley relied on Dr. Kenney who was unshakeable in his testimony. Ludeman had been shot in the back; Dr. Kenney had the clothes and the bullet to prove it.

To save himself, O'Conner took the stand. He testified the shooting was done in self-defense, as Ludeman fired the first shot. He also stated that he had fired only twice, and he was certain his first shot was a misfire. As for the threats against Ludeman, he denied them claiming, "I did not say one word to insult Ludeman." However, he did admit to using bad language against the Moose Creek men, but that was because he was under the influence of whisky.

The defense attempted to bolster the self-defense claim by producing two witnesses who testified they heard Ludeman make threats against O'Conner and then told O'Conner of those threats. But Prosecutor Hawley moved to strike their testimony, and Judge Morgan agreed.

On July 21, attorneys made their closing arguments, and Judge Morgan gave his instructions to the jury. He explained the difference between first and second-degree murder and manslaughter. He also told them that O'Conner could not claim self-defense if he provoked the fight or if Ludeman was retreating at the time of the fatal shot. With the information, the jury took little time to make its decision. O'Conner was guilty of first-degree murder.

On July 22, O'Conner's lawyers filed a motion for a new trial. They cited the usual reasons—the verdict was contrary to the evidence, the judge's directions did not follow the law—but their strongest complaint was jury misconduct.

Although the jury was supposed to be sequestered, Deputy Fuller was negligent in his duties. On one occasion he allowed three of the jurors to go into a saloon where they had drinks and visited with some of the locals. On another occasion, Fuller left the jurors on the sidewalk while he went into a saloon and had a brandy.

Judge Morgan called for a hearing to look into the allegations. Fuller admitted that he allowed the three jurors to go to the saloon to get a drink. But the saloon was right next to the deliberation room; they were gone but a short time, and they were not under the influence of liquor when they returned. As for his own drink of brandy, Fuller said he needed the drink because he was not feeling well. He was only in the saloon a minute, and he had his eyes on the jury the entire time, as they were standing on the sidewalk waiting for him. Morgan was clearly not pleased with Fuller's indiscretions, but he did not believe they were reason enough to call for a new trial. He denied the motion.

With the legal wrangling out of the way, O'Conner was back in court the next day. Judge Morgan wasted no time and sentenced O'Conner to hang. The execution would take place on September 17, 1880. As Prosecutor Hawley was concerned about the lax state of affairs in Lemhi County, he asked the judge to order Sheriff Young to provide a special guard for the Lemhi County jail, adding that the county should pay for it. Judge Morgan so ordered.

The verdict and impending execution divided Lemhi County. Letters were written and a petition with 123 signatures was sent to Territorial Governor John B. Neil, asking him to commute O'Conner's sentence to life in prison. Claiming that O'Conner did not have the means to hire an attorney to take his case to the territorial supreme court, they believed justice would be better served if his life was spared. But others, including Dr. Kenney, Frank Limpach, and John Stover, sent their own petition. Citing the recent influx of miners into Lemhi County, many of them unruly and lawless, they asked the governor to let the "law take its course and justice be done." They told the governor they could not feel secure if "desperadoes like O'Conner shall go unpunished after committing the gravest crime known to the law."

While the governor took the matter under consideration, O'Conner's case was appealed to the supreme court. It is unclear who filed the appeal, and no one appeared on O'Conner's behalf. In fact, the appeal was completely void of information; there was no bill of exceptions, no assignment of errors, nothing for the court to consider. But because of the gravity of the case, the court reviewed the indictment, the trial minutes, and the judge's instructions. The justices could find no errors and as such, affirmed the judgment.

As for O'Conner, he remained under guard in the county jail threatening everyone involved with his trial including the jury and Prosecutor Hawley. As for Judge Morgan, O'Conner wanted "five minutes of liberty, a double-barreled shot gun, and Judge Morgan before it." Then he would die happy.

He would never get the chance. Although he made one escape attempt—he used a pipe and a candle as a makeshift blowpipe to burn through a log in his cell—he was a condemned man. On September 10, Governor Neil, who was out of the territory, informed acting governor R. A. Sidebotham that the governor "would not be justified in interfering" with the decisions of the court. He would not commute O'Conner's sentence to life in prison.

With that, O'Conner's fate was sealed. On September 17, 1880, still proclaiming he was the victim, he was hanged in the county jail yard on a scaffold built specifically for him. As O'Conner stood above the trap, he told the crowd, "I die innocent of murder. I only defended my own life."

His execution went unreported by all the major newspapers in the territory, save the *Yankee Fork Herald*, who called the execution "a warning and example to all would be murderers." In case they did not get the message, Sheriff Young left the gallows intact for the next nine years, a reminder to all that murder would not be tolerated in Lemhi County.

6. Murder Most Foul

Raymond A. Snowden

September 22, 1956
October 18, 1957

Few people remember his name, but those who lived in Boise in 1956 can still remember his crime. Raymond Allen Snowden, the last man hanged in Idaho, committed one of the grisliest murders in Boise history where the lurid details of his crime still circulate.

The dark and tawdry night clubs of Garden City—favored by transients, prostitutes, and lonely men—set the scene for Snowden's final violent act. The Pink Elephant, the Lone Pine, the Alpine Club, Don & Dell's, the HiHo—to name a few—catered to those looking for a good time, with dance music and plenty of beer and hard liquor to go around. Snowden hit most of them on the night of September 22, 1956, the same night he brutally murdered and then mutilated the body of Cora Lucyle Dean. His crime was the culmination of a two-week drinking binge and a life filled with violence and despair.

Snowden was born in Middleboro, Massachusetts on October 22, 1921. While his mother would describe his childhood home as "clean, comfortable, and cheerful," Snowden saw it differently. One of eight children, he remembered much dissension in the family, calling his home "unpleasant." Times were especially difficult in 1929 when Snowden's father, who suffered from tuberculosis, was sent to a sanitarium. The family went on government assistance, and Snowden found himself disciplined by his older brothers and sisters. They beat him severely, the scars of those beatings still evident on his back on the day he died.

His life of crime began early. At eleven, he broke into a store. He was caught, and a series of foster homes followed. When a home didn't suit him, he would run away. In all, he went through twelve foster homes. He dropped out of school and was eventually sent to a reform school, the Lyman School for Boys in Westborough, Massachusetts. He had difficulties there getting along with the staff. "There was constant pushing and threats and abuse," Snowden said of the school. In 1939, he left.

In January 1940, he joined the Civilian Conservation Corps and went to Vermont. He stayed with the CCC's until 1941, then joined the

National Guard. His unit was mobilized in March of 1941, and he was sent to Florida.

The service was not a good fit for Snowden. He had a difficult time following orders, disliked the intimidation, and had trouble forming relationships. After a year in the service, he'd had enough. In an altercation with a sergeant at Camp Blanding, Snowden threw the first punch and broke his superior's jaw. He was placed in the guardhouse but promptly escaped. He was captured, dishonorably discharged, and incarcerated for one year in the Camp Blanding stockade.

He returned home to Massachusetts but was not welcome. He had difficulty finding a job because of his record, and his family offered him little support. His sister tried to get him a job, but then, according to Snowden, she continually meddled in his private affairs. "They never tried to help me through any rough spots," Snowden would say of his family. "They just didn't care." After four years of a life going nowhere, he left Massachusetts, never to return. His mother helped him pack.

He spent the next ten years as a drifter, seldom holding on to a job for more than six months. He set pins in a bowling alley, drove long haul truck, worked construction, followed the wheat harvest from Texas to the Dakotas. At almost every stop, he found himself in trouble with the law. Each offense was a little more serious, a little more violent. In South Carolina, he robbed a girl at knifepoint. He stabbed a woman in Texas. He went to jail in California on robbery charges. Each time he was released, he moved on.

Women were always the core of his problems. He always seemed to have one, although he would admit he had little or no respect for them. It wasn't that he didn't like women, but he had "a low regard for them. I would say that most of them are not worth a damn, the biggest share of them, from what I have met." Still he pursued them, but the pursuit led to guilt. He admitted if he had his way with a woman, he felt unclean and tried to get away from her. But then, if he saw her again, he would once again want her. It was a vicious circle of lust, guilt, lust.

Snowden married at least twice. His first marriage came in 1945 in New York to seventeen-year-old Vivian Fiero. The marriage lasted less than one year. During this time, Vivian gave birth, but Snowden refused to accept paternity. He next married Dorothy Farrell in Quartzite, Arizona, but the details of this marriage are vague. While one account states they married in 1947, Snowden thought it could have been 1950. The union may

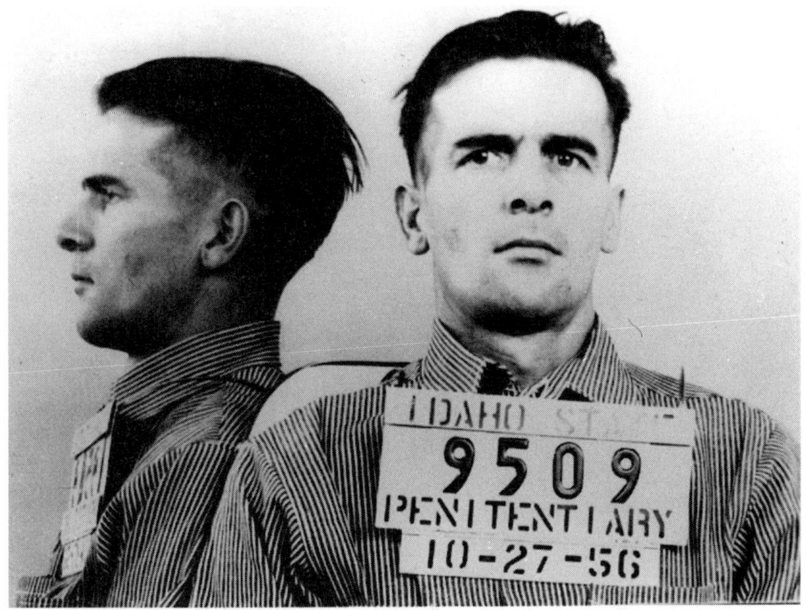

Raymond Snowden

have produced a son, Oscar Harry, although Snowden denied this. The relationship with Dorothy was like the others, short-lived. After she had him arrested for assault, he moved on to other towns and women. "I was always looking for something else," he said.

To compound his problems with women, Snowden liked to drink—a lot. He admitted to drinking "a hell of a lot every night," and if he had the money he would get "staggering drunk." For twelve days leading up to the murder of Cora Dean, he drank constantly, and on September 22, he had been drinking the entire day.

The drinking binge was initiated by his live-in girlfriend Marcell (Marcy) Cobb. The two had struck up a relationship in Portland, where Snowden had spent over a year working in the shipyards. When the work ran out, Snowden made his way to Boise and Marcy followed. The two moved into the Milner Hotel at 1005 Grove Street, and Snowden found work at a hardware store downtown.

Marcy spent most of her time drinking, which caused frequent fights between the couple. "She'd get blind every weekend," he said of her drinking. "I like to get a buzz on, but I don't like getting that blind drunk."

Unfortunately, Snowden seldom heeded his own words. In July 1956 Snowden returned home from work, expecting to find dinner ready. Instead

Chinden Avenue, Garden City, 1950s

he found an empty apartment. Tired and angry, he walked to the XXXX Club to find Marcy "sitting on a stool about half-crocked." Snowden admitted he lost his temper and "belted her and knocked her off her stool." While Marcy picked herself up and went home to make dinner, Snowden stormed off to another bar, where he proceeded to get roaring drunk. When he made it back to the apartment, he "worked her over pretty good," perhaps even pulling a knife. The police arrived, and Snowden spent the rest of the night in the county jail. The next day, Marcy refused to press charges and Snowden was released. But the fights and physical abuse continued and in September, she left him for good, running off to Montana with another man.

The move sent Snowden into a tailspin. On September 10, he had another run-in with the Boise police after he was accused of attempting to rape a pregnant woman. Supposedly he held a knife to the back of the woman's neck and threatened to cut out her child if she did not have sex with him. Somehow the woman escaped and told authorities, but when they questioned Snowden, he denied any involvement. The husband, however, took matters into his own hands. He paid a visit to Snowden's apartment and proceeded to teach him a lesson. The police were called, and when they arrived found Snowden at the mercy of the husband. Snowden wanted the man arrested, but the police let him go. No charges were ever filed against either man.

The beating put Snowden over the edge. Hotel guests remember him drinking heavily both night and day, and any mention of Marcy sent him into a tirade. Then on September 22, after a day of drinking and shooting pool with his friend Richard Carrier, he learned Marcy was back in town. It was time to track her down. He didn't count on Cora Dean getting in the way.

Cora Lucyle Bundy Dean was born in Kansas in 1908 to Lucy and Claude Bundy. Following Claude's death sometime before 1920, Lucy and Cora made their way to Boise where Lucy opened a dressmaking shop. It is unclear whether Cora attended school, but in December 1924, she married Norville Brough, a Utah native. In 1927, Cora filed for a divorce, claiming Norville had abandoned her and failed to provide the "common necessaries to live," even though he had the ability to do so.

Cora's whereabouts and activities are unknown between 1930-1950, but in 1954, she married Sinclair M. Dean in Las Vegas, Nevada. The honeymoon ended quickly as Dean abandoned her after only one month. From Las Vegas she moved to Winnemucca, Nevada and then to Pasadena, California, before returning to Boise in April of 1956. Once in Boise, she moved in with her mother at 914 Logan Street and filed for divorce from Dean, charging him with desertion. She did not find employment but found an eligible bachelor in Howard Wade, a barber.

Wade had an apartment at 1109 Jefferson Street. Early in the evening on September 22, Cora met him there. They were joined by Del and Edith Merrill. Around 7 p.m. they drove to the Merrill home on 616 S. 13th where they had hamburgers and beers. It is unclear exactly how many beers Cora had, but at some point, she and Wade argued. Wade decided to go home, but Cora refused to leave. He gave her five dollars to get a cab and then left angrily. Cora stayed at the Merrill's until 9 p.m. when she hailed a cab and headed for Garden City.

Cora stopped first at the Ranch Club. She told the cab driver to wait and went into the club. She returned shortly and instructed the driver to take her to the HiHo. After getting change from the bartender, she paid the cabbie and arranged to be picked up at midnight. The driver would later recall that Cora did not seem drunk. She was a no-show at midnight.

Once at the HiHo, Cora wasted no time in starting her party. She ordered a drink and set up camp at one end of the bar. She danced with several men and struck up a conversation with Mary Menke. According to Menke, Cora was noticeably intoxicated; she was quite friendly and talking very loudly, announcing that she was "not supposed to be out here tonight, but I am, and I'm going to have a good time."

Cora was firmly ensconced at the HiHo bar when Snowden made his fateful decision to find Marcy. Around 9 p.m., he and Richard Carrier drove to Garden City where they stopped at five different clubs. Snowden had at least one beer at each, searching the crowds for his former girlfriend.

At about 9:45 p.m., Snowden and Carrier arrived at the HiHo. Snowden ordered a drink, a Seagram's 7 with seven-up, and made his way to the end of the bar. Although Snowden would later testify that he didn't know Cora, having only seen her a few times "at joints up town," witnesses would recall that when Snowden approached her and tapped her on the shoulder, Cora seemed delighted to see him. They struck up a conversation, and Cora asked him to dance. Although he refused at first, Cora persisted, and the two danced at least twice. During this time, Carrier left the HiHo, and Snowden was on his own to find a ride home.

Tired and drunk, Snowden left the HiHo sometime after ten. An intoxicated Cora followed him, and outside the club they argued. Cora wanted to continue her partying uptown and insisted Snowden join her, paying for both the cab ride and the drinks to come. Snowden thought otherwise. A scuffle ensued in which Cora kneed Snowden in the groin, and he retaliated with a backhand to her face. The physical confrontation brought them momentarily back to their senses. They calmed down and began walking toward a Phillips 66 station on the corner of Chinden and 38th Street. Their plan was to use the phone there to call a cab.

They never reached the phone. Snowden decided he didn't want to spend the evening with Cora and turned around to go back to the HiHo. Cora, angry, hit him and kneed him again. According to Snowden, he "blew his top," and in the shadows of Kern's Paint Store, located across the street from the service station, he took out thirty-five years of anger and frustration on Cora.

His reaction was violent and swift. He pushed her to the ground, and using his pocketknife with a 2-¼ inch blade, he savagely destroyed her. An initial slash to her throat quieted her screams. Then he stabbed her once in the abdomen and several times around the eyes. Death came with one slice to the base of her skull, which severed her spinal cord. The murderous attack took less than a minute.

But Snowden wasn't through. Enraged, he continued to attack Cora's lifeless body. He cut away her clothes, leaving her exposed. He attacked her breasts, her pelvis, her vagina. He attempted to cut off her left breast, and when he failed at that, he skinned away her right nipple. Then he did the unthinkable. He ate it. Then he was done.

He left Cora's body where it fell but took her wallet. He walked out to Chinden Boulevard and tried to flag down a car. Reo Tomlinson, a barber on his way to pick up his children at the Ada Theatre, saw Snowden in his rearview mirror. Thinking someone was in trouble, he turned around. When Tomlinson rolled down his window, Snowden told him he had been in a fight in one of the clubs and wanted to get out of Garden City. Tomlinson offered him a ride. In the car, Snowden was concerned about the blood he had on him, but Tomlinson only saw blood on the inside of his hands. Snowden got out of the car on the corner of 15th and Main and gave Tomlinson fifty cents for his trouble.

Staying in the shadows, Snowden walked to Boise City Recreation, a bowling alley on 12th and Main, where he had some friends. On the way, he threw his knife into a sewer drain in front of Hannifin's Cigar Store. Once at the bowling alley, he borrowed a pair of pants from one of the employees and used the bathroom, where he changed his clothes and flushed the contents of Cora's wallet. Then he left, heading toward his hotel. In the process, he got rid of his clothes and the wallet. He arrived at the Milner sometime between 11 p.m. and midnight. He left briefly, then returned shortly after 1 a.m. He was in his room when the body of Cora was discovered and news of the brutal slaying ripped through Boise.

A young boy who had been scouring the area for beer bottles discovered Cora's body. Terrified, the boy ran into the street where he found a Garden City patrolman. Upon seeing the body, the patrolman notified county officials and the hunt for her killer commenced. Officials from the Garden City Police, the Ada County Sheriff's Department, the Boise City Police, and the Ada County Prosecutor's office were involved in the investigation.

Boise Police Chief Frank Demarest took the lead in the investigation. On Monday, after the story of the murder appeared in the *Idaho Statesman*, leads poured into his office. The most promising came from Reo Tomlinson and other witnesses who placed Cora and Snowden together at the HiHo.

Boise police also recalled Snowden's attack of Marcy just months earlier. They knew right where to find him, and by noon on Monday, he was in custody. Demarest, Ada County Sheriff Pat McCarty, and Ada County Prosecutor Blaine Evans tag-teamed the interrogation, and around 7 p.m. that evening, Snowden confessed to the crime. He was arraigned shortly before midnight and charged with first-degree murder.

Both Demarest and McCarty added to the drama of the case. Demarest told the press the crime was an "atrocious, sadistic murder, committed by an apparent sex psychopath." He added that the details of the murder were so sordid, they were only fit to come out at trial. McCarthy put his own spin on Snowden's confession, stating that Snowden killed Cora when "she refused his advances."

The police also sensationalized the murder by hinting Snowden was involved in similar cases across the country. Officials were especially curious about the 1941 murder of a Lyman, Massachusetts woman, a case that had never been solved. Later he was linked to a murder in Colorado. However, even after the FBI was brought in, police uncovered no connection between Snowden and any other murders.

While Snowden confessed to Cora's murder on his first day in custody, he was not completely forthcoming or honest with information he supplied. It took three more days of intense questioning before police finally had all the details. They recovered the knife Snowden had used but never found Cora's wallet or Snowden's clothes. They wouldn't need them. Prosecutor Evans would go to court with at least two signed confessions.

Snowden appeared in Third District Court on September 28 in front of Judge M. Oliver Koelsch. There he heard the formal charges against him. He did not enter a plea, but instead told the judge he wanted "to talk to a lawyer." Koelsch promised to appoint one and scheduled a plea hearing for October 5.

Koelsch appointed J. Fred Cromwell to represent Snowden, and from the beginning, Cromwell struggled to defend his client: the crime was too sensational, the confessions too damning, the public outcry too deafening. Snowden did little to help his case. While he pleaded not guilty at his preliminary hearing on October 5, within a week, he had changed his mind. On October 18, over the objections of his lawyer, he appeared before Koelsch again and asked to withdraw his plea. Although the judge warned him of the consequences, Snowden was insistent. He changed his plea to guilty and Koelsch set October 23 for the sentencing hearing.

Idaho Prison Warden Lou Clapp was in charge of Snowden's execution.

Prosecutor Evans made it clear from the beginning that he was seeking the death penalty. Besides Snowden's signed confessions, he had the murder weapon, Snowden's bloody shoes, and numerous eyewitnesses. Even more damning was the testimony of Ada County Coroner Joseph Beeman who described in detail Cora's wounds and presented colored pictures of her ravaged body. Although Cromwell objected to the pictures as prejudicial, Koelsch allowed them.

Evans also called Dr. Dale Cornell, a psychiatrist who had examined Snowden. Cornell testified that although Snowden had a mental illness—he was a psychopath—he was not insane and certainly knew right from wrong. Evans concluded that Snowden was impulsive, a hedonist, and a man who acted exclusively in his best interests. He also added that Snowden had no sense of responsibility for his actions. However, none of these behaviors made him crazy.

Cromwell tried to build on Cornell's testimony to save Snowden's life. In his closing statement, he acknowledged Snowden killed Cora, but argued the murder was impulsive. Based on the doctor's testimony, Cromwell claimed, "An action of impulse cannot and does not carry either deliberation or premeditation." Snowden's comment that he "blew his top" confirmed that he acted on impulse. Thus, while the murder was gruesome, it was not planned, and Cromwell asked the judge to consider the charge of voluntary manslaughter in sentencing.

But the crime was too horrific. In his sentencing comments, Judge Koelsch stated there were no extenuating or mitigating circumstances in the crime. The fact that Snowden had taken the time to remove his knife from his pocket and open it showed intent. Looking directly at Snowden, Koelsch told him that the crime was "conceived from a callous disregard of human life and carried out in utter defiance of moral and legal standards." With that, Koelsch sentenced Snowden to hang, setting December 7 as the execution date.

Snowden appealed the sentence and a stay of execution was granted. In January, Cromwell appeared before the Idaho Supreme Court and argued to save Snowden's life. He reiterated to the court that Snowden's act was not a result of malice or premeditation; it was an act of impulse caused by his mental illness. He added that Snowden's alcohol consumption that night also contributed to his impulsiveness, and in ignoring these issues, the judge had overreached in sentencing Snowden to death.

But the justices were unconvinced. On July 24, 1957, they issued their findings. Writing for the majority, Justice Henry McQuade dismissed all of Cromwell's arguments.

"The full purpose and design of the defendant's conduct was to take the life of the deceased," McQuade wrote. "The court had no other alternative than to find the defendant guilty of willful, deliberate, and premeditated killing in view of the defendant's acts of deliberately opening up a pocket knife and then hacking and cutting until he had killed Cora Lucyle Dean." He added, "This case exemplifies an abandoned and malignant heart and sadistic mind, bent on taking human life. The imposition of the death sentence was not an abuse of discretion. The judgment is affirmed."

With that, Snowden's fate was sealed and he knew it. He refused to allow Cromwell to request a new hearing before the supreme court. He did not ask for a hearing before the state pardons board. Instead, he remained in solitary confinement at the Idaho State Penitentiary waiting for a new execution date. It came soon enough, midnight, October 18.

A loner in life, Snowden remained so during his last few months of confinement, the only man condemned to death out of 712 other prisoners. He spoke little, not even to the guards. He opened up only to Orville Stiles, the prison chaplain. Stiles learned that Snowden was an avid reader and brought him books and crossword puzzles. Stiles brought him a Bible, and Snowden spent most of his final days reading it. He refused to write to his mother, but did correspond with a sister who advised him "the Bible would help him some." One member of his family came to visit, a brother. He also sent money, which Snowden spent on cigarettes and hard candy. That same brother telegrammed prison officials on October 17 to inform them that no one from the family intended to claim the body.

On the night of his execution, Snowden ordered his last meal—lobster, sweet potatoes, asparagus, a tossed salad, cranberry sauce, hot rolls, tea, and strawberry shortcake—but when the time came, he could only eat a few bites. As the night lengthened, he and Stiles waited, sharing a pot of tea and his final thoughts.

For the first time, prison officials would use their new execution chamber. Located on the second floor of the Cell Block Five, next to death row, the room replaced the outside scaffold used for earlier prison hangings. Throughout the day, guards repeatedly tested the trap door to ensure all would be ready for Snowden. The sound of the door dropping reverberated through the cell block; guards would recall the prisoners were eerily quiet that evening.

Around 11:45 p.m., prison guards arrived at Snowden's cell. They carried a backboard complete with arm, leg, and foot straps. Snowden balked at first, but with Stiles' assurances, he allowed himself to be strapped in. They delivered him to the execution room and placed him in an upright position. The hangman's noose dangled directly above his head.

Approximately ten people gathered in the observation room, among them Boise Police Chief Frank Demarest and Ada County Sheriff Pat McCarty, who had so deftly built the case against Snowden. Several newspaper reporters were also at the execution, but all declined to enter the observation room.

With Snowden in place on the trap door, Prison Warden Lou Clapp asked if he had any final words. Snowden, calm and clear, replied, "I do, but I don't know how to say it." Clapp gave him a few more minutes, then placed a black hood over his head. He stepped back and the executioner, who received $600 for his trouble, stepped forward. He placed the noose around Snowden's neck, pushed the knot close to his spine, and pulled the trap door. The backboard veered a bit, scraping the side of the trap, but the deed was done. Snowden was pronounced dead at 12:20 a.m., October 18, 1957.

While in prison, Snowden gave officials an account of his life. Nothing was ever his fault. His mistreatment at home, at school, in foster homes, in the army—all led to his bad behavior. No matter what the incident, he was never to blame. The chip on his shoulder was a forest of excuses. Only near the end did he realize he had gone too far.

"Do you think your crime was so bad that not even God can forgive you?" Chaplain Stiles asked him.

"Yes," Snowden replied.

He would be the last man hanged by the State of Idaho. His body lies in an unmarked grave in the old penitentiary cemetery.

Acknowledgments

Book ideas come to me in the middle of the night. That is my only explanation for how I chose the topic for *Hanged*. For the past six years, the men of *Hanged* have haunted my dreams and cluttered my desk. As I put the finishing touches on their stories, I hope I did them justice.

I am thankful for all the people who helped in the creation of *Hanged*. Most important is the incredible staff at the Idaho State Historical Library and Archives—Rod House, Jon Yandell, Kathy Hodges, Carolyn Bowler, Linda Morton-Keithly, among others—who searched through boxes and stacks of court records, county records, inmate files, photos, maps, and miscellaneous materials to find the evidence I needed to create this book. The work they do to preserve Idaho's history is invaluable.

I also need to thank Jim Rush, Francie Ford, and Marquita Blanton who read the early stories and gave valuable advice on what to leave in and what to take out. As for my peace-loving editor, Renee Silvus, her enthusiasm, attention to detail, and sharp pencil were much appreciated. The same can be said for JoAnn Livermore who gave this book a final proofread.

I am forever indebted to Shelly Chamberlain, a former student and now a fine teacher, who patiently answered all of my questions concerning pages and pixels and PDFs.

Finally, I must thank my husband Bob for his constant support. His encouragement and positive outlook influence me every day.

About the Author

Kathy Deinhardt Hill was raised in Idaho. She lives near McCall with her husband Bob where her other interests include gardening, cycling, and hiking.

Other books by the author

Spirits of the Salmon River—a history of the men and women buried along the banks of the Salmon River. Published by Backeddy Books.

On the Road: Twenty Great Day Trips from McCall—a travel guide for destinations near McCall. Published by Big Mallard Books.

For Better or Worse: The Legacy of William "Deadshot" Reed—the story of William Reed and his family who homesteaded on the South Fork of the Salmon River. Published by Big Mallard Books.

Biking the Backroads—a bicycle guide to recreational rides around McCall. Co-authored with Ellen McKinney. Published by Big Mallard Books.

To order any book by Kathy Deinhardt Hill, please contact:
Big Mallard Books
14068 Pioneer Road
McCall, Idaho 83638

SOURCES

History of Idaho Courts

Arrington, Leonard J. *History of Idaho*, Vol. 1. Moscow, Idaho: University of Idaho Press, 1994.

Bianchi, Carl F., ed. *Justice for the Times: A Centennial History of the Idaho State Courts*. Boise: Idaho Law Foundation, 1990.

"Capital punishment bill repeal overwhelmingly beaten in Senate. *Idaho Statesman* (Boise), Jan. 13, 1961.

Cenarrusa, Pete. *General and Special Laws of the State of Idaho*. Caldwell: Caxton's, 1973.

Death Penalty Information Center. "History of the Death Penalty." www.deathpenaltyinfo.org (accessed May 22, 2007).

------. *General and Special Laws of the State of Idaho*. Caldwell: Caxton's, 1978.

Doty, Kay. *The Old Idaho Territorial-State Prison*. Boise: Horse Publishing and Printing.

Ellinger, Charles. "Execution has strong support." *Idaho Statesman* (Boise), Dec. 27, 1993.

Fick, Bob. "Death penalty signed into law." *Idaho Statesman* (Boise), Feb. 14, 2003.

Hahn, Gregory. "Death penalty moves a step closer toward reinstatement." *Idaho Statesman* (Boise), Feb. 1, 2003.

"Idaho senate takes aim at firing squad option." *Idaho Statesman* (Boise), March 23, 2009.

"Legal Executions in Idaho." *Idaho State Historical Society Reference Series*. #1127. 1995.

Morrissey, David. "Idaho execution raises old debate." *Times-News* (Twin Falls, Idaho), July 27, 1979.

------------. "Two sit on Idaho's Death Row." *Idaho State Journal* (Pocatello), Dec. 2, 1976.

Steelwater, Eliza. *The Hangman's Knot: Lynching, Legal Executions, and America's Struggle with the Death Penalty*. Boulder: Westview Press, 2003.

Trillhaase, Martin. "Death penalty reinstated, 60-10 vote." *Idaho State Journal* (Pocatello), March 8, 1977.

Wells, Merle W. *Gold Camps and Silver Cities*. Moscow, Idaho: University of Idaho Press, 2002.

Woolheim, Peter. "A Place of Confinement: Constructing the Old Idaho State Penitentiary 1872-1973." 1993. www.idahohistorynet/OldPenConfinement.pdf (accessed March 15, 2008).

Yu, Li-hua. "Chinese Immigrants in Idaho." PhD diss., Bowling Green State University, 1991.

1. For Love

James Sidney Larkins

1870 U. S. Federal Census. Lynn, Weber, Utah Territory. *1870 United States Federal Census* [database on-line]. Provo, UT, USAL Ancestry.com Operations Inc, 2003.

"The Callihan suspects." *The Salt Lake Tribune*, Feb. 3, 1892.

"Callihan's slayer." *Utah Journal* (Logan), Jan. 27, 1892.

"Josie Hill is murdered." *The Salt Lake Tribune*, Dec. 26, 1895.

"Killed for money." *The Standard* (Ogden, Utah), June 6, 1891.

"The killing of Callahan." *The Salt Lake Tribune*, May 7, 1895.

"Larkins end." *The Salt Lake Tribune*, May 1, 1897.

"Larkins sent to jail." *The Salt Lake Tribune*, Jan. 1, 1896.

"The law vindicated." *The Blackfoot News* (Idaho), May 1, 1897.

"The mystery of Callahan." *The Salt Lake Tribune*, June 9, 1891.

Nichols, Jeffrey. *Prostitution, Polygamy, and Power: Salt Lake City, 1874-1918.* University of Illinois Press: Champaign, Illinois, 2002.

"Probably murder." *The Idaho Register* (Idaho Falls), Dec. 27, 1895.

The Salt Lake Tribune: June 6, 1891; June 10, 1891; June 21, 1891; Feb. 11, 1892; Jan. 7, 1896; Jan. 8, 1896; May, 9, 1896; April 28, 1897; April 29, 1897.

"Sid Larkins must hang." *The Salt Lake Tribune*, Feb. 4, 1897.

"Sidney Larkins hanged." *Idaho Daily Statesman* (Boise), May 1, 1897.

The Standard (Ogden, Utah). Jan. 26, 1892; Feb. 9, 1892.

State of Idaho vs. James Sidney Larkins. Transcript. Bingham County, Fifth Judicial District, March 1896. AR226. Idaho State Historical Society Public Archives and Research Library.

"State v. Larkins." *Reports of Cases Argued and Determined in the Supreme Court of State of Idaho.* Volume 5. Sol Hasbrouck, editor. San Francisco: Bancroft-Whitney Company, 1903. 200-213.

The Utah Journal (Logan, Utah), Jan. 27, 1892

Photo/Illustration Credits

Line drawing of Sidney Larkins and Josie Hill. *Salt Lake Tribune*, May 1, 1897. Provided by the University of Utah, Utah Digital Newspaper, on-line.

William Bond

1910 U.S. Federal Census. Boise, Ada, Idaho. *1910 United States Federal Census* [database on-line]. Provo, UT, USA: Ancestry.com Operations Inc, 2006.

1910 U.S. Federal Census. Silver City, Owhyhee, Idaho. *1910 United States Federal Census* [database on-line]. Provo, UT, USA: Ancestry.com Operations Inc, 2006.

"Bond begins to weaken." *Idaho Daily Statesman* (Boise), Oct. 9, 1904.

"Bond now on trial for murder." *Evening Capital News* (Boise), Oct. 7, 1904.

"Bond pays the death penalty for the murder of Charles Daly." *Idaho Daily Statesman* (Boise), Aug. 11, 1908.

Bond, William Henry (1091). Idaho State Prison File, AR42. Idaho State Historical Society Public Archives and Research Library.

"Bond's letter creates stir." *Idaho Daily Statesman* (Boise), Feb. 15, 1905.

Census Returns of England and Wales, 1881. Kew, Surrey, England: The National Archives of the UK (TNA): Public Record Office (PRO), 1881. Ancestry.com and The Church of Jesus Christ of Latter-day Saints. *1881 England Census* [database on-line]. Provo, UT, USA: Ancestry.com Operations Inc, 2004.

"Charles Daly is foully murdered." *Idaho Capital News* (Boise), Oct. 12, 1904.

Daly, Jennie (1096). Idaho State Prison File, AR42. Idaho State Historical Society Public Archives and Research Library.

Idaho Daily Statesman (Boise): Jan. 25, 1905; Feb. 8, 1905; Feb. 19, 1905; Feb. 21, 1905; Feb. 26, 1905.

"Is guilty of manslaughter." *Idaho Daily Statesman* (Boise), Feb. 23, 1905.

"Morbid women in courtroom." *Idaho Daily Statesman* (Boise), Feb. 7, 1905.

"Mrs. Daly is star witness." *Idaho Daily Statesman* (Boise), Feb. 12, 1905

"Mrs. Daly weeps at victim's bier." *Evening Capital News* (Boise), Oct. 8, 1904.

"Murder case set for trial." *Idaho Daily Statesman* (Boise), Jan. 27, 1905.

"Murder in the first degree." *Idaho Daily Statesman* (Boise), Feb. 16, 1905.

"Murdered in his own home." *Idaho Daily Statesman* (Boise), Oct. 7, 1904.

"Must answer for murder." *Idaho Daily Statesman* (Boise), Oct. 8, 1904.

"Must serve 10 years in prison." *Idaho Daily Statesman* (Boise), Feb. 26, 1905.

"Opening day of long term." *Idaho Daily Statesman* (Boise), Jan. 25, 1905.

"Out into the world after years in prison." *Idaho Daily Statesman* (Boise), May 26, 1911.

"Standing room at a premium." *Idaho Daily Statesman* (Boise), Feb. 10, 1905.

State of Idaho v William Henry Hicks Bond. Court Records. Ada County, Third Judicial District, January Term, 1905. AR202. Idaho State Historical Society Public Archives and Research Library.

"State v. Bond." *Reports of Cases Argued and Determined in the Supreme Court of State of Idaho*. Volume 12. I. W. Hart, editor. San Francisco: Bancroft-Whitney Company, 1907. 424-444.

"Sticks firmly to her story." *Idaho Daily Statesman* (Boise), Feb. 14, 1905.

"Story of Mrs. Daly's career." *Idaho Daily Statesman* (Boise), Feb. 22, 1905.

"Trial of Mrs. Daly is begun." *Idaho Daily Statesman* (Boise), Feb. 21, 1905.

"Widow held as an accomplice." *Idaho Daily Statesman* (Boise), Oct. 15, 1904.

PHOTO/ILLUSTRATION CREDITS

William Bond. Idaho State Historical Society. Inmate photo #1091.

Jennie Daly. Idaho State Historical Society. Inmate photo #1096.

Judge George Stewart. Idaho State Historical Society. Biography #107.

Fred Seward

1900 Federal Census. Republic, Ferry, Washington. *1900 United States Federal Census* [database on-line]. Provo, UT, USA: Ancestry.com Operations Inc, 2004.

1900 Federal Census. Wallace City, Shoshone, Idaho. *1900 United States Federal Census* [database on-line]. Provo, UT, USA: Ancestry.com Operations Inc, 2004.

1910 Federal Census. Spokane City, Spokane, Washington. *1910 United States Federal Census* [database on-line]. Provo, UT, USA: Ancestry.com Operations Inc, 2006.

"Case will test ordinance." *Star Mirror* (Moscow, Idaho), June 18, 1908.

"Commits murder and then attempts suicide." *Star Mirror* (Moscow, Idaho), Oct. 22, 1908.

"Moscow starts to clean town." *Spokesman Review* (Spokane, Washington), Jan. 8, 1908.

"Murderer now professes religion." *Idaho Daily Statesman* (Boise), May 3, 1909.

"Murderer Seward goes to death without a tremor." *Idaho Daily Statesman* (Boise), May 8, 1909.

"New penitentiary warden arrives." *Idaho Daily Statesman* (Boise), April 20, 1909.

Seward, Fred (1511). Idaho State Prison File, AR42. Idaho State Historical Society Public Archives and Research Library.

"Seward guilty of murder in the first degree." *Star Mirror* (Moscow, Idaho), Dec. 17, 1908.

"Seward is denied life imprisonment." *Star Mirror* (Moscow, Idaho), April 29, 1909.

"Seward lives in fear of the gallows." *Idaho Daily Statesman* (Boise), April 8, 1909.

"Seward pays penalty for atrocious crime." *Star Mirror* (Moscow, Idaho), May 6, 1909.

"Seward sentenced to be hanged February 19." *Star Mirror* (Moscow, Idaho), Dec. 31, 1908.

"Seward tells story of crime." *Idaho Daily Statesman* (Boise), May 5, 1909.

"Seward will have hearing." *Star Mirror* (Moscow, Idaho), Nov. 19, 1908.

Snook, John. *Biennial Report of the Idaho State Penitentiary: Fiscal Years 1909 and 1910.* AR42. Idaho State Historical Society Public Archives and Research Library.

State of Idaho v Fred M. Seward. Court Records, Latah County, Second Judicial District, December Term, 1908. District Court Book 6, Criminal Case #2, Registration # 331. Latah County Court Records, Moscow, Idaho.

"Stay of execution granted." *Idaho Daily Statesman* (Boise), Feb. 18, 1909.

"Three new prisoners." *Idaho Daily Statesman* (Boise), Jan. 3, 1909.

"To be hanged by neck until dead." *Idaho Daily Statesman* (Boise), May 7, 1909.

"Want Seward's sentence commuted." *Star Mirror* (Moscow, Idaho), Feb. 11, 1909.

Wegars, Priscilla. "'Inmates of Body Houses': Prostitution in Moscow, Idaho, 1885-1910." *Idaho Yesterdays*: 33, Spring 1989, 25-37.

"Will be no further delay." *Star Mirror* (Moscow, Idaho), Nov. 26, 1980.

Photo/Illustration Credits

William Seward. Idaho State Historical Society. Inmate photo #1511.

Seward Gallows. Idaho State Historical Society. Executions #78-2.58.

2. For Fortune

Herman St. Clair

"Attempted escape of St. Clair." *Idaho Semiweekly World* (Idaho City), April 26, 1898.

Barker, Reginald. "Pioneer Jailer Proves Himself a Hero Too, When Prisoner Escapes." *The Idaho Statesman* (Boise), Aug. 30, 1925.

Carrey, Johnny and Cort Conley. *The Middle Fork, a Guide*. Cambridge, Idaho: Backeddy Books, 1992.

"Dropped into eternity." *Idaho Semiweekly World* (Idaho City), June 24, 1898.

"Fight with St. Clair." *Idaho Daily Statesman* (Boise), June 26, 1898.

"Found Guilty." *Idaho Daily Statesman* (Boise), Nov. 18, 1897.

"H. C. St. Clair on trial." *Idaho Daily Statesman* (Boise), Nov. 16, 1897.

Idaho Semiweekly World (Idaho City): Nov. 2, 1892; Nov. 9, 1897; Nov. 12, 1897; Dec. 10, 1897; Jan. 4, 1898; Jan. 14, 1898; May 13, 1898; June 14, 1898.

"Murder in Long Valley." *Idaho Semiweekly World* (Idaho City), Oct. 29, 1897.

"Murderer St. Clair attempts to escape." *Idaho Daily Statesman* (Boise), April 23, 1898.

"Register and Descriptive List of Convicts under Sentence of Imprisonment in the State Prison of California." Corrections. California State Archives.

St. Clair, Herman. Death Warrant. AR205. Idaho State Historical Society Public Archives and Research Library.

"St. Clair murder trial." *Idaho Semiweekly World* (Idaho City), Nov. 19, 1897.

"St. Clair pays the penalty." *Idaho Daily Statesman* (Boise), June 25, 1898.

"St. Clair's past record." *Idaho Semiweekly World* (Idaho City), Nov. 23, 1897.

"Sentence of St. Clair." *Idaho Daily Statesman* (Boise), Nov. 21, 1897.

State of Idaho vs. Herman St. Clair. Transcript. Boise County, Third Judicial District, Nov. 1897. AR205. Idaho State Historical Society Public Archives and Research Library.

"State v. St. Clair." *Reports of Cases Argued and Determined in the Supreme Court of State of Idaho*. Volume 6. Sol Hasbrouck. San Francisco: Bancroft-Whitney Company, 1903. 109-113.

Valley County Idaho: Prehistory to 1920. Shelton Woods, ed. Roseberry, Idaho: Valley County History Project, 2001.

Photo/Illustration Credits

Herman St. Clair. San Quentin Prison. Photos of convicts under sentence of imprisonment in the state prison of California. California State Archives.

Herman St. Clair. Folsom Prison. Photos of convicts under sentence of imprisonment in the state prison of California. California State Archives.

Herman St. Clair. San Quentin Prison. Photos of convicts under sentence of imprisonment in the state prison of California. California State Archives.

Van Wyck. Idaho State Historical Society. Towns 70-42.142.

Herman St. Clair. Idaho State Historical Society. 62-14.19.

Michael Mooney

1870 U. S. Federal Census. Franklin, Cache, Utah Territory. *1870 United States Federal Census* [database on-line]. Provo, UT, USAL Ancestry.com Operations Inc, 2009.

1880 U. S. Federal Census. Cove Creek, Millard, Utah. *1880 United States Federal Census* [database on-line]. Provo, UT, USAL Ancestry.com Operations Inc, 2005.

"The Assassins." *Ogden Standard Examiner* (Utah), Nov. 11, 1881.

Bancroft, Hubert H. *Bancroft's Works, Vol. 31. History of Washington, Idaho and Montana, 1845-1889.* San Francisco: The History Company, 1890.

Barnes, Frank (6). Idaho State Prison File, AR42. Idaho State Historical Society Public Archives and Research Library.

"Captured." *Blackfoot Register* (Idaho), Nov. 5, 1881.

"Cold Blooded Murder." *Blackfoot Register* (Idaho), Oct. 28, 1881.

Conley, Cort. *Idaho for the Curious.* Cambridge, Idaho: Backeddy Books, 1982.

"Continued." *Ogden Standard Examiner* (Utah), Nov. 28, 1881.

"The Court." *Blackfoot Register* (Idaho), Nov. 26, 1881.

"The Court." *Blackfoot Register* (Idaho), Dec. 3, 1881.

Daughters Of Utah Pioneers. *The Trailblazer History of the Development of Southeastern Idaho.* Franklin, Idaho: Daughters of Utah Pioneers, 1930

"The Gallows." *Blackfoot Register* (Idaho), Jan. 6, 1883.

"Guilty." *Ogden Standard Examiner* (Utah), Nov. 25, 1881.

Hinckley, Joel Ricks. One World Tree. Ancestry.com. http://trees.ancestry.com/owt/person. Accessed Feb. 1, 2010.

Idaho Pioneer Association. *A Brief History of Franklin.* 1960.

"Malad city news." *Blackfoot Register* (Idaho), Dec. 3, 1881.

McDevitt, Thomas J., M.D. *Idaho's Malad Valley, a History.* Pocatello, Idaho: Little Red Hen, Inc, 2001.

"Michael Mooney." *Ogden Standard Examiner* (Utah), Dec. 9, 1882.

"Michael Mooney." *Ogden Standard Examiner* (Utah), Dec. 30, 1882.

"Michael Mooney." *Ogden Standard Examiner* (Utah), Jan 2, 1883.

"People v. Mooney. *Reports of Cases Argued and Determined in the Supreme Court of Territory of Idaho.* Volume 2. Sol Hasbrouck, editor. San Francisco: Bancroft-Whitney Company, 1903. 17-19.

Sexton, Lena A. "The first hanging in Idaho: The story of Mooney and Barnes." *Southern Idaho Magazine,* Dec. 1, 1982. 4.

Woodward, Lucy. One World Tree. Ancestry.com. http://trees.ancestry.com/ owt/person. (Accessed Feb. 1, 2010).

Photo/Illustration Credits

Map of Franklin. Hubert Bancroft. *Bancroft Works Vol. 21. History of Washington, Idaho, and Montana.* San Francisco: The History Company, 1890.

Joel Hinckley. Family photo provided by Laurelei Lindsay.

Henry McDonald

1880 U. S. Federal Census. Boise, Ada, Idaho Territory. *1880 United States Federal Census* [database on-line]. Provo, UT, USAL Ancestry.com Operations Inc, 2005.

1880 U. S. Federal Census. Kelton, Box Elder, Utah Territory. *1880 United States Federal Census* [database on-line]. Provo, UT, USAL Ancestry.com Operations Inc, 2005.

"District court." *Idaho Avalanche* (Silver City), June 11, 1881.

"District court." *Idaho Avalanche* (Silver City), June 18, 1881.

Hailey, John. *History of Idaho.* Boise: Syms-York Co., 1910.

Henry McDonald Collection. MS 2/289. Idaho State Historical Society Public Archives and Research Library.

"Henry McDonald: The end of a worthless life. *Idaho Tri-Weekly Statesman* (Boise), Oct. 15, 1881.

Idaho Avalanche (Silver City): Nov. 13, 1880; June 4, 1881; Sept. 17, 1881.

Idaho Tri-Weekly Statesman (Boise): March 15, 1881; March 19, 1881; March 23, 1881; May 17, 1881; May 24, 1881; June 2, 1881.

"John Hailey." *Idaho State Historical Society Reference Series.* #543. 1971.

Jones, Larry. "Boise-Kelton Stage Service Past City of Rocks." *Idaho State Historical Society Reference Series.* #849. Sept. 1995.

--- "Kelton Road." *Idaho State Historical Society Reference Series.* #74. Jan. 1972.

"McDonald interviewed." *Idaho Avalanche* (Silver City), Oct. 15, 1881.

"The McDonald jury." *Idaho Avalanche* (Silver City), June 18, 1881.

"McDonald's Capture." *Idaho Tri-Weekly Statesman* (Boise), May 26, 1881.

"People v. Henry McDonald." *Reports of Cases Argued and Determined in the Supreme Court of Territory of Idaho.* Volume 2. Sol Hasbrouck, editor. San Francisco: Bancroft-Whitney Company, 1903. 10-12.

"The people vs. Henry McDonald." *Idaho Tri-Weekly Statesman* (Boise), June 19, 1881.

"The people vs. Henry McDonald." *Idaho Tri-Weekly Statesman* (Boise), June 11, 1881.

"The people vs. Henry McDonald." *Idaho Tri-Weekly Statesman* (Boise), June 14, 1881.

"The people vs. Henry McDonald." *Idaho Tri-Weekly Statesman* (Boise), June 16, 1881.

"Retributive justice in Idaho." *Idaho Tri-Weekly Statesman* (Boise), Oct. 18, 1881.

"A stroke for liberty." *Idaho Tri-weekly Statesman* (Boise), April 17, 1881.

Territory of Idaho vs. Henry McDonald. Court Records. Owyhee County, Second Judicial District. AR1. Idaho State Historical Society Public Archives and Research Library.

United States National Park Service "The Kelton Road—the Stage Era." *City of Rocks Historic Resources Study.* 1996. http://www.nps.gov/archive/ciro/hrs/hrs.htm.

Photo/Illustration Credits

Map of Kelton Road. Chance, David. "Historical Sketch of the Kelton Road." National Park Service, 1993. Taken from Historic Resources Study, City of Rocks National Reserve Southcentral Idaho. On-line, National Park Service.

Silver City. Idaho State Historical Society. Towns 76-138.96.

Henry McDonald. Idaho State Historical Society. Biography 1312-F.

John Hailey. Idaho State Historical Socity. Biography 86-A.

Edward Rice

1880 U. S. Federal Census. Umatilla, Umatilla, Oregon. *1880 United States Federal Census* [database on-line]. Provo, UT, USA: Ancestry.com Operations Inc, 2005.

1900 U. S. Federal Census. Wallace, Shoshone, Idaho. *1900 United States Federal Census* [database on-line]. Provo, UT, USA: Ancestry.com Operations Inc, 2004.

Arrington, Leonard J. *History of Idaho.* Moscow, Idaho: University of Idaho Press, 1994.

"Awaits hangman." *Idaho Daily Statesman* (Boise), Nov. 23, 1900.

"Bad case for Rice." *The Twice Weekly Spokesman-Review* (Spokane, Washington), Oct. 29, 1900.

Conley, Cort. *Idaho for the Curious.* Cambridge, Idaho: Backeddy Books, 1882.

"Convict Edward Rice develops insanity symptoms." *Idaho Daily Statesman* (Boise), May 15, 1901.

"Ed Rice dies on scaffold. *Idaho Daily Statesman* (Boise), Dec. 1, 1901.

"Ed Rice doomed." *Idaho Daily Statesman* (Boise), June 16, 1901.

"Ed Rice must hang." *The Wallace Press* (Wallace, Idaho), Nov. 23, 1901.

Egan, Timothy. "Gambling raid angers mining town." *New York Times*, Aug. 20, 1991. http://www.nytimes.com/1991/08/20/us/gambling-raid-angers-mining-town-html (accessed Feb. 1, 2010).

"Gashed his throat." *Idaho Daily Statesman* (Boise), Jan. 2, 1901.

"Loses his wife and will lose his life." *The Twice Weekly Spokesman-Review* (Spokane, Washington), Nov. 5, 1900.

"Mailey's money was shy." *The Twice Weekly Spokesman-Review* (Spokane, Washington), Nov. 1, 1900.

"Murder at Wallace." *The Twice Weekly Spokesman-Review* (Spokane, Washington), Oct. 4, 1900.

"New Lease of Life." *Idaho Daily Statesman* (Boise), Dec. 28, 1900.

Rice, Edward. Compiled Military Service File. National Archives and Records Administration, Washington D.C.

Rice, Edward. Federal Military Pension Application File. National Archive and Records Administration, Washington D.C.

Rice, Edward (788). Idaho State Prison File, AR42. Idaho State Historical Society Public Archives and Research Library.

"Rice still lives." *Idaho Daily Statesman* (Boise), Jan. 3, 1901.

"Rice to hang this morning." *Idaho Daily Statesman* (Boise), Nov. 30, 1901.

State of Idaho v Edward Rice. Court Records. Shoshone County, First Judicial District, September Term, 1900. AR218. Idaho State Historical Society Public Archives and Research Library.

"State v Rice." *Reports of Cases Argued and Determined in the Supreme Court of State of Idaho.* Volume 7. Sol Hasbrouck, editor. San Francisco: Bancroft-Whitney Company, 1903. 762-775.

The Twice Weekly Spokesman-Review (Spokane, Washington), Nov. 5, 1900; Nov. 8, 1900.

"Wallace has a 'house' problem." *Ellensburg Daily Record* (Washington), Oct. 3, 1973

PHOTO/ILLUSTRATION CREDITS

Edward Rice. Idaho State Historical Society. Inmate photo #788, 80-2.17.

Sixth Street, Wallace, Idaho. Idaho State Historical Society. Towns, 80-40.142.

Bank Street, Wallace, Idaho. Idaho State Historical Society. Towns, 74.31.1.

Old Penitentiary Gate. Idaho State Historical Society. Idaho State Penitentiary, 68-57.30.

William Borah. Idaho State Historical Society. Biography, 2296.

NOAH ARNOLD

"$250 each offered for black bandits." *Northern Idaho News* (Sandpoint), July 23, 1923.

"Arnold calm when final hour comes." *Idaho Daily Statesman* (Boise), Dec. 19, 1924.

Arnold, Noah *aka* Ford, Robert (3301). Idaho State Prison File, AR42. Idaho State Historical Society Public Archives and Research Library.

"Black killer must pay for crime with life." *Northern Idaho News* (Sandpoint), Sept. 18, 1923.

"Black thugs rob, kill W.A. Crisp of Hope." *Northern Idaho News* (Sandpoint), July 17, 1923.

Donnelly, Mike (3302). Idaho State Prison File, AR42. Idaho State Historical Society Public Archives and Research Library.

Ford, Robert *aka* Arnold, Noah. (8432). Washington State Prison File. Washington State Archives. Olympia, Washington.

"Hangman's noose looms for Hope slayers." *Northern Idaho News* (Sandpoint), July 31, 1923.

"Murder in first degree sustained." *Northern Idaho News* (Sandpoint), Aug. 7, 1923.

"Negro bandit may not hang." *Northern Idaho News* (Sandpoint), Oct. 2, 1923.

"Negro bandits are formally charged." *Northern Idaho News* (Sandpoint), Sept. 11, 1923.

"Negro bandits seek jail escape." *Northern Idaho News* (Sandpoint), Aug. 21, 1923.

"Say Negro is Hope murderer." *The Spokesman-Review* (Spokane, Washington), July 27, 1923.

State of Idaho v Noah Arnold. Court Records. Bonner County, Eighth Judicial District, September Term, 1923. AR42. Idaho State Historical Society Public Archives and Research Library.

"State v Noah Arnold." *Reports of Cases Argued and Determined in the Supreme Court of the State of Idaho.* Volume 39. I. W. Hart, editor. San Francisco: Bancroft-Whitney, 1925. 589-607.

Photo/Illustration Credits

Noah Arnold. File of Robert Ford. Washington State Reformatory. Washington State Prison Files. Washington State Archives.

Noah Arnold. File of Robert Ford. Washington State Prison Files. Washington State Archives.

Noah Arnold. Idaho State Historical Society. Inmate photo #3301.

Kuok Wah Choi

1870 U. S. Federal Census. Idaho City, Boise, Idaho Territory. *1870 United States Federal Census* [database on-line]. Provo, UT, USAL Ancestry.com Operations Inc, 2009.

1880 U. S. Federal Census. Rocky Bar, Alturas, Idaho Territory. *1880 United States Federal Census* [database on-line]. Provo, UT, USAL Ancestry.com Operations Inc, 2005.

Elsensohn, Sister M. Alfreda. *Pioneer Days in Idaho County*, Volume 1. Caldwell, Idaho: Caxton Printers, 1947.

Hodges, Kathy. "The execution of Kuok Wah Choi." *Mountain Light: The Newsletter of the Idaho State Historical Society* 43 (Spring 2004): 12-13.

"Kwok Wah Choy." *Wood River Times* (Hailey, Idaho), Sept. 17, 1885.

"Kwong Wah Choy." *Wood River Times* (Hailey, Idaho), Sept. 18, 1885.

"People v. Kuok Wah Choi." *Reports of Cases Argued and Determined in the Supreme Court of Territory of Idaho*. Volume 2. Sol Hasbrouck, editor. San Francisco: Bancroft-Whitney Company, 1903. 90-95.

Territory of Idaho vs. Kuok Wah Choi, aka Ah Sam. Trial records. Alturas County, Second Judicial District, 1894-1895. AR200. Idaho State Historical Society Public Archives and Research Library.

Wegars, Priscilla. "Polly Bemis: Lurid Life or Literary Legend?" in *Wild Women of the Old West*, edited by Glenda Riley and Richard Etulain. Golden, Colorado: Fulcrum Publishing, 1968. 45-68.

Wunder, John. "The Courts and the Chinese in Frontier Idaho." *Idaho Yesterdays* 25 (Spring 1981): 23-32.

Yu, Li-hua. "Chinese Immigrants in Idaho." PhD diss., Bowling Green State University, 1991.

Photo/Illustration Credits

Chinese in mining camp. Idaho State Historical Society. Chinese 83-37.22.

John T. Morgan. Idaho State Historical Society. Biography 750.

Simeon Walters

1870 U. S. Federal Census. Ada County, Idaho Territory. *1870 United States Federal Census* [database on-line]. Provo, UT, USAL Ancestry.com Operations Inc, 2009.

1880 U. S. Federal Census. Boise City, Ada, Idaho Territory. *1880 United States Federal Census* [database on-line]. Provo, UT, USAL Ancestry.com Operations Inc, 2005.

"Body found." *Idaho Tri-Weekly Statesman* (Boise) Dec. 3, 1868.

"Conviction and sentence of Walters." *Owyhee Avalanche* (Silver City, Idaho), April 3, 1869.

"Coroner's inquest." *Idaho Tri-Weekly Statesman* (Boise), Dec. 5, 1868.

"District court." *Idaho Tri-Weekly Statesman* (Boise), Dec. 22, 1868.

"The People v Simeon Walters." *Idaho Reports 1866-1880: Reports of Cases Determined in the Supreme Court of Idaho Territory*, Vol. 1. H. E. Prickett, editor. San Francisco: Bancroft-Whitney Company, 1882. 271-276.

People vs. Simeon Walters. Territorial Court Records, Second District Court, Boise County, 1869. AR 205. Idaho State Historical Society Public Archives and Research Library.

"Examination." *Idaho Statesman* (Boise), Nov. 3, 1868.

"Execution of Simeon Walters." *Idaho World* (Idaho City), Dec. 16, 1869.

Records of Criminal Cases 1863-1870. Idaho Territory District Court, Second Judicial District, Boise County. Idaho State Historical Society Public Archives and Research Library.

"Sentence of Walters." *Idaho Tri-Weekly Statesman* (Boise), March 27, 1869.

"Sim Walters convicted." *Idaho Tri-Weekly Statesman* (Boise), March 18, 1869.

"Supposed Murder." *Owyhee Avalanche* (Silver City, Idaho), Nov. 7, 1868.

"Supposed murderer arrested." *Idaho Tri-Weekly Statesman* (Boise), Oct. 31, 1868.

"The trial of Simeon Walters." *Idaho World* (Idaho City), March 18, 1869.

"The trial of Simeon Walters." *Idaho World* (Idaho City), March 25, 1869.

United States IRS Tax Assessment Lists, 1862-1918. [database on-line]. Provo, UT, USAL Ancestry.com Operations Inc, 2008.

"Walters' trial." *Owyhee Avalanche* (Silver City, Idaho), March 27, 1869.

Photo/Illustration Credits

Owyhee Stage Route. Idaho State Historical Society. R.N. Preston. Maps of Early Idaho. Corvallis, Oregon: Western Guide Publishers, 1972.

Territorial Prison, Idaho City. Idaho State Historical Society. Towns, Idaho City 113.

Ernest Walrath and Troy Powell

Corlett, John. "Board of pardons denies clemency for Boise slayers." *Idaho Daily Statesman* (Boise), April 12, 1951.

----- "Condemned pair plead for lives at board hearing." *Idaho Daily Statesman* (Boise), April 10, 1951.

-----"Hearing on slayers' fate ends." *Idaho Daily Statesman* (Boise), April 11, 1951.

"Death sentence affirmed for two Boise slayers." *Idaho Daily Statesman* (Boise), Feb. 2, 1951.

Johnson, Richard. "Walrath, Powell testify in Boise murder hearing. *Idaho Daily Statesman* (Boise), June 16, 1950.

-----"Police say two youths confess to slaying grocer." *Idaho Daily Statesman* (Boise), May 10, 1950.

Klein, Sandor S. "Walrath, Powell sent to deaths at Idaho prison." *Idaho Daily Statesman* (Boise), April 13, 1951.

McMurtrey, Dale. Interviewed by Kathleen Dodson. OH 595. Boise: Idaho Oral History Center, Sept. 18, 1981. Idaho State Historical Society Public Archives and Research Library.

Powell, Troy (7986). Idaho State Prison File, AR42. Idaho State Historical Society Public Archives and Research Library.

Powell, Troy (19800). Oregon State Prison File. Oregon State Archives.

"State to ask death penalty for Boise duo." *Idaho Daily Statesman* (Boise), June 2, 1950.

"State v Powell et al." *Reports of Cases Argued and Determined in the Supreme Court of the State of Idaho*. Volume 71. Clay Koelsch, editor. St. Paul: West Publishing Co., 1951. 131-139.

State of Idaho v Troy Powell and Ernie Walrath. Court records. Ada County, Third Judicial District, Criminal Case No. 1610. June 1950. Idaho State Supreme Court.

"Two suspects in slaying retain counsel." *Idaho Daily Statesman* (Boise), May 11, 1950.

Walrath, Ernest (7987). Idaho State Prison File, AR42. Idaho State Historical Society Public Archives and Research Library.

Walrath, Ernest (19363). Oregon State Prison File, Oregon State Archives.

"Wilson, Newton." *Boise City and Ada County Directory*, Vol XVI. R. L. Polk & Company, 1927. 367.

"Youthful slayers of Boise grocer sentenced to die." *Idaho Daily Statesman* (Boise), June 17, 1950.

PHOTO/ILLUSTRATION CREDITS

Ernest Walrath (19363). Oregon State Prison file. Oregon State Archives.

Troy Powell (19800). Oregon State Prison file. Oregon State Archives.

Powell and Walrath on day of arrest. Idaho Daily Statesman (Boise), May 10, 1951.

Ernest Walrath. Idaho State Historical Society. Inmate photo #7987, 79-5.554.

Troy Powell. Idaho State Historical Society. Inmate photo #7986, 79-5.553.

Charles Winstead. Idaho State Historical Society. Biography 3655.

Robert Smylie. Idaho State Historical Society. 73.223.22.

Powell gravesite. Photo by author.

ROMAIN, RENTON, AND LOWER

Arrington, Leonard. *History of Idaho, Vol. 1*. Moscow, Idaho: University of Idaho Press, 1994.

Bailey, Robert G. *River of No Return*. Lewiston, Idaho: Lewiston Printing, 1983.

Bianchi, Carl F., ed. *Justice for the Times: A Centennial History of the Idaho State Courts*. Boise: Idaho Law Foundation, 1990.

"The Creation of Idaho Territory." *Idaho State Historical Society Reference Series*. #264. March 1969.

"Dispensing justice in territorial days." *Wallace Press Times* (Idaho), Dec. 12, 1920.

"Early Nez Perce County." *Idaho State Historical Society Reference Series*. #334. 1963.

"The end of the Magruder tragedy." *The Golden Age* (Lewiston, Idaho), March 12, 1864.

"Execution of the Magruder murderers." *Boise News* (Idaho) March 26, 1864.

"Execution of the Magruder murderers." *The Daily Oregonian* (Portland), March 10, 1864.

Hamilton, Ladd. *This Bloody Deed: The Magruder Incident*. Pullman: Washington State University Press, 1994.

"Idaho's First Year." *Idaho State Historical Society Reference Series*. #226. February 1964.

Josephy, Alvin M., Jr. "The blood of Abel: Murder most foul and justice most swift in frontier Idaho." *American West* 20, May/June 1983: 31-37.

Magruder Collection. Court Records, Nez Perce County. AR216. Idaho State Historical Society Public Archives and Research Library.

"Magruder murder is recalled." *Wallace Press Times* (Idaho), Feb. 8, 1920.

"Magruder murder is recalled." *Wallace Press Times* (Idaho), Feb. 15, 1920.

"Magruder murder is recalled." *Wallace Press Times* (Idaho), Feb. 22, 1920.

McConnell, W. J. *Early History of Idaho*. Caldwell, Idaho: Caxton Printers, 1913.

"Pocatello woman recounts details in the early day murder of her grandfather, Lloyd Magruder, by cutthroat gang." *Idaho Statesman* (Boise), Oct. 11, 1942.

Welch, Julia Conway. *The Magruder Murders: Coping with Violence on the Idaho Frontier*. Helena, Montana: Falcon Press, 1991.

Photo/Illustration Credits

Map of Magruder route. Created by Shelly Chamberlain.

Lewiston. Idaho State Historical Society. Towns 2771.

Hill Beachy. Idaho State Historical Society. Biography 2709.

3. For Honor

Alexander Woods

"Annual jail delivery." *Idaho Register* (Eagle Rock), July 14, 1888.

"Another jail delivery." *The Idaho News* (Blackfoot), July 14, 1888.

"A black deed." *Idaho Register* (Eagle Rock), May 14, 1887.

Idaho Daily Statesman (Boise), July 25, 1888.

Idaho Register (Eagle Rock), May 21, 1887; May 28, 1887; July 2, 1887.

"Jerked to death." *The Idaho News* (Blackfoot), Aug. 18, 1888.

"People v. Woods." *Idaho Reports: Reports of cases of the Supreme Court of the Territory of Idaho 1881-1890, Vol. 2*. Sol Hasbrouck, editor. San Francisco: Bancroft-Whitney Company, 1903. 364-365.

Territory of Idaho v. Alexander Woods. Court Records. Bingham County, Third Judicial District, May Term, 1887. AR226. Idaho State Historical Society Public Archives and Research Library.

"Throw up your hands." *Idaho Register* (Eagle Rock), July 2, 1887.
"Wife murderer hanged." *Deseret News* (Salt Lake City), Aug. 22, 1888.
"Woods execution at Pocatello." *Idaho Daily Statesman* (Boise), Aug. 22, 1888.

PHOTO/ILLUSTRATION CREDITS

Pacific Hotel. From Bannock County Images Project. Contributed by ISU
   Special Collections. On line at Idaho Digital Resources.

GEORGE PIERSON

1880 U. S. Federal Census. Atlanta Mining Camp, Alturas, Idaho Territory. *1880
   United States Federal Census* [database on-line]. Provo, UT, USA: Ancestry.
   com Operations Inc, 2005.
"Banjo Nell must go!" *Wood River Times* (Hailey, Idaho), Dec. 4, 1882.
"The condemned man." *Wood River Times* (Hailey, Idaho), July 31, 1884.
"The escaped murderer." *Wood River Times* (Hailey, Idaho), Aug. 17, 1883.
"The escaped murderer." *Wood River Times* (Hailey, Idaho), Sept. 4, 1883.
"The fugitive captured." *Wood River Times* (Hailey, Idaho), Sept. 10, 1883.
"George Pearsons." *Wood River Times* (Hailey, Idaho), Aug. 30, 1893.
"Governor Bunn's action in the Pierson case." *Idaho Tri-Weekly Statesman*
   (Boise), July 31, 1884.
"Is this another murder!" *Wood River Times* (Hailey, Idaho), Aug. 18, 1882.
"The law of murder." *Wood River Times* (Hailey Idaho), Oct. 25, 1882.
"The other side." *Wood River Times* (Hailey, Idaho), Sept. 5, 1883.
"Pearson executed." *Wood River Times* (Hailey, Idaho), Aug. 1, 1884.
"Pearsons re-captured." *Wood River Times* (Hailey, Idaho), Sept. 8, 1883.
"People v. Pierson." *Idaho Report: Reports of Cases Argued and Determined in
   the Supreme Court of Territory of Idaho. 1881-1890, Vol. 2.* Sol Hasbrouck,
   editor. San Francisco: Bancroft-Whitney Company, 1903. 76-82.
Russell, Jo Anne. A Necessary Evil: prostitutes, patriarchs, and profits in Boise
   City 18631915 (master's thesis, Boise State University, 1991).
Territory of Idaho v. George Pierson. Trial transcript and related materials. Alturas
   County, Second Judicial District. AR42, AR200. Idaho State Historical
   Society Public Archives and Research Library.
Wells, Merle. *Gold Camps and Silver Cities*. Moscow, Idaho: University of Idaho
   Press, 2002. 150.
Wood River Times (Hailey, Idaho): Aug. 18, 1883; Aug. 25, 1883.

PHOTO/ILLUSTRATION CREDITS

Wood River Mines. From Gold Camps and Silver Cities by Merle Wells.
   Reprinted by permission of the Idaho State Historical Society.
Vienna. Idaho State Historical Society. Towns 19-17/A.B.
Henry Prickett. Idaho State Historical Society. Biography 64.74.1.
William Bunn. Idaho State Historical Society. Biography 442.q.

John Jurko

1920 U.S. Federal Census. Twins Falls Ward 1, Twin Falls, Idaho. *1920 United States Federal Census* [database on-line]. Provo, UT, USA: Ancestry.com Operations Inc, 2009.

"Autopsy shows brain of Jurko was affected." *Idaho Daily Statesman* (Boise), July 10, 1926.

"Death Sentence is pronounced on Jurko." *Twin Falls Daily News* (Idaho), Sept. 24, 1924.

"Defense scores in second day of Jurko trial." *Twin Falls Daily News* (Idaho), Sept. 19, 1924.

"In the Matter of the Application for Pardon and Commutation of Sentence of John Jurko." Minutes, State Board of Pardons, July 7-8, 1926. AR 42/5-7. Idaho State Historical Society Public Archives and Research Library.

"Jurko asserts fatal shooting was provoked." *Twin Falls Daily News* (Idaho), June 27, 1925.

"Jurko battles for life; fate is not decided." *Idaho Daily Statesman* (Boise), July 8, 1926.

Jurko, John (3416). Idaho State Prison File, AR42. Idaho State Historical Society Public Archives and Research Library.

"Jurko loses his last battle to avoid gallows." *Idaho Daily Statesman* (Boise), July 9, 1926.

"Jurko waives first hearing." *Twin Falls Daily News* (Idaho), July 1, 1924.

"Local man faces murder prosecution as a result of death of A.B.W. Vandenmark in affray in pool room." *Twin Falls Daily News* (Idaho), June 26, 1924.

"Plans made to appeal verdict." *Twin Falls Daily News* (Idaho), Sept. 21, 1924.

"State rests in Jurko trial on murder charge." *Twin Falls Daily News* (Idaho), Sept. 18, 1924.

"State v Jurko." *Reports of Cases Argued and Determined in the Supreme Court of State of Idaho.* Volume 42. I.W. Hart, editor. San Francisco: Bancroft-Whitney Company, 1927, 319-338.

State of Idaho v John Jurko. Court Records. Twin Falls County, Eleventh Judicial District, September Term, 1924. AR1. Idaho State Historical Society Public Archives and Research Library.

"Time near for Jurko to face murder charge." *Twin Falls Daily News* (Idaho), Sept. 14, 1924.

United States, Selective Service System. *World War I Selective Service System Draft Registration Cards, 1917-1918.* Washington, D.C.: National Archives and Records Administration. *World War I Draft Registration Cards, 1917-1918* [database on-line]. Provo, UT, USA: Ancestry.com Operations Inc, 2005.

Photo/Illustration Credits

John Jurko. Idaho State Historical Society. Inmate photo #3416.

John Taylor. Idaho State Historical Society. Biography 73.223.19.

Headstone. Photo by author.

4. In Desperation

Tambiago

"The Bannock Indians." *Idaho Tri-Weekly Statesman* (Boise), Jan. 22, 1878.

Crowder, David. "Nineteenth-Century Indian-White Conflicts in Southern Idaho." *Idaho Yesterdays* 23, Summer 1979: 13-18.

-------*Tendoy, Chief of the Lemhis*. Caldwell, Idaho: Caxton Press, 1969.

d'Easum, Dick. "Bannock War at Camas Prairie." Idaho State Historical Society Reference Series, #474. 1969.

"The end of the Bannock war, capture of the last hostile band." *New York Times*, Sept. 15, 1878. The New York Times Archives Online. www.query.nytimes.com. accessed Feb. 21, 2010.

"The hanging of Tambiago." *Idaho Tri-Weekly Statesman* (Boise), June 29, 1878.

Idaho Tri-Weekly Statesman (Boise), Dec. 20, 1877.

"Idaho's Indian Wars." *Idaho State Historical Society Reverence Series*, #23.

Illustrated History of the State of Idaho. Chicago: Lewis Publishing Company, 1899.

"An Indian murderer caught." *Idaho Tri-Weekly Statesman* (Boise), June 19, 1878.

Madsen, Brigham. *The Northern Shoshoni*. Caldwell, Idaho: Caxton Press, 1980.

McDevitt, Thomas J., M.D. *Idaho's Malad Valley, a History*. Pocatello, Idaho: Little Red Hen, Inc, 2001.

McKenzie, Michael. "To the Brink and Back." *Columbia* Summer 2008: 19-27.

"Murderer arrested—trouble at Fort Hall Indian Agency. *Idaho Tri-Weekly Statesman* (Boise), Nov. 29, 1877.

"Not afraid to die, but unwilling to talk much." *Idaho Tri-Weekly Statesman* (Boise), June 27, 1878.

People of the United States vs Tambiago (an Indian). Court Records, Oneida County, Third Judicial District. AR243. Idaho State Historical Society Public Archives and Research Library.

"Reports of Prisoners Confined 1876-1884." Idaho Territorial Prison Records, AR42/2. Idaho State Historical Society Public Archives and Research Library.

Photo/Illustration Credits

Bannock Indians. Nation Anthropological Archives, Smithsonian Institution. gn_01712A.

Joseph Pinkham. *Illustrated History of the State of Idaho*. Chicago. Lewis
Publishing Company, 1899.

James Ellington

"Capture of Ellington." *Idaho Daily Statesman* (Boise), Dec. 23, 1894.

"Charles Briggs dead." *Idaho Daily Statesman* (Boise), Dec. 26, 1894.

"Charles Briggs shot." *Idaho Daily Statesman* (Boise), Dec. 21, 1894.

"Coroner's jury verdict." *Idaho Daily Statesman* (Boise), Dec. 21, 1894.

"Ellington has nerve." *Idaho Daily Statesman* (Boise), March 26, 1896.

"Ellington must hang." *Idaho Daily Statesman* (Boise), Feb. 11, 1895.

"Ellington on the stand." *Idaho Daily Statesman* (Boise), Feb. 9, 1895.

French, Hiram Taylor. *The History of Idaho: A Narrative Account of its Historical
Progress, Its People, Its Principal Interests, Vol. 2.* Chicago: Lewis Publishing
Company, 1914. 764-765.

"He must die." *Idaho Daily Statesman* (Boise), Dec. 13, 1895.

"His last hope vanished." *Idaho Daily Statesman* (Boise), May 21, 1896.

"It hinges on a knife." *Idaho Daily Statesman* (Boise), March 18, 1895.

"James A Ellington hanged." *Idaho Daily Statesman* (Boise), May 28, 1896.

"The jury cannot agree." *Idaho Daily Statesman* (Boise), Feb. 10, 1895.

"Last hours on earth." *Idaho Daily Statesman* (Boise), May 27, 1896.

"Mrs. Briggs' statement." *Idaho Daily Statesman* (Boise), May 23, 1896.

"On trial for his life." *Idaho Daily Statesman* (Boise), Feb. 7, 1895.

"People v Ellington. *Idaho Reports: Reports of cases argued and determined in
the Supreme Court of the State of Idaho Vol. 4.* Sol Hasbrouck, editor. San
Francisco: Bancroft-Whitney Company, 1903. 529-538.

"Sentence of Ellington." *Idaho Daily Statesman* (Boise), March 26, 1895.

State of Idaho v James A. Ellington. Court Records. Ada County, Third Judicial
District, January Term, 1895. AR202. Idaho State Historical Society
Public Archives and Research Library.

"That knife in court." *Idaho Daily Statesman* (Boise), March 20, 1895.

"Trial of Ellington." *Idaho Daily Statesman* (Boise), Feb. 8, 1895.

Photo/Illustration Credits

James Ellington, line drawing. Idaho Daily Statesman (Boise), May 28, 1896.

Frank Martin. Idaho State Historical Society. Biography 73-2237.

William McConnell. Idaho State Historical Society. Biography 80.37.88.

William Reynolds (aka Frank Williams)

"Annual jail delivery." *Idaho Register* (Eagle Rock), July 14, 1888.

"A hard trip." *Idaho Register* (Eagle Rock), Jan. 8, 1887.

"Bingham County Idaho 1895." *1895 U. S. Atlas.* CFC Productions 2003.
www.livgenmi.com/1895/ID/County/bingham.htm.

"Frank Williams the Cariboo murderer." *The Idaho News* (Blackfoot), July 21, 1888.

"Gold Mines of Caribou Mountain." *Idaho Yesterdays* 19 no. 4 (1976): 10.

"Homicide." *Idaho Register* (Eagle Rock), Dec. 25, 1886.

"The last hours of Frank Williams." *The Idaho News* (Blackfoot), July 28, 1888.

"Pays the penalty." *Idaho Register* (Eagle Rock), July 21, 1888.

"People v. Williams." *Idaho Report: Reports of Cases Argued and Determined in the Supreme Court of Territory of Idaho. 1881-1890, Vol. 2.* Sol Hasbrouck, editor. San Francisco: Bancroft-Whitney Company, 1903. 366.

"Returned." *Idaho Register* (Eagle Rock), April 23, 1887.

Territory of Idaho v. Frank Williams. Court Records. Bingham County, Third Judicial District, May Term, 1887. AR226. Idaho State Historical Society Public Archives and Research Library.

"Throw up your hands." *Idaho Register* (Eagle Rock),, July 2, 1887.

"To examine the bodies." *Idaho Register* (Eagle Rock), April 16, 1887.

U. S. Army, Register of Enlistments, 1798-1914 [data base on-line]. Provo, Utah. Generations Network, Inc. 2007.

Photo/Illustration Credits

Map of Cariboo Mines. Idaho State Historical Society.

Theodore Warlich

1880 U. S. Federal Census. Lewiston, Nez Perce, Idaho. *1880 United States Federal Census* [database on-line]. Provo, UT, USA: Ancestry.com Operations Inc. 2005.

1880 U. S. Federal Census. Washington, Idaho, Idaho. *1880 United States Federal Census* [database on-line]. Provo, UT, USA: Ancestry.com Operations Inc. 2005.

Aiken, Katherine G. *"Idaho's Bunker Hill: The rise and fall of a great mining company, 1885-1891.* Norman, Oklahoma: University of Oklahoma Press, 2005.

"Hanged for murder." *Idaho County Free Press* (Grangeville), June 18, 1886.

"Idaho Territory v Theodore Warlich. Court Records. First Judicial District, Idaho County, April 1886. AR 42/3, Box 15. Idaho State Historical Society Public Archives and Research Library.

Nez Perce News (Lewiston, Idaho): March 11, 1886; April 8, 1886; May 27, 1886.

Rickard, T. A. *The Bunker Hill Enterprise.* San Francisco: Mining and Scientific Press, 1921.

"Sentenced to death." *Nez Perce News* (Lewiston, Idaho), April 22, 1886.

Photo/Illustration Credits

Mount Idaho Courthouse. Idaho State Historical Society. Towns 2750.

Edward Stevenson. Idaho State Historical Society. Biography 46-B.

5. The Demon Rum

James Conners

"Blackfoot shooting." *The Pocatello Tribune* (Idaho), Sept. 26, 1904.

"Condemned man is indifferent." *Idaho Daily Statesman* (Boise), Dec. 16, 1904.

"Conners found guilty." *Idaho Republican* (Blackfoot), Nov. 5, 1904.

Conners, James (1050), Idaho State Prison File, AR42. Idaho State Historical Society Public Archives and Research Library.

"Connors meets death bravely." *Idaho Daily Statesman* (Boise), Dec. 17, 1904.

"Hoboes hold up section gang." *Idaho Daily Statesman* (Boise), Sept. 26, 1904.

"In the district court." *Idaho Republican* (Blackfoot), Oct. 28, 1904.

"James Connors must die on scaffold." *Idaho Daily Statesman* (Boise), Nov. 3, 1904.

"Mob plans to lynch murderer while victim is being buried." *Idaho Daily Statesman* (Boise), Sept. 29, 1904.

"Murder at Blackfoot." *Idaho Falls Times*, Sept. 30, 1904.

"Murder follows Hobo's holdup." *The Salt Lake Herald*, Sept. 26, 1904.

"No danger of mob violence at Blackfoot this morning." *The Pocatello Tribune* (Idaho), Sept. 27, 1904.

"Prisoners sentenced." *Idaho Republican* (Blackfoot), Nov. 11, 1904.

"The rope was ready to hang the murderer." *The Pocatello Tribune* (Idaho), Sept. 28, 1904.

"A shooting affray at Blackfoot Sunday." *Idaho Republican* (Blackfoot), Sept. 30, 1904.

State of Idaho v James Conners. Court Records. Bingham County, Sixth Judicial District, October Term, 1904. AR226. Idaho State Historical Society Public Archives and Research Library.

State of Idaho v James Conners. Probate Court Records. Bingham County, Sept. 26, 1904.

Photo/Illustration Credits

James Conners. Idaho State Historical Society. Inmate photo #1050.

Anthony McBride

Bancroft. Hubert H. *Bancroft's Works, Volume 31, History of Washington, Idaho, and Montana, 1845-1889.* San Francisco, The History Company, 1890.

"Execution of Anthony McBride." *Boise Semi-weekly Democrat*, Jan. 25, 1868.

"Execution of McBride." *Idaho Tri-Weekly Statesman* (Boise), Jan. 25, 1868.

Idaho Tri-Weekly Statesman (Boise), Nov. 21, 1867; Jan. 25, 1868.

McBride, Anthony. Compiled military service file. National Archives & Records Administration, Washington, DC.

Mills, Nelle Ireton. *All Along the River: Territorial and Pioneer Days on the Payette*. Payette Radio Limited, 1963.

"Prisoner escaped." *Idaho Tri-Weekly Statesman* (Boise), Nov. 19, 1867.

"Sentenced." *Idaho Tri-Weekly Statesman* (Boise), Nov. 30, 1867.

Territory of Idaho vs. Anthony McBride. Court Records. Ada County, Third Judicial District. Old Criminal Records. AR 202. Idaho State Historical Society Public Archives and Research Library.

U. S. Army, Registry of Enlistments, 1798-1914. [database on-line]. Provo, UT, Ancestry.com Operations, Inc. 2007.

Photo/Illustration Credits

Map of Payette Valley. Hubert Bancroft. Bancroft Works, Vol. 31: History of Washington, Idaho, and Montana, 1845-1889. San Francisco: The History Company, 1890.

Timothy O'Connor

1880 U. S. Federal Census. Salmon City, Lemhi, Idaho Territory. *1880 United States Federal Census* [database on-line]. Provo, UT, USAL Ancestry.com Operations Inc, 2005.

"Home scraps." *Yankee Fork Herald* (Bonanza City, Idaho), Sept. 18, 1880.

"Home scraps." *Yankee Fork Herald* (Bonana City, Idaho), Sept. 25, 1880.

Lemhi County History Committee. *Centennial History of Lemhi County Vol. 1*. Salmon, Idaho: 1992.

"Lemhi Placers." *Idaho State Historical Society Reference Series*. # 383. 1980.

"Our Salmon City letters." *Yankee Fork Herald* (Bonanza City, Idaho) Feb. 28, 1880.

"Our Salmon City letters: full particulars of the Leesburg tragedy." *Yankee Fork Herald* (Bonanza City, Idaho), Feb. 14, 1880.

"The People v Timothy O'Conner." *Idaho Reports 1866-1880: Reports of Cases Determined in the Supreme Court of Idaho Territory, Vol. 1*. H. E. Prickett, editor. San Francisco: Bancroft-Whitney Company, 1882. 759-760.

People vs. Timothy O'Conner. Territorial Court Records, Third District Court, Lemhi County, AR 1. Idaho State Historical Society Public Archives and Research Library.

"Tim Conner's last statement." *Yankee Fork Herald* (Bonanza City, Idaho), Oct. 9, 1880

Photo/Illustration Credits

Map of Lemhi Mines. From *Gold Camps and Silver Cities* by Merle Wells. Reprinted by permission of the Idaho State Historical Society.

Leesburg. Idaho State Historical Society. Towns 443-D.

James Hawley. Idaho State Historical Society. Biography 73-87.4.

6. Murder Most Foul

Raymond Snowden

1910 U. S. Federal Census. Salina Ward 3, Saline, Kansas. *1910 United States Federal Census* [database on-line]. Provo, UT, USA: Ancestry.com Operations Inc. 2006.

1930 U. S. Federal Census. Boise, Ada, Idaho. *United States Federal Census* [database on-line]. Provo, UT, USA: Ancestry.com Operations Inc. 2002.

"Accused killer queried again by officials." *Idaho Daily Statesman* (Boise), Sept. 26, 1956.

Ada County Marriage Records, Vol. 19, p 77. *Idaho Marriages, 1842-1996* [database on-line]. Provo, UT, USA: The Generations Network, Inc., 2005.

"Boisean admits mutilation murders as police solve case in quick time." *Idaho Daily Statesman* (Boise), Sept. 25, 1956.

"Court to set death date for Snowden." *Idaho Daily Statesman* (Boise), Aug. 15, 1957.

"Date nears for execution of Snowden." *Idaho Daily Statesman* (Boise), Oct. 16, 1957.

Day, Sam. "The Execution of Raymond Snowden: 'An abandoned and malignant heart.'" *Intermountain Observer* (Boise), Oct. 5, 1968.

--- "The Execution of Raymond Snowden: 'Blood on his hands.'" *Intermountain Observer* (Boise), Sept. 28, 1968.

---"The Execution of Raymond Snowden: The last of a vanishing breed." *Intermountain Observer* (Boise), Oct. 12, 1968.

"Death weapon in Garden City murder found." *Idaho Daily Statesman* (Boise), Sept. 27, 1956.

"Execution for Snowden upheld by Supreme Court." *Idaho Daily Statesman* (Boise), July 25, 1957.

Gunn, Ira. Interviewed by Kathy Hodges. OH1174 a-b. Boise: Idaho Oral History Center, May 22, 1992. Idaho State Historical Society Public Archives and Research Library.

"Killer orders final meal before death." *Idaho Daily Statesman* (Boise), Oct. 17, 1957.

Maxwell, Mark. Interviewed by Kathleen Dodson. OH0739. Boise: Idaho Oral History Center, Oct. 21, 1981. Idaho State Historical Society Public Archives and Research Library.

"Mutilation murder suspect claims innocence in court." *Idaho Daily Statesman* (Boise), Oct. 6, 1956.

"Mutilation slayer suspect asks court for attorney." *Idaho Daily Statesman* (Boise), Sept. 29, 1956.

National Archives and Records Administration. *U.S. World War II Army Enlistment Records, 1938-1946* [database on-line]. Provo, UT, USA: Ancestry.com Operations Inc, 2005.

"Services are held at penitentiary for executed man." *Idaho Daily Statesman* (Boise), Oct. 20, 1957.

"Snowden dies on gallows for murder." *Idaho Daily Statesman* (Boise), Oct. 18, 1957.

"Snowden doomed to hang for mutilation murder." *Idaho Daily Statesman* (Boise), Oct. 27, 1956.

"Snowden pleads guilty to mutilation slaying." *Idaho Daily Statesman* (Boise), Oct. 19, 1956.

Snowden, Raymond (9509). Idaho State Prison File, AR42. Idaho State Historical Society Public Archives and Research Library.

"State asks death penalty at hearing for Snowden." *Idaho Daily Statesman* (Boise), Oct. 24, 1956.

State of Idaho v Raymond Allen Snowden. Court Records. Ada County, Third Judicial District, Criminal Case No. 2253. October 1956. Idaho State Supreme Court, Boise, Idaho.

"State v Snowden." *Reports of Cases Argued and Determined in the Supreme Court of the State of Idaho.* L. J. Bideganeta, editor. St. Paul, Minnesota: West Publishing Co., 1957, 266-275.

"Woman's body found Sunday in Garden City." *Idaho Daily Statesman* (Boise), Sept. 24, 1956

Photo/Illustration Credits

Raymond Snowden. Idaho State Historical Society. Inmate photo 9509, 79-5.552.

Chinden Avenue. Idaho State Historical Society. Ms 281 Box 11/22.

Lou Clapp. Idaho State Historical Society. P1984-15.49.

Index

Ackley, D. W. 35, 207
Agnew, J. D. 18, 23
Allen, Charles 131, 134
Ammond, George 158
Arney, Charles 81
Aronson, A. T. 89
Asher, Allen P. 88
Babcock, William 166
Bacon, Joseph 100-107
Bainbridge, Augustus 175
Baird, A. B. 171
Ballard, David W. 108, 173, 214
Barnes, Frank 51-55
Beachy, Hill 130-139, 141
Bennett, H. M. 52, 148, 187
Bivens, David 209-210, 212
Black, Mike 4
Borah, William 71, 80
Bowers, Thomas 105
Brady, James 33
Briggs, Charles 179-181
Britton, Frank 108-109
Broderick, Case 97, 150, 161
Buck, Norman 161, 199
Budge, Alfred 12
Bunn, William 159, 161
Cahalan, Thomas 61, 210
Chalfant, Charles 33
Chalmers, Horace and Robert 134-139
Chinese 2, 94-96, 98
Clapp, Lou 126-127, 233, 235
Collister, Dr. George 19, 79, 181, 186
Conner, A. H. 91
Cooper, Barbara 116-121
Crawford, Willard 52, 193
Crisp, William 82, 86-89, 93
Cromwell, J. Fred 232-234
Crook, General George 178
Cummings, Henry 31
Cummins, John 212-214
Curtis, E. J. 105, 212
Daly, Charles 15-19
Daly, Jennie 15-26
Davis, George 147-148, 191

Dean, Cora 225, 227, 229
Decker, John 39-43
Delana, Benton 169, 171
Delana, Elbert 169
Demarest, Frank 231-232, 235
Donnelly, Mike 86-93
Dunbar, William 19-20
Duvall, John 211-212
Fain, John S. 220
Fisk, James 132, 137, 139, 141
Fleming, Grace 28-32, 36
Forney, James H. 199
Fulton, Hugh 184-185
Glenn, Gus 57, 61, 66-67
Gray, John 176
Guthrie, W. P. 166, 168
Hailey, John 56, 61, 68-69
Hall, John T. 152-162
Harriman, P. O. 166
Hawley, James 12-13, 157-158, 161, 220-223
Hawley Jr., Jess 119-126
Hays, Charles 43-44
Hays, James B. 148-149, 191, 193
Hill, Josie 6-7, 10
Hinckley, Joel 49, 51, 53
Homer, W. H. 50-53
Hough, George C. 106
Hunt, Frank 80, 186
Huston, John 97, 157
Kelton Road 56, 60, 71-72, 75
Kempthorne, Dirk 4
Kinney, James 204
Kinyon, Frank 19-21, 26
Kirkpatrick, William 82, 87-89
Koelsch, Charles 20-24, 26
Koelsch, Oliver 232-234
Lindsey, L. B. 106
Ludeman, William 215-221
Magruder, Lloyd 129-141
Mailey, Matthew 72-76, 80
Marcus, Claude 119-120, 122, 124-126
Marlatt, William 59-60
Martin, Frank 181-186

Martin, Henry 66, 68
Masters, Ira 126
Mayhew, Alexander E. 76, 78
McCarty, Pat 232, 235
McConnell, William 185-186
McNaughton, W. F. 89-91
McNicoll, Robert 216-220
McQuade, Henry 234
McQuillan, James 47
Miller, Charles F. 76-77, 79-80
Mills, Homer C. 166-167
Moody, Silas 20, 25
Morgan, John T. 52-54, 97, 99, 148-149, 161, 220-223
Morgan, William M. 90, 92
Mosher, Clay 43, 48
Myers, George 56-68
Myers, William 209-212
Neil, John B. 54, 222-223
Noggle, David 108
No Ho Wah 175-176
Onderdonk, James L. 220
O'Neill, Clara 27-30, 36
Page, William (Billy) 132-136, 139-142
Parker, J. W. 199-201
Parks, Samuel 139-140
Parsons, George M. 161
Patterson, J. B. 156-158
Perky, Kirtland 20-25
Phillips, William 134-135, 139, 141
Pinkham, Joseph 176-177
Poe, James 199-201
Prickett, Henry E. 66-68, 106, 108, 157-161, 176
Reed, Charles 187-194
Rhoden, Alex 173, 175
Richards, J. H. 181-183, 186
Riebold, George 197-199
Risch, Jim 4
Roberts, Moses 208-213
Robins, C. A. 125-126
Samuels, Henry F. 76-78
Savage, Henry C. 196-199, 201
Sibletts, Simon 190-192
Smith, Alanson 158, 162
Smith, H. W. 148-149
Smith, J. Edward 12-13

Smylie, Robert 124-126
Snook, John 34-36, 93, 169
Snow, Edwin 33
Standrod, D. W. 12-13
Steele, Edgar C. 31-32
Stevens, James M. 206
Stevenson, Edward 94, 150, 200-201
Stewart, George 24-26, 44-45, 47
Stiles, Orville 234-236
Stover, John 216, 218-219, 221-222
Sutherland, Angus 74-76
Sweet, Elbert P. 203-206
Talkington, Albert 201
Taylor, J. W. 166-167, 169
Taylor, Samuel 190-194
Tot Kee 96-97
Truitt, Warren 31-33
Vandenmark, A. B. W. 163-171
Waters, G. L. 97-98
Wells, Keith 4
Wester, J. R. 181, 184
Wheeler, J. W. 170
White, B. F. 176
Whitney, E. L. 26, 34
Wilson, Newton 110, 116-121, 125
Winn, John 188-194
Winstead, Charles 120-125
Woods, Sarah 144-149
Wyatt, Anneas 39